Designing timber buildings

Fausto Sanna

Designing timber buildings

THE CROWOOD PRESS

First published in 2022 by
The Crowood Press Ltd
Ramsbury, Marlborough
Wiltshire SN8 2HR

enquiries@crowood.com
www.crowood.com

British Library Cataloguing-in-Publication Data
A catalogue record for this book is available from the British Library.

ISBN 978 0 7198 4077 7

Cover design by Sergey Tsvetkov

Front cover image: Congress and Exhibition Centre in Agordo (Italy), designed by Studio Botter and Studio Bressan. (Photo: Simone Bossi)

Back cover images: top left: house in Haute-Nendaz (Switzerland), designed by Jean-Michel Martignoni, Ma Maison Bois. (Photo: Franck Paubel, Ma Maison Bois, Switzerland & Kontio, Finland); top right and middle left: new FINSA Headquarters in Santiago de Compostela (Spain), designed by MRM Arquitectos. (Photo: MRM Arquitectos, Spain); bottom: Congress and Exhibition Centre in Agordo (Italy), designed by Studio Bressan and Studio Botter. (Photo: Simone Bossi)

Frontispiece: Spinelli Refugee Centre, Mannheim Germany, designed by the students of Atelier U20, Faculty of Architecture, Technische Universität Kaiserslautern. (Photo: Yannick Wenger – Mannheim)

Disclaimer
The information contained in this book is for guidance only and should only be used in conjunction with professional advice. The author and publisher disclaim all liability for any loss or damage, whether direct or indirect, arising as a result of the use of this book or the information contained in it.

Dedication
To my mother and Josema

Typeset by Simon and Sons
Printed and bound in India by Parksons Graphics

Contents

I AM GRATEFUL TO THE PEOPLE WHO HAVE contributed to the preparation of this book: Annalaura Fornasier, Adam Primmer, Eleonora Piga, Liisa Murd and Alex Boyce.

A big thank-you to Nick Evans, Senior Lecturer at Cardiff School of Art & Design, for his very useful suggestions, and to The Crowood Press, for advice on, and insight into, the content and structure of this publication.

Finally, I would like to thank all the architectural practices, construction companies and institutions that have provided images and information on their projects:

ABCP architecture (Canada); Alma-nac (United Kingdom); Anton Varela García arquitecto (Spain); Andreas Kretzer, Hochschule für Technik Stuttgart (Germany); Atelier U20, Department of Architecture, Technische Universität Kaiserslautern (Germany); BGLA architecture + urban design (Canada); Catnic (United Kingdom), a Tata Steel Enterprise, in particular Charmaine Dean; Dietrich | Untertrifaller Architects (Austria); Dow Jones Architects (United Kingdom); Feilden Fowles (United Kingdom); Hemsec Manufacturing Ltd (United Kingdom), in particular Lizz Clarke; HK Architekten (Austria); Kontio Log Houses (Finland), in particular Pierre Vacherand; Lacol | arquitectura cooperativa (Spain), in particular Carles Baiges Camprubí and Cristina Gamboa; MAAJ Architectes (France); Ma Maison Bois – Jean-Michel Martignoni (Switzerland); Mirko Franzoso architetto (Italy); MRM Arquitectos (Spain), in particular Miguel Alonso Flamarique; Neumann Monson Architects (United States); Scotts Timber Engineering Ltd (United Kingdom); Studio Botter (Italy), in particular Andrea Botter; Studio Bressan (Italy), in particular Emanuele Bressan; Studio Weave (United Kingdom); Woodknowledge Wales (United Kingdom), in particular Gary Newman and Diana Waldron.

AP	acidification potential
BRE	Building Research Establishment
BS	British standard
BSI	British Standards Institution
CAD	computer-aided design
CEN	European Committee for Standardization (Comité Européen de Normalisation)
CFCs	chlorofluorocarbons
CLT	cross-laminated timber
CML	Institute of Environmental Sciences (Centrum voor Milieuwetenschappen), Leiden University
CNC	computer numerical control
DLT	dowel-laminated timber
DPC	damp-proof course
EC	European Commission
EMC	equilibrium moisture content
EN	European Standards
EP	eutrophication potential
EPD	environmental product declaration
EPS	expanded polystyrene
eq.	equivalents
EU	European Union
FMB	Federation of Master Builders
FSC	Forest Stewardship Council
GHGs	greenhouse gases
glulam	glued laminated timber
GWP	global-warming potential
HFCs	hydrogenated halocarbons
IES	Institute for Environment and Sustainability
IPCC	Intergovernmental Panel on Climate Change
ISO	International Organization for Standardization

LoW	list of waste
LSL	laminated-strand lumber
LVL	laminated veneer lumber
MC	moisture content
MDF	medium-density fibreboard
MMC	modern methods of construction
NLT	nail-laminated timber
OSB	oriented-strand board
ODP	ozone-depletion potential
OPC	ordinary Portland cement
PCR	product-category rules
PD	published document (BS, ISO, CEN standards)
PE	primary energy
PEFC	Programme for the Endorsement of Forest Certification
PIR	polyisocyanurate
POCP	photochemical ozone-creation potential
POE	post-occupancy evaluation
PSL	parallel-strand lumber
PUR	polyurethane
PVC	polyvinyl chloride
RIBA	Royal Institute of British Architects
Sb	antimony
SCL	structural composite lumber
SIP(s)	structural insulated panel(s)
SO$_2$	sulphur dioxide
TF	timber frame
TPP	Timber Procurement Policy
UK	United Kingdom
UN	United Nations
US or USA	United States of America
VCL	vapour-control layer
VOCs	volatile organic compounds
XPS	extruded polystyrene

Bring out the nature of the materials, let their nature intimately into your scheme. Strip the wood of varnish and let it alone – stain it. [...] Reveal the nature of wood, plaster, brick or stone in your designs; they are all by nature friendly and beautiful. No treatment can be really a matter of fine art when these natural characteristics are, or their nature is, outraged or neglected.

Frank Lloyd Wright (1908, p.157)

Timber Architecture Today

Over the last three decades, timber has undoubtedly known a renaissance as a building material, especially when used structurally. However, an important distinction should be made between mainstream and one-off projects. The latter have enjoyed a very positive reception by critics and the profession at large, and favourable coverage in the media, such as magazines, journals and TV programmes, aimed at a variety of audiences. Timber architecture is also encouraged by numerous *ad hoc* initiatives and awards[1], organized by research institutions and professional or trade associations, which tend to reward the overall merit of timber-built projects, but also the level of innovation, experimentation and environmental responsiveness that they demonstrate.

One-off projects are often commissioned by open-minded clients, who wish to use sustainable resources and can appreciate the aesthetic qualities of timber as a construction material. Conversely, in the UK, mainstream timber architecture, especially in the residential field, tends not to exhibit its loadbearing structure but to mimic masonry construction instead. Many dwellings constructed of timber-framed or structural insulated panels adopt heavyweight cladding systems, such as brickwork or rendered blockwork (the former being particularly popular in England, the latter in Scotland). This results in timber dwellings not being easily identifiable as such, at least not at first glance and not from the outside. The reason for this preference is, on the one hand, a true appreciation for the appearance of masonry cladding and, on the other hand, a perception of masonry houses as more robust, more durable, and thus safer than their timber counterparts. This type of perception was reinforced in the 1980s, when a couple of accidental fires destroyed timber houses in Britain. This was widely covered by the media, resulting in negative publicity for the timber housebuilding sector. Unsurprisingly, developers involved in the delivery of mainstream housing – and related large schemes – need to expand their clientele, maximize their profit and therefore aspire to accommodate people's perceptions and expectations of what a 'good home' (or a 'good investment') is and looks like.

A problem often encountered by designers leading a timber-based project arises from structural standards and building regulations. Every time a project adopts materials or techniques that are not conventional, meeting performance requirements might not be straightforward and may need special calculations or *ad hoc* assessments, as there is no common practice or modus operandi to rely on. This has immediate repercussions on how easily and quickly planning permissions can be obtained from relevant authorities. The same problem is also encountered in countries where, for instance, timber construction is mainstream in the residential low-rise sector, but is still much less developed for tall residential buildings or for non-domestic projects.

Another obstacle for those who embark on a timber-based project is finding the relevant expertise needed for each of its phases: requesting specialist consultancy at the design stage, ordering and stocking materials through the supply chain and using the skilled labour necessary to guarantee the desired level of workmanship.

Many of the architects that we have interviewed for the case studies presented in the book have lamented some form of difficulty or delay associated with obtaining approval for their proposed design, meeting the requirements of local building codes or finding the right expertise from amongst local tradesmen.

Structure of the Book

The first two chapters provide an introduction to wood, by explaining its natural properties and contemporary silvicultural practice (Chapter 1) and by exposing current developments in treated, modified and engineered timber (Chapter 2). Chapter 3 deals with the environmental aspects of timber architecture and illustrates some practical tools and resources to interpret the ecological credentials of wood-based products.

The remainder of the book delves into timber building techniques. Chapter 4 discusses timber-framed panels, Chapter 5 deals with structural insulated panels (SIPs), and Chapter 6 offers guidance on massive timber techniques, including cross-laminated timber (CLT).

Selection of Case Studies

The selection of cases studies presented throughout this book aims to illustrate recent developments in timber architecture, and spans different constructional techniques, building types and geographical regions.

While some of the case studies employ construction methods discussed in Chapters 4 to 6 (sometimes offering interesting variations on those themes), others employ hybrid methods or structural systems. For instance, we will see hybrid systems whereby timber-based techniques are complemented by steel or reinforced-concrete members, either to augment the overall rigidity of the building or to create an artificial platform, raised from the ground, that supports the upper storeys.

The budgetary constraints within which the buildings proposed were realized vary widely from case to case. For instance, Case Study 7 revolves around social sustainability and affordability of homes, and around novel living/housing models that can encourage these.

Although, as mentioned, the choice of projects aspires to illustrate the variety of present-day timber architecture, there are also some common denominators, one of these being the design team's attempt to establish a strong connection between the building and its place. This connection has been achieved through different approaches: while some projects make reference to local building typology and provide an original re-interpretation of traditional building types, others create an interesting nexus with vernacular tradition by 'citing' just some of its elements or forms in a more abstract or metaphorical fashion.

All the selected projects, in addition, respond attentively to the characteristics of the site and often offer ingenious solutions to challenges such as very dense urban areas (with poor accessibility and consequent logistical problems for the construction phase), plots of irregular geometry, or humble surroundings (car parks, for instance, as in Case Study 9). Another aspect shared by all the projects is that the architects have resisted the temptation to conform, uncritically, to current design trends that leave little room for consideration of the *genius loci* and the architectural and constructional past of the place that hosts them.

For each case study, we will provide some general information first, and explain the context in which the design was commissioned and the brief generated, so

Table 0.1 Summary of the case studies, showing building type, timber techniques and geographical region.

Case study	Name	Building type	Timber techniques							Region
			post-and-beam / skeleton	timber-frame panels	SIPs	log construction	CLT panels	DLT panels	hybrid	
1 (Ch.2)	Congress and Exhibition Centre	non-residential – recreational	■							Europe – Italy
2 (Ch.4)	Feilden Fowles' Studio	non-residential – offices		■					(steel posts)	Europe – United Kingdom
3 (Ch.4)	Maggie's Centre Cardiff	non-residential – healthcare centre		■					(steel skeleton)	Europe – United Kingdom
4 (Ch.4)	Woodland Classrooms	non-residential – educational	■							Europe – United Kingdom
5 (Ch.4)	Taverny Medical Centre	non-residential – healthcare centre					■		(blockwork)	Europe – France
6 (Ch.5)	House in the Woods	residential – single family			■					Europe – United Kingdom
7 (Ch.6)	La Borda Apartment Block	residential – apartment block					■			Europe – Spain
8 (Ch.6)	Three Sisters Footbridge	non-residential – footbridge					■		(steel cables and shafts)	America – Canada
9 (Ch.6)	111 East Grand Avenue	non-residential – offices						■	(concrete core)	America – USA
10 (Ch.6)	House in Haute-Nendaz	residential – single family				■			(concrete core)	Europe – Switzerland

that the most salient aspects of the design strategy can be appreciated. Then, we will deal with the technical aspects, to explain the materiality of the designs and how these were physically realized. We will discuss both the building techniques employed and the construction processes adopted, and how these were decided as part of a bespoke response to the unique conditions posed by the brief.

As regards the locations, some of the buildings are immersed in a rural landscape, while others attempt to make the most of the precious space within high-density urban areas. As a consequence, the residential buildings we propose are of diverse types and sizes: from detached, self-sufficient houses to flats that benefit from shared services and spaces, thus encouraging the occupants to live closely with one another and become part of a micro-community at the apartment-block level.

Finally, some of the case studies have – though to a different extent – an experimental nature and thus offer a unique and valuable contribution to the advancement of timber architecture. The details of the architectural practices that have led the projects can be found in the 'Useful Contacts' section towards the end of the book.

Notes

[1] Timber competitions around the world include (but are not limited to): the Wood Awards organized by TRADA (UK), the Structural Timber Awards by the Structural Timber Association (UK), Deutscher Holzbaupreis by Holzbau Deutschland (Germany), Holzbaupreis Südtirol – Premio Archilegno Alto Adige by South Tyrol Architects' Council (Italy), various regional awards in Austria (Holzbaupreis Steiermark, Oberösterreichischer Holzbaupreis, Niederösterreichische Holzbaupreis), Prix Nationale de Construction Bois (France), Træprisen (Danish Wood Award) by Træinformation (Denmark), Träpriset (Swedish Wood Award) by Svenskt Trä (Swedish Wood), Puupalkinto (Finnish Wood Award) by Puuinfo (Finland), the Wood Design Awards by WoodWorks (USA), the Building Excellence Awards by the Structural Insulated Panel Association (USA), the Wood Design & Building Awards by *Wood Design & Building* magazine (Canada), and the Australian Timber Design Awards by the Timber Development Association (Australia).

Chapter One

Solid Wood and Silvicultural Practice

Wood Species and Anatomy

Classification of woods

Trees can be divided into two broad categories: softwoods and hardwoods. However, this terminology can be misleading, in that not all hardwoods are harder than softwoods, and not all softwoods are less hard than hardwoods. From a botanical point of view, softwoods are gymnosperms (or conifers): they generally produce cones and their leaves are evergreen and shaped as needles or scales. The woody material produced by softwoods is non-porous. Hardwoods are angiosperms, as the ovaries of their flowers contain the seeds; they have broad leaves and are usually deciduous – they lose their leaves in the autumn or winter. The wood produced by hardwoods is porous.

Anatomy – macroscopic level

A tree trunk is composed of different parts, from the centre out:

- pith, which originated in the early growth of the trunk, prior to wood formation;
- heartwood, which is made of dead cells but nonetheless stores extractives (different types of biochemicals produced by the plant);
- sapwood, which conducts sap from the roots to the leaves, and also produces and stores

substances that are fundamental for the living plant. In sapwood, parenchyma cells (which store nutrients) are alive;

- vascular cambium, a very thin layer that produces wood and bark via cell division, and is thus responsible for the growth of the tree;
- inner bark, through which the sugars produced by photosynthesis are transported from the leaves to the roots;
- outer bark, which protects the inner bark.

Heartwood and sapwood together constitute the largest part of the trunk; however, their mutual proportions vary greatly across wood species. Some species have a very thin sapwood band, while in others these two types of tissue are present in almost equal parts. When the cross-section of a trunk is observed with the naked eye, the distinction between heartwood and sapwood is very obvious in some species, as the two tissues have different colours: typically, sap is yellow and lighter, while heartwood is brown and remarkably darker. In other species, however, colour differentiation is much less pronounced and it is more difficult to distinguish one type of tissue from the other. The sapwood-heartwood proportion is important for applications in the construction industry, since the physical and mechanical properties of the two component parts are quite different. Sapwood tends to have lower density and lower strength than heartwood. Furthermore, in preservative treatments, sapwood tends to be more treatable than heartwood; consequently, the effectiveness and level of penetration of the preservative chemicals used depend on the proportion of these two types of tissue within the piece of wood to be preserved.

OPPOSITE: **Fig. 1.1.** Redwood Grove at Leighton, in the Welsh county of Powys. (Photo: Woodknowledge Wales & Rosie Anthony)

1 pith
2 heartwood
3 sapwood
4 vascular cambium
5 inner bark
6 outer bark

Fig. 1.2. Cross-section of a trunk (pine tree) showing the component parts of the woody material.

The anatomical axes and sections

It is very useful to consider the structure, physical properties and mechanical behaviour of wood by analysing the trunk relative to three different planes of section, which reflect its anatomy:

- transverse plane, which shows the cross-section of the trunk;
- radial plane, which is parallel to the longitudinal axis of the trunk and passes through its centre (the pith);
- tangential plane, which is parallel to the longitudinal axis of the trunk and tangent to any of its growth rings.

Anatomy – microscopic level

At the microscopic level, the anatomical structure of wood changes between softwoods and hardwoods, as these are made of different cell types. Softwoods have two basic cell types: tracheids and parenchyma cells. Tracheids are very long cells (the length being around 100 times the width) and form about nine-tenths of the woody material.

Hardwoods have a more complex structure, with a larger number of basic types of cells, which show greater variation in shape and dimension. Hardwoods have vessels, which conduct water and are formed by cells (vessel elements) aligned in the longitudinal direction of the trunk. Vessels are much shorter than the tracheids present in softwoods, can have a small or large diameter and can be arranged in different patterns. The porous nature of hardwoods is due to the abundant presence of vessels. Fibres are another important cell type and offer mechanical support within the woody material; this is why the density and strength of timber depends upon the thickness of the fibres' cell walls. Parenchyma cells are arranged in a more complex and varied manner than in softwoods.

Cell walls mostly consist of three different types of materials: lignin, cellulose and hemicellulose. In very simple terms, cellulose can be considered as a very long molecule with great tensile strength, which makes up macromolecules (microfibrils) that are part of the cell wall. Lignin is a matrix material in which the microfibrils are distributed; and hemicellulose is made of smaller molecules that improve the bond between lignin and cellulose.

Durability

Wood is vulnerable to different types of biological attack, by bacteria, insects, fungi and marine borers.

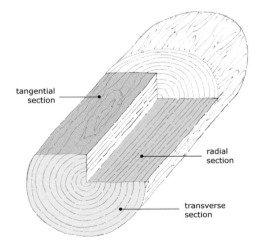

tangential section

radial section

transverse section

Fig. 1.3. The thermo-physical and mechanical properties of wood are better understood in reference to the three anatomical sections: transverse, radial and tangential.

Some insects attack wood because they feed on it (for example longhorn beetles and common furniture beetles); others because they form their nest inside it, but do not eat it. Fungi can cause different types of rot, depending on the components of the woody material that they can decompose and consume. For instance, brown rot is caused by fungi that break down cellulose and hemicellulose, and leave lignin intact; white rot, conversely, is caused by fungi that decompose lignin. Most types of fungi can only proliferate in moist wood: this means that the level of vulnerability of wood is directly proportional to its moisture content.

Natural defects

Wood is a highly variable material and can contain a number of natural defects, most of which originate from the history of the plant in the forest and the environmental conditions under which it grew and lived. Among other important factors that can be related to the presence of defects in the woody material sourced from a tree are: its growth on flat or sloping terrain, prolonged exposure to strong winds, and wide seasonal or diurnal variations in hygrothermal conditions (temperature and relative humidity of the air).

The size and number of natural defects have a noticeable effect on the properties of wood, especially mechanical ones: this is the reason why wood needs to be attentively inspected, graded and selected for structural applications. In each country, codes and structural standards set out the rules for the structural classification of wood and dictate what defects, and in what size or concentration, can be accepted for each structural class. The method by which the presence of defects is quantified can also vary from country to country.

In structural applications of wood, the presence of defects becomes particularly critical in the proximity of connections between members, where high stresses can form and need to be adequately resisted by the wood to avoid damage or failure.

Knots

The presence of knots is associated with the growth of branches from the trunk. A knot is the part of a branch that is incorporated in the trunk. Knots can be grouped into two types: encased and intergrown.

The extent to which knots can affect the mechanical response of a structural member depends on many parameters, such as their size, whether they are isolated or clustered, their soundness and their position within the member itself, and the type and magnitude of stresses in that location.

The detrimental effect of knots is much more evident in tension than it is in compression. For instance, in a simply supported beam that is subjected to gravitational loads and is bending as a consequence, a knot will have much greater impact if it is located at the bottom of the member (which is in tension) than at the top (which is in compression). In long columns, knots have been demonstrated to lower stiffness values. The influence of knots in roundwood is less pronounced than in sawnwood, chiefly because of the material discontinuity in the latter.

Cross grain

In the idealized tree, the direction of grain is perfectly parallel to the longitudinal direction of the trunk. However, this is often not the case in reality and cross grain is a common defect where the grain is at an angle to the longitudinal direction. Cross grain can be found in both softwoods and hardwoods and can present itself in a variety of configurations; spiral grain is one of the most common and is caused by spiral growth of the fibres around the trunk. Sometimes, cross grain is localized and limited to the area where the growth of a branch disturbed the regular orientation of the fibres around the longitudinal axis of the trunk. This is also the reason why the grain appears deviated around knots. Cross grain heavily affects the mechanical properties of wood, and experimental studies have demonstrated the relationship between the angle of slope and property loss.

Cracks and fissures

Cracks and fissures consist in discontinuity within the woody material. They can be caused by a variety of factors, some of which are associated with the felling and drying processes, others with the history of the living plant in the forest and related events. Once a trunk has been felled, the magnitude and distribution of internal stresses change and might result in cracks. Similarly, when wood loses part of its moisture content during the drying season or process, it is prone to the formation of cracks.

Reaction wood

Reaction wood is abnormal tissue that can grow within the leaning trunk of a tree. This tissue is called compression wood in softwoods, and tension wood in hardwoods. Compression wood forms on the lower side of the inclined trunk, while tension wood forms mostly, but not exclusively, on the upper side. Unsurprisingly, the tendency to develop reaction wood differs across species. Although not all the mechanical properties of reaction wood are poorer than those of clear wood, it is generally preferable (if not compulsory) to eliminate it, due to its abnormal behaviour and altered workability.

A pitch pocket (or resin pocket) is an opening within the woody material that contains resin; they can be found in some softwoods such as pine, spruce and larch. Since pitch pockets cause discontinuity within the woody material, they can result in loss of mechanical strength.

Thermo-Physical Properties

Anisotropy

Wood is a strongly anisotropic material, in that most of its physical and mechanical properties vary in the three anatomical directions that have been previously described: the longitudinal direction (parallel to the grain) and the two directions across the grain, radial and tangential. Therefore, when describing a property, especially in quantitative terms, it is in most cases necessary to specify to which direction it refers, or in which direction it has been measured. A sound understanding of the effects of anisotropy is key for designers to specify timber components correctly and to design buildings that employ timber constructional techniques.

Anisotropy noticeably affects the way in which timber changes volume due to fluctuations in its moisture content, and the way in which a structural member responds to external actions exerted in the three different directions.

Hygroscopicity and dimensional movement

Wood is a very hygroscopic material, which means that it can easily exchange moisture (both liquids and vapour) with the surrounding environment. The rate at which wood exchanges moisture with the air depends essentially on three factors: the quantity of water currently contained inside the wood, and the temperature and relative humidity of the air. The same piece of wood exhibits different thermophysical properties and mechanical response to external actions depending on the amount of water that it contains, referred to as moisture content. More precisely, moisture content (MC) is defined as the mass of water contained in the wood divided by the mass of the ovendry wood. Although MC is expressed as a percentage, its maximum value can be much more than 100 per cent: for instance, the MC of green (unseasoned) wood can range greatly, between about 30 per cent and over 200 per cent. In green wood, MC can have different values between heartwood and sapwood, which depend on the species. It is normal for wood to undergo changes in MC as environmental conditions vary over time: a wood component in a building is exposed to fluctuations in the air around it (relative humidity and temperature) not only throughout the year (changes between one season and the next) but also throughout the day. Therefore, a wood component will undergo variations in MC as a result of these environmental variations, and the rate at which it does so will depend on whether it is has been previously treated or modified. Good design and specification should always take into account the possible variations of MC within timber building components, both structural and non-structural. The MC value at which timber is not exchanging moisture with the surrounding environment (neither absorbing nor releasing moisture) is called equilibrium moisture content (EMC).

While the exchange of moisture between wood and air is a relatively slow process, the exchange between wood and liquid water can be much faster. This means that wood can undergo rapid changes in MC if exposed to water, due to capillary action, especially if water is in contact with the end-grain. Unlike absorption of vapour, absorption of liquid water can even increase MC above fibre-saturation point.

Wood is dimensionally stable when its MC is above fibre-saturation point. Conversely, if MC is below this threshold, wood will undergo changes in volume as it exchanges moisture with the environment: it will expand (swell) during adsorption and contract (shrink) during desorption. The macroscopic variation in volume reflects the same phenomenon at the microscopic level: due to exchange of moisture, the walls of the cells undergo changes in volume.

The extent to which wood shrinks and swells as a result of changing MC varies greatly along the three anatomical axes, due to its anisotropy. Volume changes are minimal along the longitudinal axis of the trunk, but they are much greater in the radial direction and even greater in the tangential direction. Shrinking or swelling in the tangential direction is indeed about twice as great as in the radial direction. Due to this complex behaviour and marked differentiation between the three anatomical axes, a piece of wood can become distorted when it dries, especially if the drying process is rapid. It can, for instance, warp or split and this could compromise its suitability for

the fabrication of a building component. Distortion and the appearance of splits and checks in a timber component can also happen during its service life, with repercussions that can vary from poorer appearance to decreased structural performance.

Thermal behaviour

Thermal conductivity of any given type of wood will vary, like most of its properties, depending on its MC. The conductivity of softwoods at 12 per cent MC is around 0.12-0.14 W/(m·K): this is an order of magnitude greater than materials typically used for thermal insulation, whose conductivity is around 0.020-0.035 W/(m·K).

Wood that has been completely dried (ovendry wood) expands when its temperature increases and contracts when it decreases, similar to most materials. The coefficient of thermal expansion reflects the anisotropic nature of wood: species and specific gravity do not affect the coefficient in the direction parallel to the grain (longitudinal direction) but do affect it in the radial and tangential directions. The dimensional change of wood that contains some moisture (as opposed to ovendry wood) follows a more complex mechanism. If the temperature of moist wood increases, the wood will initially tend to expand slightly following normal thermal expansion, but it will soon start to release part of its moisture and to contract as a consequence. These two behaviours combined will ultimately result in shrinkage as net dimensional change (because contraction due to desorption will prevail over expansion).

Mechanical Properties

Instantaneous behaviour

The structural response of timber members is rather complex. An initial simplification can be made for short-term loading conditions that cause low stress levels: wood can be considered as a material that fully adheres to the principles of elasticity. Therefore, we can assume that, in a wood member, deformation is directly proportional to the level of stress induced by the loads applied and is completely reversible. In other words, we assume the member to deform instantaneously when loaded and to revert to its original configuration immediately after unloading. This also means that we expect the wood member to respond instantaneously to both loading and unloading, without any changes in deformation if there are no changes in the loading conditions and no associated changes in stress levels.

Under this simple, elastic model, the constant of proportionality between stress and strain (or deformation) is the modulus of elasticity, which, due to wood being anisotropic, needs to be differentiated between the three anatomical axes. This means that three moduli of elasticity are to be considered: in the longitudinal direction (highest), radial direction (intermediate) and tangential direction (lowest).

When heavy loads are applied on a timber structural member that induce high stress levels, it will stop obeying the laws of elasticity and will exhibit a plastic response: this means that part of the deformation will remain after the loads have been fully removed. If the exerted loads are even greater, the wood member will eventually fail by breaking.

The modulus of rupture is the parameter used to measure the strength of wood in bending up to the elastic limit (but not beyond it). Other measures of strength must, once again, take into account the different behaviour along the anatomical axes. For instance, compressive strength is generally examined under two criteria: parallel to grain and perpendicular to grain. The former, for any given wood species, tends to be one order of magnitude greater than the latter. For example, for Sitka spruce at 12 per cent MC, compressive strength is 38.7MPa parallel to grain, but only 4.0MPa perpendicular to grain (experimental data from Forest Products Laboratory, 2010).

Structural classes

Standard BS EN 338 defines the structural classes of timber, in terms of its characteristic strength, stiffness and density. Different groups of classes are introduced: the classes for softwoods all have a C prefix (for coniferous), while the classes for hardwoods have a D prefix (for deciduous). The number following the C or D prefix designates the characteristic bending strength of the wood.

For instance, class C24 is for softwood with characteristic bending strength of 24N/mm². Classes prefixed T (for tension) apply to softwoods used to fabricate engineered wood in which tension will be the predominant stress.

Creep: time-dependent behaviour

While the idealized assumption of elasticity for timber structures is very convenient for its simplicity and for computational purposes, it does not reflect their complex behaviour and can lead to poor, if not unsafe, design decisions. In reality, timber is a viscoelastic material and its mechanical response to external forces is the combination of two different properties, elasticity and viscosity, which yield immediate and slow responses, respectively, to the same actions.

Let us imagine that a timber member is subjected to a prolonged, constant load: it deforms as soon as the load is applied, and this instantaneous response is governed by the laws of elasticity. The deformation keeps increasing over time, governed by the laws of viscosity; this time-dependent behaviour is called creep. The rate at which the deformation increases over time however is not constant: initially the deformation increases more rapidly; then more slowly, until no more deformation occurs. If the load is removed from the timber member, a similar phenomenon will be observed. Part of the deformation will recover immediately (instantaneous, elastic response); then the deformation will continue to decrease over time, initially more rapidly and then more slowly until no changes in deformation will happen (time-dependent, creep response). However, at the end of this process, the deformation will not have completely recovered: a small portion of it is irreversible.

Creep occurs even when small loads are applied and low levels of stress are induced inside the structural members. Under typical service conditions and when constant loads have been applied for numerous years, the creep component of the total deformation can be equal to the instantaneous component. If the prolonged loads are sufficiently high, creep deformation can even lead to failure of a structural member.

Structural standards in different countries allow designers to account for creep behaviour for permanent or prolonged loads in a straightforward manner, without making calculation procedures too lengthy or onerous. It is important that designers appreciate this time-dependent behaviour of timber structures, when working on new buildings or when consolidating existing ones.

Silviculture

Global trends in the timber industry

A reliable source of information for world trends in the timber industry is the Global Forest Products, Facts and Figures report from the Food and Agriculture Organization of the United Nations[1]. It divides timber production into the following categories: roundwood (used for any purposes other than energy), sawnwood, wood-based panels, fibre furnish and paper, and wood fuel.

Roundwood

Roundwood comprises pulpwood, sawlogs and veneer logs. The five largest producers of industrial roundwood are the United States of America, the Russian Federation, China, Brazil and Canada, which, combined, account for 53 per cent of global removals of roundwood.

Exports of roundwood are exiguous compared to other industries. New Zealand became the largest exporter in 2018, followed by the United States, Canada and the Czech Republic. The major producers of roundwood are also its largest consumers, with the Asia-Pacific region being the major importer, due to its relatively small production base.

Sawnwood

Sawnwood is wood that has been processed through sawing or chipping. The major producers of sawnwood are China, the United States of America, Canada, the Russian Federation and Germany, with a combined 58 per cent share of world production in 2018.

The largest exporters are Canada, the Russian Federation, Germany, Sweden and Finland. The major importers are China, the United States, the United Kingdom, Japan and Germany. China, the United States, Germany and Japan are also the major consumers, alongside Canada.

Wood-based panels

This category includes plywood, laminated veneer lumber, particleboard, oriented-strand board (OSB) and fibreboard (all described in Chapter 2). The largest producers are China, the United States, the Russian Federation, Germany and Canada, with a 69 per cent share of global production. These countries are also the major consumers alongside Poland.

The largest exporters are China, Canada, Germany, the Russian Federation, Malaysia and Thailand. The main importers are the United States, Germany, Japan, Poland and the United Kingdom.

Other forestry products

Other silvicultural activity is dedicated to the production of paper and paperboard, mainly used for packaging in the building industry. The United States and China dominate this market. Wood destined for fuel, instead, mostly originates from Africa and Latin America.

The timber industry in the United Kingdom

The United Kingdom (UK) does not play a key role in the global timber trade. Softwood accounts for the majority of British silvicultural practice: for instance, it constituted 92 per cent of total wood production in 2020[2]. The UK, for this reason, does not have the natural capacity to meet its own demand for hardwood and runs a timber-trade deficit with other countries: in 2020, it imported 7.2 million m³ of sawnwood but produced 3.4 million m³ [2]. It is worth noting that, out of 157 sawmills currently operating in the UK, 104 are exclusively dedicated to softwood[3].

The production of softwood and hardwood is dominated by Scotland and England, respectively. Climate affects the quality of wood: British softwood tends to exhibit lower mechanical properties than its Canadian and Scandinavian counterparts. This is because colder climates encourage a slower growth rate in trees, which has been demonstrated to favourably influence density and structural properties. As a result, UK-grown softwood tends to be used more for fencing and packaging than in construction[4].

Imports of sawn softwood mostly come from the European Union, with Sweden, Latvia and Finland providing the largest portion of trade. The UK imports particleboard from Germany, France and Latvia; fibreboard from Ireland, Germany and Spain; and hardwood from Estonia. By contrast, other products arrive from outside the European Union, with China and Brazil contributing most of the plywood, and the US and Canada most wood-pellets[5].

The management of UK forests is overseen by several entities: Forestry England, Forestry Commission (England), Natural Resources Wales, Forestry and Land Scotland, Scottish Forestry and the Forest Service (Northern Ireland). These bodies ensure the long-term sustainability of forests by issuing felling licences and Forest Management Plans, which set out the future development and strategies for individual woodlands.

Timber trade is regulated by the Timber Procurement Policy (TPP), which ensures the legality and sustainability of wood products, by asking producers to achieve official certification (such as FSC or PEFC, both explained in Chapter 3) or to present a case study

Type of ownership	England	Wales	Scotland	Northern Ireland	UK total
Conifers					
FE/FLS/NRW/FS	151	98	426	55	730
Private sector	190	54	653	8	905
Total	**341**	**152**	**1079**	**63**	**1635**
Broadleaves					
FE/FLS/NRW/FS	64	19	41	7	131
Private sector	907	138	347	48	1440
Total	**971**	**157**	**388**	**55**	**1571**

Table 1.1 Woodland area in the UK, by ownership and forest type, in thousand hectares. FE: Forestry England, FLS: Forestry and Land Scotland, NRW: Natural Resources Wales, FS: Forest Service Northern Ireland. (Source: Forestry Commission, 2020)

Year	Softwood			Hardwood		
	FE/FLS/NRW/FS	Private	Total softwood	FE/FLS/NRW/FS	Private	Total hardwood
2000	4,850	2,572	7,422	130	524	654
2001	4,604	2,891	7,494	145	486	632
2002	4,650	2,793	7,443	118	502	620
2003	4,817	3,091	7,907	117	445	562
2004	4,894	3,246	8,141	113	399	513
2005	4,579	3,499	8,077	101	492	593
2006	4,582	3,661	8,243	45	392	438
2007	4,653	4,083	8,736	40	400	440
2008	4,415	3,823	8,238	43	388	431
2009	5,126	3,266	8,392	87	449	536
2010	4,625	4,633	9,258	70	464	534
2011	4,870	5,186	10,056	75	465	540
2012	4,836	5,259	10,095	55	478	533
2013	5,084	5,852	10,936	78	453	531
2014	4,900	6,627	11,527	71	465	536
2015	4,691	5,968	10,659	73	492	565
2016	5,011	5,734	10,745	68	528	596
2017	4,761	6,075	10,836	85	652	737
2018	4,522	6,827	11,349	88	746	835
2019	3,937	5,890	9,828	68	801	869
2020	4,616	5,434	10,050	84	830	913

Table 1.2 Roundwood removals in the UK, by ownership and wood type, in thousand green tonnes. FE: Forestry England, FLS: Forestry and Land Scotland, NRW: Natural Resources Wales, FS: Forest Service Northern Ireland. (Source: Forestry Commission, 2021)

Fig. 1.4. A semi-automated sawmill in Scotland. The trees have been felled and the trunks limbed and bucked (cut to the same length). The logs thus obtained are now loaded onto a conveyor belt that takes them into the building where they will be further processed.

with credible evidence, which will then be assessed on an individual basis[6]. This framework is complemented by the European Union Timber Regulation and the Forest Law Enforcement, Governance and Trade, which prohibit trading with products from unlawful logging.

The timber industry in North America

The United States has become one of the largest traders in the global timber industry, which is one of the top ten employers across forty-eight American states. Oregon is the top producer of softwood[7], followed by Georgia, Arkansas, Mississippi, Alabama and North Carolina[8], while Pennsylvania, Tennessee, Kentucky, North Carolina and Virginia produce most of the hardwood[9].

The United States Forest Service is the agency of the US Department of Agriculture that administers 154 national forests and 20 national grasslands. It sells permits for wood removals. Additionally, individual states have their own forestry bodies and regulations.

Given its wealth of natural resources, it is not surprising that Canada's timber industry plays a key role in the nation's economy. In 2019, Canada produced 978,600m³ of hardwood and 57,653,200m³ of softwood[10]. Of the total area of woodland in Canada, 90 per cent is publicly owned by the provinces or territories, 4 per cent belongs to the federal government, and 6 per cent is privately owned[11]. By law, forest management plans must be put in place before any harvesting can start. These plans must be approved by the province or territory and should emphasize community participation and respect for indigenous peoples.

Responsible forestry management

Woodland occupies 31 per cent of the earth[12] and plays a key role in keeping a balanced ecosystem, especially because trees absorb carbon dioxide. Appropriate forest management can contribute towards mitigating climate change, with approaches that include reforestation (replacing harvested trees with new trees) and afforestation (planting trees where there are none). A wider palette of tree species ensures diversity and the long-term security of forests against climate change and pests. Finally, wood harvesting does not necessarily translate into complete disruption to wildlife, as careful planning can incorporate habitat maintenance and enhancement, for example by leaving soft edges (a gradual transition from open ground to forest) or by facilitating the juxtaposition of habitats (ensuring that habitat elements are located next to other critical components for the enhancement of wildlife)[13].

The UK Forestry Standard[14] includes the following elements in its requirements for responsible wood management: contribution to biodiversity, mitigation of climate change, respect for historic environments, preservation of landscape, inclusion of people and preservation of water and soil. National protection frameworks are supported by the United Nations' six Global Forest Goals: the reversion of forest loss, the enhancement of forest economies, the increase in protected woodland, the mobilization of investment in sustainable forestry, the promotion of governance frameworks at national and international level for the sustainable management of forests, and the establishment of international collaboration[15]. The United Nations places strong emphasis on the inclusion and respect for local communities and indigenous people in forest management. The World Heritage initiative, by the United Nations Educational, Scientific and Cultural Organization, also ensures that places of outstanding cultural and natural beauty are maintained, many of which include woodlands. Several protective international treaties and conventions are in force, such as the International Tropical Timber Agreement, Convention on Biological Diversity and the International Arrangement on Forests[16].

Although the rate of deforestation is decreasing, agricultural expansion continues to drive the reduction in woodland mass[15]. More worryingly, illegal logging remains a huge risk to the long-term sustainability of forests with a share of 15 per cent and 30 per cent of global timber trade, with special incidence in the Amazon Basin, Central Africa and Southeast Asia, where some of the most important ecosystems are located[17]. In the UK and the European Union, the requirements set by the Timber Procurement Policy and the European Union Timber Regulation fully ban trading timber products originating from illegal logging. In the United States, the Lacey Act of 1900, which forbids trading with plants and animals of illegal origin, was amended in 2008 to include timber[18]. These legislative measures show that there is political will to eradicate illegal timber activity worldwide, with its devastating effects on the environment, human rights and wildlife.

Fig. 1.5. Example of stump regeneration in a coniferous forest. This process ensures the long-term sustainability of felling by replacing harvested trees with new ones. (Photo: Woodknowledge Wales & Rosie Anthony)

Notes

[1] Food and Agriculture Organization of the United Nations, 2018

[2] Forest Research, 2021

[3] Forest Research, 2019

[4] Ross, 2011; Davies, 2013; Forest Research, 2021

[5] Forest Research, 2012

[6] Department for Environment, Food and Rural Affairs, 2013

[7] Oregon Forest Resources Institute, 2016

[8] United States Forest Service, 2021

[9] Luppold et al., 2017

[10] Canadian Forest Service, 2020

[11] Natural Resources Canada, 2020

[12] Roux et al., 2020

[13] McEvoy, 2012

[14] Forestry Commission, 2017

[15] United Nations, Department of Economic and Social Affairs, 2019; Food and Agriculture Organization of the United Nations, 2020

[16] Sotirov et al., 2020

[17] Interpol, 2019

[18] U.S. Fish and Wildlife Service, ca.2008

Chapter Two

Treated, Modified and Engineered Wood

Preservative Treatments

Assessing the need for treatment

Preservative treatment is performed to increase the durability of timber and make it less susceptible to biological attack and consequent deterioration by insects, fungi, bacteria or marine borers. Thus, preserving timber lowers replacement costs and contributes to better, more efficient and sustainable utilization of forest products. The necessity for treatment should be evaluated against a variety of factors: the natural durability of the wood species, the service conditions under which the wood components will be used (expected levels of relative humidity and exposure to moisture), the presence or absence of sapwood, the expected service life of the components, and the other materials with which the timber components will be in contact (for example metal fixings or flashings, which might be prone to accelerated corrosion).

Fungal attack is more likely to occur in sapwood than in heartwood, therefore it is important to understand whether any sapwood is contained in the wooden product for which treatment is to be decided. Since different wood species show different proportions of heartwood and sapwood (as discussed in Chapter 1) and different levels of heartwood penetrability, they also exhibit different levels of treatability.

In Europe, standard BS EN 350 defines five classes of natural durability of the heartwood relative to

fungal decay: these range from class 1 (very durable) to class 5 (not durable). Sapwood is always considered as class 5, unless evidence has shown that for some species this is incorrect. The same European standard also deals with resistance to insect attack (with two classes: durable and not durable) and with resistance to attack by termites and marine borers (with three classes: durable, moderately durable and not durable).

From a chemical point of view, preservatives can be divided into two main categories: water-borne and oil-borne. The number of possible active ingredients in water-borne preservatives is very large, and includes copper, chromium, zinc, boron and arsenic compounds. The chemicals permitted for timber preservation vary between countries and are subject to changes in the legislation over time, as more research is conducted into their impact on the environment and on human and animal health. Creosote, for example, is a category of chemicals that are very efficacious as active ingredients in oil-borne preservatives and were widely used in numerous countries. However, due to its toxicity (associated with hazards for human health and ecosystems), use of creosote has been widely reduced since the 2000s. The level of protection obtained through a treatment process depends upon the chemicals used, their degree of penetration into the woody material and their retention over time.

Wood composites based on flakes or fibres are generally protected from biological attack during their manufacturing process, when preservatives are used. Other composite wood products such as glulam or plywood can be treated similarly to sawn timber after they have been manufactured.

OPPOSITE: **Fig. 2.1.** Roof constructed of trussed rafters. (Photo: Woodknowledge Wales & Rosie Anthony)

Material compatibility

When specifying metal fixings for preservative-treated timber, designers should ensure that they are chemically compatible with the substances contained in the preservative used. Some treatments can corrode metals, therefore stainless- or galvanized-steel fixings should be utilized, or in some instances it might be possible to separate the fixings from the wood by interposing plastic spacers. Other incompatibilities are possible, for example, some water-borne preservative treatments can diminish the effectiveness of PVA-based adhesive.

Whole-section treatments

Whole-section treatments typically involve the insertion of timber pieces into large metal cylinders; here, vacuum is applied and subsequently the wood is immersed into preservative solutions. Inside the cylinder, impregnation can be performed under low or high pressure.

For exposed timber components, it is important to consider that treatments might affect the colour or appearance of the wood. There are processes whereby the wood is not only treated but also pigmented, to eliminate the need to apply colour during the installation phase.

Localized supplementary treatments

If, after preservative treatment, a timber member is subjected to localized on-site operations such as cross-cutting, drilling or notching, then it might be necessary to reinstate protection in the affected areas by applying products compatible with the previous treatment, either with a brush or by spraying. Areas around mechanical fixings and exposed end-grain in joints should also receive further protection on site.

Various types of sealants are available, with different chemical formulations; for instance, they can be based on natural oils and waxes, on paraffin or on acrylic substances, and can be mixed with water-repellent additives and siccatives (drying agents).

Modification of Timber

Modification of wood is aimed at improving its properties and performance over time: increasing durability by reducing its vulnerability to biological attack (fungi or insects), increasing hardness, dimensional stability and resistance to acids, bases or ultraviolet radiation, and enhancing appearance. However, some modification processes can also have undesired effects, such as the reduction of some mechanical properties; therefore, designers and specifiers should carefully assess the advantages and disadvantages associated with the type of modified wood that they select. Manufacturers should always be able to provide clear, evidence-based data on both the benefits and disadvantages that arise from their processes. Due to the cost of the industrial processes and the chemicals needed for modification, modified wood and wood-based products tend to be more expensive than solid timber, which results in them being specified only when the benefits are sufficient to justify the additional cost.

All types of permanent modification make the woody material less hygroscopic and reduce its equilibrium moisture content. The result is wood with increased dimensional stability. This is particularly beneficial for timber components exposed to wide fluctuations in relative humidity or to the elements if in exterior locations. If wooden building components change less in dimension, then the coatings applied on their surfaces (if any) will remain effective for a longer time: this means that maintenance cycles and re-application of coatings will need to be less frequent, with economic and environmental benefits.

Among the mechanical properties that can be enhanced by modification processes is hardness; that is, the resistance to abrasion – which is crucial in applications such as decking or flooring.

In a sense, strength can also be augmented, in that modified wood is less prone to absorb water and strength is higher when internal moisture content is lower.

One mechanical property that can be negatively affected by modification is brittleness. For instance, acetylation can render the woody material more brittle, and this should be an important aspect to consider in structural applications.

Chemical processes

In chemical processes, timber is impregnated with suitable substances at high-pressure levels. Sapwood is generally easier to modify than heartwood, therefore permeable species are preferred (such as radiata pine), as the whole section can be modified. If, conversely, less permeable species are used (such as Southern yellow pine or redwood), modification will only involve the outer surfaces of the sections. Established methods include acetylation and furfurylation, which are based on the use of acetic anhydride and furfuryl alcohol, respectively. The choice of species and level of modification (full or partial) would depend on the type of application envisaged for the building products. In some applications, partial modification can be sufficient to achieve the desired performance level.

Chemical processes result in augmented dimensional stability and resistance to fungal attack but might increase brittleness. Some manufacturers produce medium-density fibreboard (MDF) from acetylated fibres: this noticeably increases its dimensional stability and broadens its range of suitable applications.

Thermal processes

Thermal processes involve heating timber sections in a controlled environment. Temperature and duration of treatment vary across methods. During the process, the wood can either be kept in an atmosphere with reduced oxygen, or under oil or steam.

The thermal treatment irreversibly changes the structure of the polymers contained in the wood. Dimensional stability and durability are generally improved, but some processes tend to impoverish the mechanical properties of wood: they can reduce modulus of rupture, impact toughness or abrasion resistance, and increase brittleness and the occurrence of cracks or splits. The appearance of wood also changes: woods that are naturally pale tend to acquire a darker colour.

Impregnation processes

Wood can be impregnated at high pressure with substances that, by creating compounds inside its tissues, yield enhanced durability, stability and density. Permeable species are preferred for impregnation. If performed on species with low permeability, these processes might only be effective on the surfaces of the timbers and have minimal impact on the innermost layers; hence, they become more similar to the preservative treatments seen above than to the other types of modification processes.

Engineered Timber

Engineered wood allows improvement of the properties of sawn wood and the fabrication of efficient products – for both structural and non-structural purposes – with augmented mechanical properties (such as strength and stiffness), lower economic cost and increased environmental sustainability. Cutting wood with natural defects into smaller parts that can be re-arranged into a new product means that the defects become less important and affect the properties of the final product much less than they would the original sawn section.

Engineered wood products can be made from smaller trees than their sawn-timber counterparts;

this permits shorter growing times for trees, with an advantage for sustainable forest management. In addition, as will be seen in the next sub-sections, wood-based composites can also use invasive timber species, and by-products and waste generated in sawmills.

The parts of wood that can be used in engineered products vary widely in size and shape: from boards and lamellae to veneers, flakes, shavings, wafers, fibres and particles. The most common adhesives used are thermosetting resins (for example formaldehyde compounds and isocyanate). Some adhesive types cannot be exposed to water for sustained periods of time and are incompatible with some chemicals used for preservative or fire-resistant treatments. Most wood-based products have lower hygroscopicity than natural wood, thanks to additives such as wax and to the pressure and heat treatments that they receive during manufacturing. Other additives can be used to increase resistance to fire and biodeterioration.

The properties of wood-based composites are more homogeneous than those of solid timber, which as discussed in Chapter 1 are variable even within the same log. Most engineered products are the result of the ingenious rearrangement and combination of different parts and layers of wood to obtain the desired characteristics and performance levels.

Structural composite lumber (SCL)

Structural composite lumber is a group of materials fabricated from strands or layers (lamellae) of timber connected by means of structural adhesives. Cross-laminated timber (CLT) is one of these materials, but is dealt with in Chapter 6, along with other types of massive panels. SCL members often have sizes comparable to those achievable with solid wood and can be produced from wood species that are not generally used for structural purposes (for example, aspen). However, SCL structural members generally have better mechanical properties than sawn wood. SCL can also be employed to fabricate components of I-joists (or of other engineered-wood products), doors and windows, as an alternative to solid timber.

Laminated veneer lumber (LVL)

LVL consists of parallel lamellae bonded with adhesive, and is relatively similar in appearance to plywood. It can be employed for posts and flexural members (beams, joists, flanges of I-joists and so on). The thickness of the veneers typically ranges between 2 and 3mm.

Parallel-strand lumber (PSL)

PSL is fabricated from narrow strips of wood that are at least 0.6m long and can be sourced from waste material generated during the manufacturing of LVL or plywood. The strips are mainly arranged parallel to the length of the member and glued together. PSL is used for applications that entail high axial loads (for example posts), but also in flexural members.

Laminated-strand lumber (LSL)

LSL consists of flaked wood strands glued together. It is utilized for studs, posts and joists.

Engineered boards and panels

Oriented-strand board (OSB)

OSB panels are formed by blending dry wood strands with resins and then pressing and heating them. The strands are obtained from tree logs or from waste materials produced in sawmills; they are of different sizes and are clearly visible on the faces of the boards. Both softwoods (for example pine or spruce) and hardwoods can be utilized for OSB production. In

North America, aspen is the most utilized species. In the typical aspect ratio, the width of the strands is one-third of the length.

OSB consists generally of three layers: in the two outer layers, the strands are longer and arranged in the longitudinal direction of the panel; in the middle layer, the strands are arranged either in the transverse direction or randomly. This results in the panels having higher bending strength and stiffness parallel to their longitudinal axis.

Over time, the manufacturing process of OSB has been refined and panels with better mechanical properties than in the past can now be produced. Although OSB does not have as good properties as plywood, it is more economical and, as a consequence, has replaced plywood in applications in which structural requirements are not too high. OSB is widely employed as a sheathing material and for structural decks.

Plywood

Plywood is fabricated by gluing together very thin sheets (or veneers) of wood, typically 1–2mm thick. It consists of an odd number of layers: in every layer, the grain is oriented perpendicular to the adjacent layers. Each layer can consist of one or more veneers. Plywood is a very flexible and versatile material and can be given a curvature. Plywood sheets can be used in a wide range of applications, to form structural decks or surfaces between joists or rafters, in floor and roof elements, or as sheathing components in wall construction. Plywood can also be utilized as a component in other engineered-wood products, such as I-joists, roof/floor panelized systems or box beams. The physical and mechanical properties of plywood depend on a number of factors, including the quality of the plies and of the glue, the layer arrangement and the achieved level of bonding between the veneers.

Thanks to the alternating direction of grain in its layers, plywood exhibits good bending strength and rigidity both in the longitudinal and transversal directions of the panels. The properties in the longitudinal direction are generally slightly higher, as there is one more layer orientated in this direction; however, the difference is much less significant than in sawn timber. In other words, alternating the direction of grain compensates, at least partially, for the anisotropy of solid wood (*see* Chapter 1).

Plywood has very good dimensional stability and minimal tendency to swell along the edges: this makes glued tongue-and-groove joints very successful even under service conditions that include some exposure to water. Thanks to its good resistance to splitting, a plywood panel can receive mechanical fixings near its edges. Special types of plywood are fabricated to be exposed: the outer layers have improved appearance and sometimes are pigmented.

The species used to fabricate construction plywood are typically softwoods (especially Douglas fir or Southern yellow pine), but hardwoods are also employed (for example beech, birch and alder), especially where the panels are exposed.

Brief history of plywood

Plywood constitutes one of the earliest forms of modified wood. Ancient Egyptians used veneer from good-quality wood to give furniture or caskets a luxurious finish[1]. Pliny the Elder remarks on the superior strength of this material compared to solid wood in his volume dedicated to the history and properties of timber[2], although its main use in Ancient Rome continued to be decorative. Classical Chinese manufacturers also made use of plywood for furniture, especially as it allowed them to create pieces in elaborate shapes and colours.

In Europe, the eighteenth century welcomed a boom in expensive and intricate furniture that relied on plywood and expert craftmanship[3]. A prime example of plywood design during this period is the cylinder desk commissioned by King Louis XV of France. This piece, called *Bureau du Roi* and located in the Palace of Versailles, took advantage of the varied natural patterns of wood grain and the flexibility afforded by plywood to offer a sumptuous, yet practical, solution.

It was not until the advent of the Industrial Revolution that mass production of veneer became possible, especially with the introduction of mechanized tools such as the bandsaw or the Bentham planer. It was common practice to improve the appearance of lower-grade furniture by covering it with glued plies of better-quality wood. Mass-produced plywood was employed for packing boxes or sawing machines[3].

Moulded plywood was another remarkable development during the nineteenth century. Bending plywood allowed designers to create elegant and comfortable furniture that fitted the human anatomy, as illustrated by the chair prototypes created by American furniture-makers John Henry Belter and Isaac Cole[3]. In the twentieth century, Alvar Aalto and Charles and Ray Eames capitalized on the techniques and knowledge earned during the previous century to create striking collections of moulded plywood furniture that followed the principles of ergonomic and minimalist design.

Right until the 1900s, the evolution of plywood was divided between the need to serve the creation of elaborate and opulent designs that required careful craftsmanship, and the introduction of mass-produced veneer into everyday objects. The twentieth century opened new frontiers for plywood with its application to buildings and transport. The Great Depression and its associated housing crisis of the 1930s encouraged the production of low-cost, prefabricated houses with plywood, thanks to its versatility and speed of manufacturing. A significant technological development was the invention of waterproof glues, patented by Dr James Nevin, which facilitated the use of plywood for boats, cars and aviation. Plywood proved to be an elastic and lightweight material that was still strong enough to hold engines. For instance, plywood was adopted for the design of British war aircraft during the Second World War, thanks to its lightness, which resulted in faster aeroplanes[4].

Today, plywood continues to be at the forefront of technological advances, which include the option of operating in virtual design environments.

Particleboard

Particleboard is fabricated from cut wood flakes and, nowadays, also from humbler materials such as sawdust, shavings or sawmill waste, which make the final product economical. The particles are mixed with a sufficient quantity of adhesive and consolidated with heat and pressure. Each board is built up of different layers: unlike OSB, finer particles are concentrated in the outer layers and coarser ones in the core. This type of arrangement produces smooth surfaces that lend themselves to other operations such as lamination or painting.

Particleboard is available in different levels of density and mechanical properties. Low-density board can be used to fabricate sound-absorbing panels, while higher-density board for structural decking in floor construction. The mechanical characteristics of particleboard are generally lower than those of fibreboard.

Cement-bonded particleboard

In this type of particleboard, the wood components are bonded by mixing with cement and water.

Different types of cement can be used, Portland being the most common and magnesia cement a viable alternative. This material is denser than other wood-based products. Low-density board can be used for ceiling panels, while high-density board is more suited to flooring and roofing applications.

Fibreboard

Fibreboard is available in a wide range of densities: hardboard (high density), medium-density fibreboard (MDF) and softboard (low density).

Fibreboard can be produced either by dry or wet processes. Heat and pressure treatments are used to enhance the mechanical properties of the panels, and to make them more water-repellent and dimensionally stable.

Hardboard is employed for wall and floor construction. MDF is used predominantly in the furniture industry and, to a lesser extent, in construction (for example, the manufacturing of doors). Softboard is used in a range of applications: thermal insulation, sound-absorbing panels, sheathing and roof decking.

Composite joists

I-joists

I-joists can be made from different combinations of materials. The flanges can be fabricated from solid sawn wood or from LVL, whereas the webs can be

Fig. 2.2. Child's chair designed by Gardner & Company (ca.1872). The full possibilities of moulded plywood were investigated during the mid-nineteenth century, when furniture designers took advantage of the strength and flexibility of this material to create furniture that better fitted the human body. (Photo: Brooklyn Museum, CC BY 3.0)

Fig. 2.3. Early photograph of the Beach Pneumatic Train (ca.1873). To solve New York's increasing transport issues, A.E. Beach proposed an underground train whose lightweight and flexible plywood frame could be moved by means of very large fans. The potential of plywood for the transport industry was fully realized in the twentieth century, with its incorporation into the design of automobiles and aeroplanes. (Photo: Public Domain)

made from plywood or OSB. This choice of materials follows structural considerations: normal (bending) stresses are highest in the flanges, so this is where the materials with highest strength are used. The web is mostly subjected to tangential stresses, while normal stresses tend to be very low (near the neutral axis). The flanges have a groove into which the web is inserted and glued.

Open-web joists

Open-web joists consist of wood-based flanges and a discontinuous web. The latter can be made of timber sections or metal components nailed to the flanges. The sections used for the flanges are either made of solid wood or LVL (similarly to I-joists). Thanks to this configuration, open-web joists have reduced weight and make it possible to easily run services through them.

Glued laminated timber (glulam)

Glulam is one of the oldest types of engineered wood. A glulam member is made from timber lamellae with the grain aligned with the length of the member itself, and bonded with structural adhesives. Typical applications include columns, beams, portal frames, rafters and three-hinged arches. The overall structural performance of glulam depends on the quality and structural grade of the wood utilized and the effectiveness of the adhesive bonds. For the latter, it is important to plane the surfaces of the lamellae, because smooth surfaces can more easily be laminated and glued together.

In flexural members such as beams, the lamellae are generally arranged flatwise, which means that the cross-section consists of different layers glued one on top of the other. The lamellae at the top and bottom of beams are generally made from higher-strength wood, while the middle lamellae (near the neutral axis) are made from lower-strength timber, following the distribution of bending stresses under typical loading conditions. This type of configuration (referred to as 'bending combination') permits optimal use of materials and makes the glulam members more economical. Typical thicknesses for the lamellae are 40 or 45mm. The advantage of using thicker lamellae is that less adhesive is consumed; however, the mechanical properties might be impoverished, as the material becomes more variable.

In the fabrication of axial members (for example columns), all the lamellae have the same structural grade, so the cross-section has consistent properties (axial combination).

In the fabrication of both bending and axial members, the lamellae that will be in tension need to be made from higher-quality wood, in terms of knots, slope of grain and stiffness. The requirements for the wood to be used in compression are less stringent. This reflects the different behaviour of wood in tension and compression.

Glulam can be fabricated from a broad variety of both softwoods and hardwoods; the wood must have been previously seasoned or dried. Manufacturers can produce glulam members in straight or curved shapes: for the latter, thin lamellae are preferable, as they are more flexible and easier to bend. Long lamellae can be produced by finger-jointing sections of timber. To fabricate a very large cross-section, two (or more) glulam beams can be glued together (each of which is composed of various lamellae).

Glulam members can have a varying cross-section along their length, following structural requirements. One of the advantages of this engineered material lies in the opportunity it offers to build structural members that are much bigger than the trunks from which their wood has been sourced. This is particularly important in contemporary silvicultural practice, whereby relatively small trees are felled in order to shorten forest rotations, with benefits for environmental sustainability.

Modern Methods of Construction

Chapters 4, 5 and 6 will illustrate the principles of some timber Modern Methods of Construction (MMC), which employ the types of treated, modified and engineered products so far discussed. An exhaustive definition of MMC can be found in *Modern Methods of Construction: Introducing the MMC Definition Framework*[5], commissioned by the UK Government. This report does not provide a single definition but captures a set of construction practices that can be included in MMC, such as pre-manufacturing of three- and two-dimensional structural units and non-structural components. As can be gathered from this framework, modified wood and offsite construction play a key role in the implementation of MMC.

A useful categorization[6] of offsite approaches might be based on the level of completeness of building components before they reach a construction site: category 0 encompasses panels or pods with their first skin installed offsite; category 1 designates insulated panels or pods; category 2 includes elements that are finished either inside or outside; category 3 is reserved for panels and pods that are fully finished. Furthermore, plants that produce offsite elements might be categorized into those relying on manual production, those that are semi-automated and those that are fully automated[7]. These categories give an indication of the variety and complexity of MMC. Customers and designers should therefore be aware of the offer available to them and how each solution might respond to their needs.

Uptake

According to the *Annual Survey of UK Structural Timber Markets*[8], an estimated 68,000 new houses were built using timber frames in 2020 in the UK. The 2016 timber frame (TF) share of the total housing stock in each UK country was thus distributed: 83 per cent in Scotland, 22.8 per cent in England, 30.7 per cent in Wales and 17.4 per cent in Northern Ireland[8]. On top of that, the rainy climate in Scotland encourages the adoption of offsite construction as it facilitates more controlled conditions within a factory's protected environment and the erection of buildings that become weather-tight sooner[9]. As of 2020, there are thirty-three companies serving offsite construction in Scotland. In the UK, it is estimated that 7 per cent of the construction sector uses some sort of offsite solutions; this compares to a noticeable 84 per cent of TF houses in Sweden and 7 per cent in the United States[8].

The Timber Utilisation Report [10] reveals an interesting correlation between the rise of single-family dwellings (as opposed to blocks of flats) and the increase of sawn softwood entering the construction industry: detached or semi-detached houses are more likely to be built in wood, therefore driving demand for softwood.

Advantages and disadvantages

The House of Commons' Housing, Communities and Local Government Committee reports the following benefits from MMC: quicker and more predictable delivery, reduction in costs, fewer people on site with improved health and safety for workers, more diverse workforce with an increased proportion of factory-based staff and standardized hours, more efficient use of materials, overall reduction in energy consumption, fewer deliveries to the site with associated reduction in noise, disruption and pollution, and shallower foundations with less ecological disturbance[11].

Furthermore, offsite construction also contributes to resource efficiency, as it facilitates the management of quantities and waste, with fewer storage requirements. Present-day prefabrication also allows for greater customization than it did in the past, when it was characterized by scarce flexibility and generally led to poor architectural results[12].

The advantages of offsite construction ought to be weighed against some disadvantages such as the need for extensive structural testing to analyse performance under different loads and usage. Architects and builders must also adapt to a new set of skills, demands and workflows to utilize offsite construction to its full capacity.

Drivers and barriers

The UK legislature has been favourable to MMC as a viable solution to the pressures arising from the housing crisis, since the Barker Report (a review of housing supply conducted in 2006) encouraged the use of MMC[13]. MMC is indeed seen as a key component in the development of affordable and sustainable housing. By way of illustration, initiatives from Scottish government support MMC through the introduction of additional modern apprenticeships, the Greener Homes Innovation Scheme and extra funding for research[14]. In 2020, the Ministry of Housing, Communities and Local Government confirmed that the UK government views MMC as a large-scale solution to the need to increase the housing stock[15]. The Welsh government also prioritizes MMC as the most effective way to respond to housing demands[16].

A major driver for the implementation of MMC is its potential to alleviate the current skills shortage within the construction industry. Offsite construction requires a lower number of staff with a traditional skills set, such as bricklaying. It can, however, be argued that the skills shortage is displaced rather than solved, with traditional tradespersons (such as carpenters, electricians and plasterers) still needed for building maintenance and site preparation[17]. Additionally, new skills demanded by MMC include project management, quality control procedures and computing to operate automated tools.

However, some barriers to the implementation of MMC, and offsite construction in particular, do still exist. There are high initial costs associated with an MMC project, and the supply chain is ineffective due to low demand – this, in turn, affects transport logistics[14]. In general, lack of investment and knowledge and inertia to innovation are also key barriers for the adoption of MMC[14]. Architects, on the other hand, are sometimes resistant to MMC due to the need to commit to a final design earlier than with on-site techniques that allow for some degree of flexibility during the construction process[18].

The offsite construction market is affected by lack of certainty, difficulties adjusting the property and repairs after damage, barriers for homeowners to secure warranties, insurance and mortgages for MMC homes, a perceived lack of proof of resilience to flood and fire, a less clear planning-permission pathway for MMC projects, and difficulties complying with building regulations and accessing capital. All these factors contribute to the public's perception of offsite houses, which is perhaps the most salient issue affecting the uptake of MMC.

Social aspects

Social perception of MMC continues to be one of the major barriers to adoption. Offsite construction, especially for domestic buildings, is poorly received by the general public. This phenomenon arose from the experience of prefabrication during the post-war period, based on low-cost, temporary solutions[19]. As a result, timber houses tend to be clad in blockwork or brickwork, as these are deemed to provide the building with a safer or more robust appearance. Innovative solutions to satisfy the public include brick slips mechanically fixed to the façade to mimic masonry.

In summary, it is safe to say that more traditional building techniques (such as brick and block) are still widely preferred by the public. By contrast, the uptake and acceptance of MMC in non-domestic projects is higher due to greater levels of investment and knowledge. In this climate, promoting the environmental credentials, cost-effectiveness and speed of MMC is of paramount importance to ensure that its acceptance by the public translates into more governmental support and investment.

Project: Community Centre, Spinelli Refugee Shelter
(*Gemeinschaftshaus Flüchtlingsunterkunft Spinelli*)

Location: Spinelli Barracks, Mannheim, Baden-Württemberg, Germany
Building type: non-residential – recreational
Completion date: 2016
Architectural design: students of Atelier U20, Faculty of Architecture, Technische Universität Kaiserslautern, Germany (under the supervision of Jun. Prof. Stefan Krötsch, Prof. Dr.-Ing. Jürgen Graf and Jun. Prof. Andreas Kretzer). Chosen design by Sandra Gressung, Sascha Ritschel and Tobias Vogel.
Key words: trusses, grid structures, CLT, untreated timber

When refugees arrive in Germany, they have to undergo a long period of inactivity, due to lengthy bureaucratic procedures. The refugee camp located in the former American Spinelli Barracks in Mannheim provided its guests with all the essentials but lacked architectural merit, especially in the communal areas. In order to address this problem, a collaborative initiative was launched at TU Kaiserslautern's Faculty of Architecture: a cohort of eighteen students, supervised by their tutors, started a design-and-build project with twenty-five refugees. The work provided not only the students, but also the refugees, with many opportunities to learn and to acquire new skills. The client was the Regional Council Karlsruhe. Students constructed their building, with the only exception of groundwork and roofing, which were conducted by local contractors. Overall construction only took three months. The larger components were fabricated in an unoccupied hangar of the former military facility, for protection from the weather.

The main building has two open spaces: a smaller and quieter courtyard, fully enclosed and with covered niches, and a larger yard that can accommodate social events. Seating booths are located along the southern and western edges.

The project did not utilize large or advanced machinery, so as to reduce economic costs. Walls and trusses were mostly fabricated from 30 × 50mm timber sections screwed together: they consist of five layers in which the timbers are orientated either vertically or diagonally. The result is a robust structure that becomes unique thanks to its rich architectural expression. In particular, the manner in which these walls and trusses filter sunlight and cast patterned shadows makes the building lively and exciting.

The walls are built up of a timber frame planked with CLT panels and clad in Douglas fir boards. In the roof, timber beams support CLT panels waterproofed with bituminous membranes. The two beams span 7 and 14.5m respectively, and employ different systems. The shorter beam uses a grid structure, and its diagonals (which are in compression) utilize 40 × 50mm timber sections. The longer beam could not employ a grid structure, due to the considerably higher forces acting on it; it uses 80 × 200mm sections for the diagonals and vertical tensile bars made of threaded rod. In order to create an architecturally uniform image, filigree battens were added to the structural components of the longer beam.

Fig. 2.4. Community Centre at the Spinelli Refugee Shelter in Mannheim (Germany), designed by the students of Atelier U20, Faculty of Architecture, Technische Universität Kaiserslautern. This timber building aims to provide the refugees with a welcoming and high-quality space during the first stages of their permanence in the country. (Photo: Yannick Wenger – Mannheim)

Fig. 2.5. The small courtyard is the Centre's most private and introverted space. It is delimited on one side by a grid wall, while on the opposite side is a series of seating booths. (Photo: Yannick Wenger – Mannheim)

Fig. 2.6. The main courtyard is designed for social events. On the left is a truss constructed with timber and steel members. On the right is a space protected by a flat canopy made of CLT panels supported by timber beams. (Photo: Yannick Wenger – Mannheim)

Fig. 2.7. The corridor leading to the small courtyard. The grid wall on the left is made of five layers of timber battens of standard section (30 × 50mm) connected by means of screws. The perforation of the grid casts lively shadows on the opposite wall, which is opaque and clad in Douglas fir boards. (Photo: Yannick Wenger – Mannheim)

Fig. 2.8. Diagram illustrating the construction of the building as a joint effort: all the students and a group of twenty-five refugees contributed. No heavy or advanced machinery was utilized during the building process. The largest building elements were fabricated in the protected environment offered by a nearby hanger no longer in use and then transported to site. (Drawing: Atelier U20)

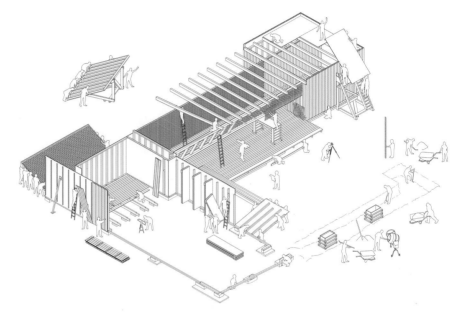

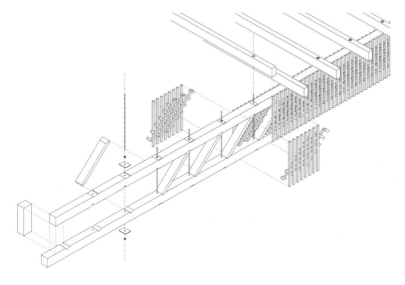

Fig. 2.9. Exploded view of the longer beam, which spans 14.5m. The top and bottom chords are made of solid timber sections. The web is comprised of diagonal timber struts and vertical steel ties. The beam is decorated with additional battens so as to achieve a similar appearance to the grid walls. (Drawing: Atelier U20)

Project: Caltron Civic Centre (*Casa Sociale Caltron*)

Location: Cles, Province of Trento, Italy
Building type: non-residential – community
Completion date: 2015
Architectural design: Mirko Franzoso architetto, Italy
Key words: larch glulam, larch cladding, CLT wall panels, woodfibre & hemp insulation

Caltron Civic Centre is located in the small Trentin town of Cles. It aims to be an important meeting point for the entire local community and for people of any age. The centre offers a new perspective onto the landscape, but at the same time enjoys high visibility from the town and serves as an attraction. This compact building lies at the boundary between the historic town and the rural landscape with its numerous apple-tree orchards.

The superstructure is almost entirely made of wood. Larch is widely used for both structural and cladding purposes. The northern and southern elevations are clad in vertical larch slats, while the eastern and western ones are defined by a series of larch columns of variable height.

The bottom volume supports and wraps the entire building. The plan layout follows the programmatic requirements set out by the local council. The entrance leads directly into a meeting room, which can easily be adapted to different needs as and when they arise. From this room, one can enter the others (kitchen, bathroom and storeroom) through sliding doors. On the top floor is a large, covered terrace, which overlooks the valley. The wooden columns that support the roof provide solar shading and privacy within this space (*see* Fig. 2.11).

Larch boards of different thicknesses are widely used for external cladding, internal lining, flooring (on the terrace) and roof covering. External walls use 95mm-thick CLT panels, finished on either side with 32mm-thick larch boards (on the outside, these are fixed to the panels by means of vertical counterbattens and horizontal battens).

The roof's timber rafters span between the external walls (on the uphill side) or larch columns (on the downhill side) and a ridge beam (240mm × 680mm), (*see* Fig. 2.14). The rafters and the ridge beam are fabricated from larch glulam. Under the larch-slat covering, set on timber battens and counterbattens, is a layer of galvanized-steel sheets laid on 25mm-thick timber boarding. The internal lining uses 20mm-thick larch slats. The gutter is concealed, sitting on top of the foot of the rafters and is lined in galvanized steel. The beam connecting the top of the columns is made from a solid larch section, which has been notched to form a drip.

The terrace is supported by 320mm-deep spruce beams, between which four layers of wood-fibre insulation have been fitted. The beams are sheathed with OSB sheets both at the top and the bottom. A layer of extruded polystyrene is laid on top of the OSB sheathing. Waterproofing is achieved with a 1.8mm-thick, single-ply PVC membrane. Larch boards laid on 40 × 40mm battens form the flooring. Since, on the downhill side, the terrace floor can be hit by wind-driven rainwater, a gutter is needed: this is concealed immediately behind the edge beam, made from a larch glulam section (440 × 60mm). The ceiling consists of larch slats fixed to battens, the gaps between which have been filled with hemp fibre.

Fig. 2.10. Caltron Civic Centre, Cles (Italy), designed by Mirko Franzoso architetto. The building is located on a hillside and overlooks a valley with numerous apple-tree orchards. (Photo: Mariano Dallago – Torino)

Fig. 2.11. The terrace on the top floor is completely covered by a roof, but open on the downhill side, from which visitors can enjoy a view towards the valley. The primary structure is exposed and consists of glulam members fabricated from larch. Larch boarding is used for the flooring, ceiling and wall lining. (Photo: Mariano Dallago – Torino)

Fig. 2.12. The timber staircase leading to the top floor. (Photo: Mariano Dallago – Torino)

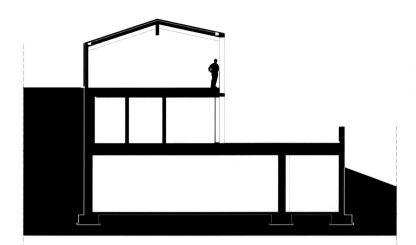

Fig. 2.13. Cross-section of the building, showing its three storeys and how it sits on the hillside. (Drawing: Mirko Franzoso architetto, Italy)

Fig. 2.14. Construction of the top floor. On the left is one of the accesses to the building. The loadbearing structure is comprised of glulam columns on steel supports, CLT panels (visible in the wall on the left) and glulam beams for the roof. (Photo: Mariano Dallago – Torino)

Project: Unterdorf Elementary School

Location: Höchst, Austria

Building type: non-residential – educational

Completion date: 2017

Architectural design: Dietrich | Untertrifaller Architects

Key words: glulam, timber framework, vertical cladding

Unterdorf Elementary School has been designed and optimized for modern pedagogical approaches. It blends harmoniously with the neighbourhood, which mainly consists of single-family houses. Some of the school's facilities and outdoor areas can be used not only by the pupils, but also by local residents; for instance, local sports clubs can use the gym out of school hours.

The school is a one-storey building whose plan layout encourages an educational culture based on playful learning in small groups of pupils. There are four identical teaching clusters, each comprised of a lounge, two classrooms, a multi-purpose room, toilets and a relaxation room. All these spaces are accessed from the lounge, which is placed at the centre of the cluster. Due to this position, the lounge cannot have windows but has a large, rectangular skylight at the top of its pyramidal roof, complete with motorized windows on the short sides, which facilitate cross-ventilation.

The school has an elongated plan laid out around a north-south axis: it is 100m long and 40m wide. While the teaching clusters are located on the east side of the building, the west side accommodates special classrooms, offices, a gymnasium and an auditorium.

The building is mostly timber-constructed, one of the few exceptions being the ground-bearing concrete slab. Wood is visible in every space, both internally and externally.

Not only is the green roof aimed at improving the building's thermal performance and avoiding overheating in summer, but also at increasing the vegetation within the property. Several measures were taken towards sustainability, including high levels of thermal insulation, triple-glazed windows, underfloor heating, and a ventilation system with heat recovery. Thanks to its use of renewable, regional building materials, the school has received recognition for its low environmental impact.

Fig. 2.15. Unterdorf Elementary School in Höchst (Austria), designed by Dietrich | Untertrifaller Architects. The main entrance is sheltered by a cantilevering canopy. (Photo: Bruno Klomfar)

Fig. 2.16. The school has an elongated shape, laid out around a north-south axis. All external surfaces are clad in vertical timber boards. (Photo: Bruno Klomfar)

Fig. 2.17. A large patio with informal seating and planters, where pupils and teachers can spend time together. (Photo: Bruno Klomfar)

Fig. 2.18. The gym is partially sunk into the ground, so that its eaves are level with the remainder of the building. The exposed roof beams show the regular grid that governs the structural strategy. (Photo: Bruno Klomfar)

Fig. 2.19. The lounge of one of the four teaching clusters. From this central space, the others can be accessed: two classrooms, a relaxation room, a multi-purpose room and toilets. The roof over the lounge is shaped as a pyramid with a large skylight at the top. (Photo: Bruno Klomfar)

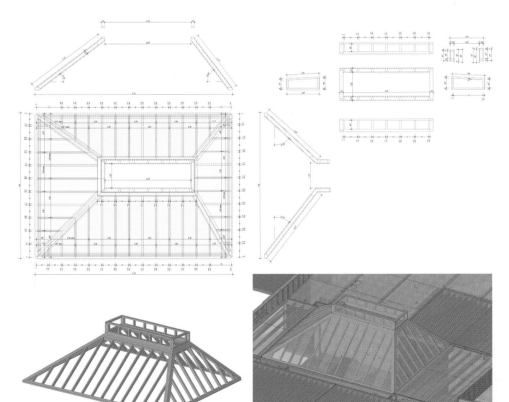

Fig. 2.20. Structural diagrams of the pyramidal roof over the central lounge of each teaching cluster. (Drawing: Dietrich | Untertrifaller Architects)

Project: New FINSA Headquarters (*Nueva Sede Servicios Centrales* FINSA)

Location: Santiago de Compostela (A Coruña), Galicia, Spain
Building type: non-residential – offices
Completion date: 2017
Architectural design: MRM Arquitectos (Miguel Alonso Flamarique, Roberto Erviti Machain and Mamen Escorihuela Vitales)
Key words: glulam, suspended floor, steel tie-rods, acetylated timber, oak flooring

The new FINSA Headquarters intervention included the full refurbishment of the existing offices and the construction of a new building, La Conexión, which connects all the others. The project aimed to modernize the company's image and values. The building complex is a space designed to allow numerous employees, visitors, customers and suppliers to gather. The transparent surfaces of the new building connect it with the surrounding landscape, thus forming a link between the pine forest from which FINSA sources its raw materials and the factory where these are processed.

The building is comprised of two storeys, both with an open-plan layout and in constant dialogue with the exterior and natural light. Smaller spaces, often delimited by glazed partitions, are dedicated to meeting rooms, a patio and various services. In La Conexión, wood is extensively used, for applications ranging from structural members to finishes and decoration. The roof consists of 22m-spanning beams of glulam, whose very large sections are exposed on the upper storey and convey a sense of grandness (*see* Fig. 2.24). Between the primary beams, a smaller frame is constructed, with 60 × 200mm timber joists, sheathed at the top and bottom with structural wood-based sheets (produced by FINSA itself). The warm roof is insulated with 200mm-thick mineral wool (fitted between the joists) and cellular-glass boards on top of the deck. Waterproofing is obtained with a double layer of bituminous membranes.

The intermediate floor is a timber framework and is suspended from the roof beams by means of steel tie-rods (*see* Fig. 2.25). The result is a very luminous and airy space.

The external cladding is made of acetylated-timber boards (100 × 18mm) laid vertically and screwed to horizontal pine battens. The interior walls are mainly lined in woodfibre boards. The suspended ceiling is acoustically improved with woodfibre boards finished with pine slats. The ground floor is finished in 30mm-thick oak boarding, while PVC flooring was specified for the first floor in the interest of acoustic comfort and hygiene (the employees continuously circulate between the offices, the factory and the sawmill, so an easy-to-clean flooring solution was therefore highly desirable).

Fig. 2.21. Construction of one of the teaching clusters. (Photo: Dietrich | Untertrifaller Architects)

Fig. 2.22. New FINSA Headquarters, Santiago de Compostela (Spain), designed by MRM Arquitectos. (Photo: MRM Arquitectos, Spain)

Fig. 2.23. The ground floor is laid out as an open-plan space. There are no vertical supports for the upper floor, as this is suspended on the roof. Wood has been specified for all the interior finishes, for instance oak for the flooring and pine for the suspended ceilings. The staircase is hanging from the roof, with a series of steel rods. (Photo: MRM Arquitectos, Spain)

Fig. 2.25. The roof consists of glulam beams whose noticeable depth was dictated by the long span, the cantilever over the main entrance and the suspended intermediate floor. Steel rods connect the timber floor structure to the roof. Within the floor framework, we can distinguish the primary beams from the joists that span between them. (Photo: MRM Arquitectos, Spain)

Fig. 2.24. The first floor, with its suspended staircase and its small patio enclosed by glazed surfaces. The roof structure, made up of very deep glulam beams, is exposed and carries the load of the floor and the staircase. In the background, a series of meeting rooms overlook the pine forest. (Photo: MRM Arquitectos, Spain)

Project: St Gerold Provostry Riding Hall (*Reithalle St Gerold*)

Location: St Gerold, Vorarlberg, Austria
Building type: non-residential – recreational
Completion date: 1997
Architectural design: HK Architekten, Austria
Key words: hybrid structures, glulam, space frame, post and beam

The Riding Hall is situated on a slope in the village of St Gerold, in Austria's Vorarlberg State, and serves people with cognitive or physical disabilities. It is an elegant, lightweight building with a gross area of 880m², which mostly uses engineered timber. The riding space is largely glazed on three sides and thus retains the feeling of being part of the open landscape, while on the fourth side it is delimited by the ancillary rooms. The fenestration on the south-east façade offers views towards the snow-capped mountain tops and conifer forest on the opposite side of the valley.

The hall uses a post-and-beam structure and is covered with a monopitch roof based on a very interesting and expressive timber-steel hybrid solution. The roof is supported by a modular space truss, each element of which is built up of three rafters, six glulam struts (two per rafter) and a steel tie-rod connected to the ends of the rafters. The struts form an upside-down pyramid whose apex is very-elegantly resolved. Steel plates are used to connect the glulam members with one another (for instance, to connect the columns with the rafters, and the struts with the rafters). The ceiling is composed of exposed timber boards, whose pale colour reflects the natural light which floods in through the glazed surfaces on the uphill side of the building. The ingenious structural solution adopted for the roof allows for long spans without the need for intermediate vertical supports (which would have been incompatible with the building's function) and minimum use of materials.

Cross-bracing against wind forces is achieved with steel diagonals set in front of the glass surfaces on the inside, which are almost invisible in back-lit conditions. The building envelope is uninsulated, since there was no thermal requirement for the hall.

Fig. 2.26. Riding Hall in St Gerold (Austria), designed by HK Architekten. The pitched roof of the building follows the slope of the terrain. The large, glazed surfaces allow users to enjoy the views out towards the mountains, villages and forests across the valley. (Photo: Ignacio Martínez)

Fig. 2.27. The roof employs an ingenious structural system thanks to which a long distance can be spanned using a small amount of materials (timber and steel). (Photo: Ignacio Martínez)

Fig. 2.28. Structural node at the apex of the inverted pyramid: here, six glue-laminated-timber struts and a metal tie-rod are elegantly jointed. (Photo: Ignacio Martínez)

Project: Domaine-Vert Nord Cultural Centre
(*Centre Culturel du Domaine-Vert Nord*)

Location: Mirabel, Quebec, Canada
Building type: non-residential – community
Completion date: 2017
Architectural design: BGLA, Canada
Key words: hybrid structures, glulam, steel structures, bolted connections

This is a multi-purpose cultural centre, arising from Mirabel Town Council's intention to create a cultural and sports centre for the community. A hall runs along the whole building and provides access to multi-purpose rooms, a kitchen, an atrium, a library and a park.

The project is conceived as an inviting point of reference for the whole area of the town, where citizens are encouraged to join and create content. The large glazing offers views onto the landscape and the sky, while the timber components (columns and ceiling lining) contribute to the centre's warm atmosphere and architectural quality. The building and its canopies realize the new physical and visual relationship between the centre and the surrounding landscape, internal spaces and exterior areas. On three fronts, the canopies create exterior spaces that are convivial, comfortable, safe and sheltered from adverse weather conditions. The canopies and their associated spaces are meant to function as a pleasant transition area for the visitors, enriched with well-crafted paving, lighting fixtures, greenery and outdoor furniture. A heat-recovery system and attentive choice of materials contribute to the building's energy efficiency. Over the main entrances is a green roof.

The glulam columns are used to provide vertical support in two different locations: outside, to carry the load of the canopies and inside, in the longitudinal hall that provides access to all the rooms. In the latter application, the columns support roofs at different heights (*see* Figs 2.29 and 2.30). For the higher roof, steel I-sections sit on top of the glulam posts, while for the lower roof the column-to-beam connection is realized with steel angle cleats bolted into the columns and into the metal webs of the beams. The ceiling is built up of wooden boards. The timber columns sit on reinforced-concrete foundations and have steel supports at the foot. All the timber columns, both inside and outside, are exposed.

The remainder of the centre is constructed around a steel skeleton. Columns and cross-bracing members use square hollow sections. The roof employs different steel sections that support a shallow profiled deck: in most cases, I-beams for shorter spans and lattice beams for longer spans.

Fig. 2.29. Domaine-Vert Nord Cultural Centre, Mirabel (Canada), designed by architectural firm BGLA. The building has several canopies that create portico-like spaces around its perimeter and are supported by exposed timber columns. (Photo: David Boyer)

Fig. 2.30. A wide corridor connects the main entrance to the rear of the building and provides access to all of the Centre's facilities. The structural system combines timber and steel members. Glulam columns support steel-constructed roof surfaces placed at different heights, which makes it possible to form clerestory windows at the top of the corridor. (Photo: David Boyer)

Case Study 1: Congress and Exhibition Centre

Fausto Sanna & Annalaura Fornasier

Location: Agordo (Belluno), Veneto, Italy
Building type: multi-purpose hall
Completion date: 2018
Design Team:
    Architects: Studio Botter, Agordo (Belluno), Italy – Andrea Botter & Sandro Botter; Studio Bressan, Montebelluna (Treviso), Italy – Emanuele Bressan
    Structural engineer: Fabio Valentini
    Building-services engineer: S.I.I.S. Srl, Padova, Italy – Michele Melato
Client: private company
Gross floor internal area: 6,400m²
Awards:
    Winner – Big See Awards, 2020
    Finalist – Constructive Alps, 2020
    Nominated – Archilovers Best Projects, 2019
    Nominated – *Architizer* Project of the Day, 15.10.2019
Keywords: glulam, Pratt truss, post and beam, snow load, multi-purpose building, flooding risk

Fig. 2.31. Construction of the longitudinal hall: we can observe the structural combination of timber columns and steel members (I-sections, lattice beams, hollow sections and so on). (Photo: BGLA, Canada)

Fig. 2.32. The Congress and Exhibition Centre designed by Studio Bressan and Studio Botter is located in the mountainous town of Agordo, in north-eastern Italy. The structural and formal appearance of the building, especially its roof, takes inspiration from vernacular architecture and the peaks of the Dolomites. (Photo: Simone Bossi)

Brief and design process

The Congress and Exhibition Centre is located in the mountainous town of Agordo, in the province of Belluno. It sits at the boundary between the urban fabric and the Alpine landscape, near the River Cordevole, and is strategically connected to public infrastructure – coach station, motorway, leisure and sports centres, stadium and schools.

The design of the Centre was jointly commissioned to two architectural firms, Studio Botter and Studio Bressan, by a well-known local company. The client requested a large, multi-purpose hall near their headquarters, to be used for private events and recreational activities for the local community. The programme required the interior to be a single, open-space hall, free of any walls or columns, with capacity for 5,000 people and able to host concerts, conferences, performances, exhibitions and fairs. The large hall is the heart of the design and is orientated on a north-south axis; it can be subdivided and partitioned into smaller units, if needed. The services (for example toilets, storage space and plant room) are all located on the eastern side of the building, to allow flexible management and use of the main hall.

The project took inspiration from Agordo's landscape and urban morphology to form an architectural language. The Centre is characterized by a geometrically complex pitched roof with several surfaces, which resemble the surrounding mountain peaks and the town's man-made forms. The roof cantilevers over the large curtain walls that make up the façades, protecting the visitors' entrance and the timber superstructure from the elements.

The structural strategy is inspired by *tabià*, a vernacular building type of the Dolomites, many examples of which can be found in the Agordo valleys, which prospered for centuries thanks to their strategic position and influences from both Veneto and South Tyrol[20]. *Tabià* are agricultural buildings located in proximity to, or attached to, family houses and were used primarily for hay and food storage. The materials utilized for their construction were mainly timber and stone. The latter was generally employed to build the basement (used as a cowshed) and, sometimes, also the living area. Timber was typically used for the construction of a barn on the upper floor, where hay was stored. These buildings were constructed with the *blockbau* – or framework – system. A similar language was adopted by the architects in the design of the Congress and Exhibition Centre: this has a slender timber skeleton whose diagonal members resemble those of *tabià* and might at first sight appear ornamental, but are in fact an integral part of the loadbearing structure.

The two architectural firms have collaborated since 2010, when Emanuele Bressan and Andrea Botter graduated from Iuav University in Venice.

They wish to design with attention to context, structural aspects and sustainability, while combining innovation and tradition. The centre's design and the architects' choice of constructing with timber has been well received by the local community and public bodies for its vernacular influences and harmonious integration into Agordo's natural and built environment.

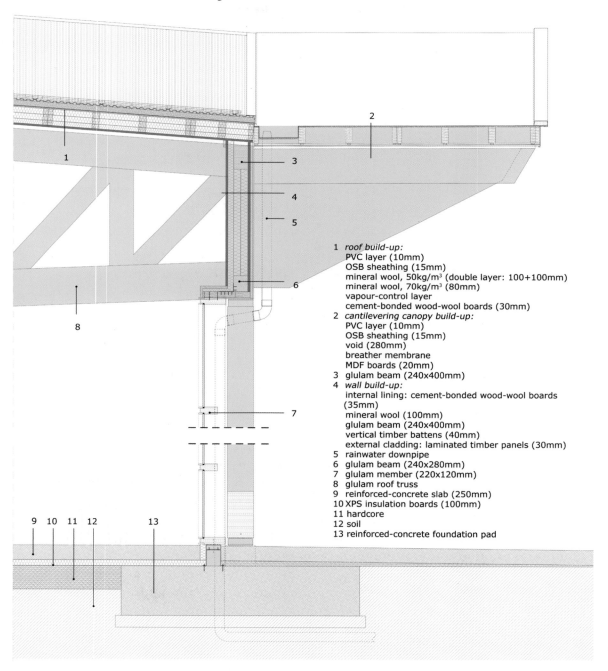

1 roof build-up:
   PVC layer (10mm)
   OSB sheathing (15mm)
   mineral wool, 50kg/m³ (double layer: 100+100mm)
   mineral wool, 70kg/m³ (80mm)
   vapour-control layer
   cement-bonded wood-wool boards (30mm)
2 cantilevering canopy build-up:
   PVC layer (10mm)
   OSB sheathing (15mm)
   void (280mm)
   breather membrane
   MDF boards (20mm)
3 glulam beam (240x400mm)
4 wall build-up:
   internal lining: cement-bonded wood-wool boards (35mm)
   mineral wool (100mm)
   glulam beam (240x400mm)
   vertical timber battens (40mm)
   external cladding: laminated timber panels (30mm)
5 rainwater downpipe
6 glulam beam (240x280mm)
7 glulam member (220x120mm)
8 glulam roof truss
9 reinforced-concrete slab (250mm)
10 XPS insulation boards (100mm)
11 hardcore
12 soil
13 reinforced-concrete foundation pad

Fig. 2.33. Detailed section through the western façade and its overhanging canopy. (Drawing: adapted and translated from Studio Botter + Studio Bressan)

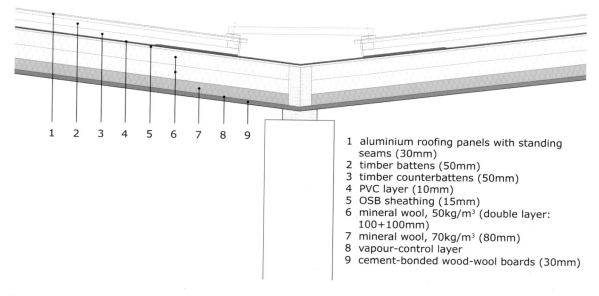

1 aluminium roofing panels with standing seams (30mm)
2 timber battens (50mm)
3 timber counterbattens (50mm)
4 PVC layer (10mm)
5 OSB sheathing (15mm)
6 mineral wool, 50kg/m³ (double layer: 100+100mm)
7 mineral wool, 70kg/m³ (80mm)
8 vapour-control layer
9 cement-bonded wood-wool boards (30mm)

Fig. 2.34. Detailed section of the roof through the valley between two sloping surfaces. (Drawing: adapted and translated from Studio Botter + Studio Bressan)

Fig. 2.35. The multi-purpose hall is the heart of the design and can host up to 5,000 people. The glulam roof trusses span 44.8m. The western façade (pictured) is a curtain wall positioned immediately behind the vertical and diagonal supports of the primary structure. (Photo: Emanuele Bressan)

Fig. 2.36. The western façade, being a long curtain wall, is very luminous and offers views out towards the Alpine landscape; while the southern façade is windowless and lined in tobacco-coloured wooden panels. (Photo: Simone Bossi)

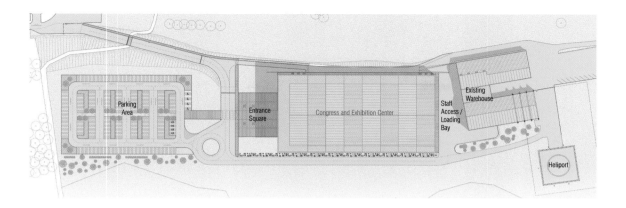

Fig. 2.37. Site plan. The project sits at the edge of the town of Agordo, near other amenities and the client's headquarters. The hall is at the centre of the site, between the car park on the north side and an existing building and heliport on the south side. (Drawing: Studio Botter + Studio Bressan)

Construction

Structural system:
Foundations: concrete pad foundations combined with raft foundations
Vertical supports: glulam columns
Ground floor: concrete raft
Roof: Pratt trusses (glulam made from red spruce)
Thermal insulation:
External walls: mineral wool (200mm);
Ground floor: extruded-polystyrene (XPS) boards (100mm) under concrete raft foundation;
Roof: 50kg/m³ mineral wool (200mm) + 70kg/m³ mineral wool (80mm)
Acoustic insulation: wood-fibre boards

Studio Botter and Studio Bressan devised a structural grid that defined the building's interior and exterior appearance. They chose to build in timber from an early stage, to strengthen the centre's relationship to the Alpine context and to propose a sustainable and prefabricated lightweight building that could be erected in a short time span, as the client

desired. The loadbearing structure is chiefly made of glued laminated timber (columns, diagonals and roof trusses), in combination with some steel hollow sections and tie-rods.

The most critical part of the design is the roof's structure, comprised of a series of parallel trusses, which are set 6.8m apart and span 44.8m. These trusses are very similar in configuration to a Pratt truss and are statically determinate. The lower chord is horizontal, while the upper chord is angled to provide an adequate slope for the roof, unlike the Pratt model proper, in which both chords are horizontal (*see* Fig. 2.40). As a result, the depth of the trusses varies between 2.56m (at the ends) and 4.45m (at midspan, at the ridge). Each truss

Fig. 2.38. The western façade, with its structural diagonals inspired by vernacular buildings (*tabiàs*) and its generous glazing to allow visitors to enjoy the views of the valley and surrounding mountains. (Photo: Simone Bossi)

Fig. 2.39. Positioning of one of the glulam trusses on its supports. The components of the primary load-bearing structure (roof trusses and their supports) were transported to the site on a lorry and assembled over the course of two months. The trusses are symmetrically tapered and reach a depth of 4.45m at the ridge. (Photo: Studio Botter + Studio Bressan)

Fig. 2.40. Along the western façade, the roof trusses are alternatively supported by columns and pairs of abutting diagonals. Each truss is connected to the ones on either side by means of *ad hoc* members positioned at the nodes along the upper and lower chords. (Photo: Studio Botter + Studio Bressan)

Fig. 2.41. The roof trusses are 44.8m long and positioned at regular intervals of 6.8m. The modular and lightweight structural strategy has achieved a very large hall, the roof of which is only supported along the edges, and thus free of any internal columns. (Photo: Studio Botter + Studio Bressan)

is supported at both ends, but the type of support alternates: every other truss is supported by glulam columns, while the remaining trusses rest on the connections between pairs of abutting diagonals, also made of glulam. Timber binders of smaller cross-section connect the trusses in the transverse plane, to stabilize them. In an idealized Pratt truss subjected to a balanced load, all members exclusively carry axial forces: the internal diagonals and the lower-chord members are all in tension, while the verticals and the upper-chord members are all in compression. In the real truss, the members also carry non-axial internal forces, but the predominant forces remain the same as in the idealized truss.

The trusses sit at three different heights, thus generating a zig-zag verge on the centre's longitudinal elevations and creating surfaces that slope diagonally with respect to the two main axes of the building. This geometrical configuration facilitates rainwater runoff, by channelling the water towards large downpipes located at the lowest points of the roof surfaces. Above the trusses, the roof slopes are built with prefabricated timber panels, lined internally with mineral wool and covered externally with aluminium sheets able to withstand horizontal seismic actions.

Portions of the trusses were fabricated in the factory, then transported to site, assembled on the ground, and finally erected with very tall cranes. The individual members of the trusses are joined by means of steel flitch plates. Steel plates are also used to connect the columns and diagonals of the façades to both the ground structure and the roof trusses.

Structural calculations were performed according to the Italian standard, which tends to be more stringent than Eurocode 5 (the European code for timber structures). The roof has been designed to withstand a $3kN/m^2$ snow load, which is higher than the nominal value prescribed for this geographical region. After completion, the roof trusses were structurally tested with a load corresponding to the design snow load: under this weight, maximum deflection (at midspan) was close to 1/1,000 of the span. The structure is designed to offer sixty-minute fire resistance. Air-conditioning ducts are easily positioned within the depth of the trusses and supported by them.

The north and west façades of the building are curtain walls that sit behind the primary structure described above (columns and diagonals); they are divided into smaller glazed panes by evenly spaced timber mullions. The east and south façades, by contrast, are opaque, clad externally in metal sheets (like the roof) and lined internally with 35mm tobacco-coloured wood-fibre boards. The combined presence of these boards and timber structural members yields excellent acoustic performance, which is key for this type of building. The top surface of the concrete raft has been polished with industrial quartz, which creates non-slip surfaces.

Environmental sustainability

Due to the large size of the building, use of timber for the loadbearing structure was chosen for its sustainable and recyclable qualities. It was essential for the architects that the structure would be recyclable at its end of life and would contribute to the reduction of greenhouse gases. The use of prefabricated elements shortens on-site construction times and reduces material waste, especially thanks to the precision achieved with computer numeric control (CNC) machinery.

The architects took some design measures towards adaptation to climate change, particularly to reduce flooding risk. Since the centre is located near the River Cordevole, several computer simulations of its potential overflow were carried out: these showed that the building is in a safe area and that the chosen ground level is appropriate.

Environmental control within the building relies on a combination of passive and active heating and cooling systems. The roof overhang on the western

SECTION C-C'

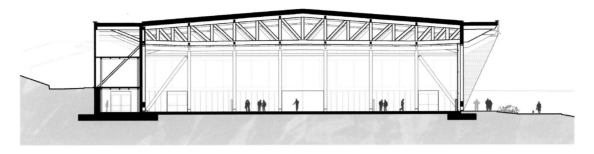

SOUTH ELEVATION

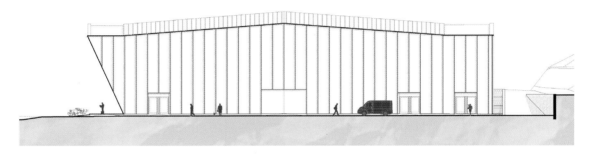

Fig. 2.42. Cross-section and south elevation. The south and east façades are externally clad with metal sheets, like the roof. The ancillary spaces (changing rooms, toilets, geothermal-energy plant and so on) are located on the ground and first floors, on the uphill side of the building. (Drawing: Studio Botter + Studio Bressan)

façade shields the hall from the sun in the summer months, thus reducing air-cooling costs. While the curtain walls of the north and west aspects allow visitors to admire the surrounding landscape, the east and south elevations are blank and fronted by a green hill slope. The building's plant, located at the rear, uses renewable, geothermal energy for its heating, ventilating and air-conditioning (HVAC) system. The HVAC system is equipped with heat-recovery devices in the air-handling units, and employs sensors to monitor indoor parameters such as temperature, humidity and CO_2 levels.

Fig. 2.43. The overhangs along the two fully-glazed façades serve a twofold function: they shield the hall from sunlight in the summer and protect visitors from rainwater or snow when they enter or leave the building. (Photo: Simone Bossi)

Notes

[1] Dixon, 1975

[2] Pliny the Elder, *Natural History*, 16

[3] Kollmann *et al.* 1975; Wilk, 2017

[4] Connor, 2009

[5] Ministry of Housing, Communities and Local Government, 2019

[6] Hairstans and Sanna, 2017

[7] Mitchell and Hurst, 2009

[8] Structural Timber Association, 2017

[9] Taylor, 2010; Steinhardt and Manley, 2016

[10] Moore, 2015

[11] House of Commons, Housing, Communities and Local Government Committee, ca.2019

[12] Owen, 2007; Lu and Liska, 2008; Hairstans, 2010

[13] Barker, 2006

[14] Scottish Government, 2011

[15] Ministry of Housing, Communities and Local Government and Esther McVey MP, 2021

[16] Welsh Government, 2020

[17] Goodier and Gibb, 2007; McCallie et al., 2015

[18] Lu and Liska, 2008

[19] Owen, 2007; Hairstans, 2010; Hamilton-MacLaren, 2013

[20] Franco and Chiapparini, 2013

Chapter Three

Environmental Aspects

International and National Responses to Environmental Impacts

Emissions that harm the environment are at an all-time high. The 2020 Emissions Gap Report, produced by the United Nations Environment Programme, makes for sobering reading, with carbon, methane and nitrous oxide emissions continuing an upward trend since the 1990s. This situation has resulted in scientific and political consensus (despite some outlier views) on the need to control emissions arising from human activity in order to protect the environment and ensure the long-term sustainability of economic growth.

Consequently, several international agreements have been introduced. The Montreal Protocol (1989), signed by United Nations members, was effective in reducing the emission of substances that deplete stratospheric ozone and was set in place in the wake of the discovery of an ozone hole over Antarctica. The Gothenburg Protocol (effective from 1999) is designed to reduce emissions of sulphur dioxide, nitrogen oxides, volatile organic compounds and ammonia, all of which cause acidification and eutrophication (explained later in this chapter). The Kyoto Protocol (effective from 2005) was the first major international instrument to control greenhouse emissions, which contribute to global warming. The Paris Agreement (2015) replaces the Kyoto Protocol from 2020 onwards with improved coverage and more stringent reduction targets.

In the European Union, the National Emission Ceilings Directive (2016/2284) imposes emission budgets on sulphur dioxide, ammonia, volatile organic compounds, nitrogen oxides and fine particulate matter for each member state, all to be achieved by 2030. The Climate Change Act 2008 enforces a reduction target of greenhouse gas emissions by at least 100 per cent of 1990 levels for all UK nations. Recent political developments mean that there is now more potential for the United States to fully participate in the Paris Agreement and to establish federal legislation to tackle climate change.

What transpires from these initiatives is that environmental protection is very much at the forefront of the political and scientific agenda and all industries ought to find strategies to adapt to more stringent legislation. In addition, greater public awareness of environmental impacts, and of climate change in particular, translates into customers pressurizing companies to offer eco-friendly products and services.

The Building Industry and Its Environmental Impact

The building industry has a significant effect on the environment, with impacts arising from its heavy reliance on non-renewable materials and energy. This aspect becomes particularly apparent if one analyses the whole life-cycle of a construction project from material production to a building's end of life.

Many of the products used in the construction sector originate from mineral extraction with significant contribution to soil and water pollution. The fabrication processes of materials such as brick, cement or concrete demand high energy-consumption and

OPPOSITE: **Fig. 3.1.** Passageway in the Community Centre at the Spinelli Refugee Shelter (Mannheim, Germany), designed by the students of Atelier U20, Technische Universität Kaiserslautern. (Photo: Yannick Wenger – Mannheim)

depend on fossil fuels for calcination. Transportation of heavy building materials carries high environmental costs. Site planning and preparation disrupt ecosystems and the actual construction phase produces greenhouse emissions. Finally, demolition might emit harmful substances back to the atmosphere and requires energy. Another source of impact is the level of waste emerging from building projects, mostly due to miscalculations arising from procurement errors, poor craftsmanship, changes in design, damage, equipment malfunction, off-cuts and packaging.

Bearing these factors in mind, it is safe to say that the construction industry has a key role to play in environmental protection and has responded by proposing materials that are less harmful to the ecosystem or more energy-efficient: for example, alternative building materials with lower environmental loads or which are by-products of other fabrication processes, such as fly ash or silica fume; or natural materials that can act as insulants, instead of fully man-made products.

Environmental advantages and disadvantages of timber architecture

Timber is deemed to constitute a more sustainable choice for building projects. As a natural material, it does not require manufacturing processes that are as energy-intensive as the ones required for artificial materials such as cement or brick. Wood products are usually biodegradable at the end of their lifespan and less impactful. Furthermore, haulage of forestry products often poses lower transportation requirements than heavier or more cumbersome materials, resulting in fewer emissions from road, rail, air and sea traffic.

Another advantage of timber is that it contributes to the reduction of carbon emissions through a process called carbon sequestration. Wood-based products contain depositories of the carbon dioxide that trees have absorbed during their growth. This, in practice, means that the timber industry contributes positively to the prevention of climate change by dint

of its reliance on a natural product that retains banks of a major contributor to global warming. Such are the perceived benefits of carbon sequestration that it is now standard practice to include it in the calculation methodology for the environmental impacts of building materials[1]. However, some researchers[2] argue that this phenomenon should not be accounted for as negative carbon emissions from timber products, in that wood will eventually release its carbon content back to the atmosphere when it naturally decomposes or when it is incinerated. In addition, the period of growth of a forest is too long for its trees to be able to offset this end-of-life carbon release. This relates to the principle that, as explained in Chapter 1, the long-term sustainability of wood strictly relies on sustainable forest management.

Offsite construction is usually deemed to improve the speed of building projects, thus reducing economic costs and the environmental burdens associated with construction sites. Building projects that benefit from an offsite approach tend to offer a more transparent and efficient management of the amount of material needed to meet construction targets, which, in turn, reduces waste and its associated environmental loads.

Despite the many undoubted benefits of timber architecture in ecological terms, it is important not to fall prey to the greenwashing generated around wood: a tendency to express unfounded claims that a timber product or technique must *necessarily* be the best choice for the environment, without robust evidence. Bold statements about the suitability of timber to reduce environmental impacts are sometimes based on an oversimplification of complex phenomena and on the consideration of some impacts only, without a full understanding of trade-offs or of the bigger picture. Indeed, environmental trade-offs in building products are inevitable: for example, a material that might be beneficial towards reducing greenhouse gases might nevertheless produce more toxic waste or require components that pollute the water.

Moreover, timber may undergo chemical treatment for preservation purposes (as was seen in Chapter 2) with substances that can exhibit a degree of toxicity for the environment. Additionally, the incorporation of several layers into timber panels (such as vapour barriers and other membranes) to meet hygrothermal and weather-protection requirements can carry a further environmental burden and energy load. As a matter of fact, the production of some insulants still widely used in timber buildings, such as mineral wool, require extensive mineral extraction, which in turn might contribute towards hazardous waste, soil and water pollution, and disruption to ecosystems. Adhesives used for many wood panels are another possible source of environmental impacts.

Another potential issue with timber construction arises from the amount of wastage produced, especially from packaging and off-cuts in the fabrication of panels or other products made from timber. This additional waste is not only an environmental hazard in itself, the energy and emissions associated with the production of materials that are then discarded impact the environment with zero benefit for the completed building.

Therefore, it becomes necessary to take a rigorous, holistic approach to the evaluation of the environmental impact of timber architecture, by analysing the different stages of manufacturing and by evaluating its effect not only on global warming but also other environmental burdens.

Analysing the Environmental Impact of Timber Architecture with Environmental Product Declarations

Life-Cycle Thinking

Life-Cycle Thinking takes into consideration the whole lifespan of a product, from manufacturing to end of life. It is a holistic approach whereby design, costs, management and the environment are assessed to evaluate the sustainability of a product. The first mention of a life-cycle methodology comes from a 1959 report for the Rand Corporation entitled Resource Allocations and Future Weapon Systems, authored by David Novick; however, the first environmental life-cycle assessment (LCA) study was conducted by the Midwest Research Institute (US) in 1969 for the analysis of the impact of Coca-Cola packaging. This study was termed Resource and Environmental Profile Analysis and focused on resource-consumption and emissions. The first German LCA dates from 1972 and was conducted by the Battelle Institute. Further LCA studies took place in the United Kingdom and Sweden throughout the 1970s[3].

Modern life-cycle assessment methods were developed by the Society of Environmental Toxicology and Chemistry with the key differentiation between inventory (quantification of emissions and materials) and impact assessment (where the effect of those emissions on the environment and human health are calculated). The first international standard came with the publication of ISO 14040, Life Cycle Assessment – Principles and Framework in 1997 and successive documents (known as the ISO 14040 series). ISO 14040 established the required sections of an LCA: goal and scope (where the product and boundaries are defined), life-cycle inventory analysis (where flows to and from nature are counted: inputs of raw materials and energy use, products, emissions to the air, water and land), life-cycle impact assessment (where potential harmful effects are analysed), interpretation and reporting of results, and critical review.

ISO 14040 does not prescribe a specific methodology to analyse impacts, yet the common factor in the selection of impact categories is that they all have the potential to damage the environment and/ or human health or to deplete natural resources. Each substance follows a path until it reaches an endpoint (or end of the cause-effect chain): whilst midpoint impacts, which lie somewhere in the chain, are useful to identify reduction targets and measures to implement them, endpoint impacts support decision making. There are several available methodologies for the assessment of these impacts, all taking a midpoint or an endpoint approach to the selection of performance indicators. The preferred methodology for LCAs in the building industry is the CML method[4], from the Institute of Environmental

Standard number	Title	Summary
ISO 14040:2006	*Environmental management. Life cycle assessment. Principles and framework.*	It sets out the parts and principles of an LCA.
ISO 14044:2006	*Environmental management. Life cycle assessment. Requirements and guidelines.*	It sets out the main components and requirements of an LCA.
ISO 21930:2017	*Sustainability in buildings and civil engineering works. Core rules for environmental product declarations of construction products and services.*	It sets out the layout and components of Environmental Product Declarations.
BS EN 15804:2012+ A2:2019	*Sustainability of construction works. Environmental product declarations. Core rules for the product category of construction products.*	It provides a framework to incorporate LCAs to the analysis of environmental impact at building level. It also states that Environmental Product Declarations are the main sources of information to assess impacts.

Table 3.1 International standards that define the main principles and components of a Life-Cycle Assessment (LCA). Environmental Product Declarations (EPDs) are the standard eco-label to communicate the results of an LCA-compliant assessment. ISO: standards of the International Organization for Standardization; EN: standards of the European Union; BS: standards of the British Standards Institution.

Sciences at Leiden University. This framework takes a midpoint approach and establishes a standard list of impact categories (all explained in this chapter) covering not only climate change, but also other aspects such as water pollution and waste production.

Eco-labelling

The environmental impact of a product is of interest not only to the scientific community but also to a public increasingly attuned to ecological concerns. As a result of this growing demand for clearly communicated environmental values, eco-labelling has evolved from individual initiatives in the 1970s to current standardized procedures. ISO 14020 is the international standard for environmental labelling with a broad definition of the type of content that such labels must contain.

Later standards have become even more stringent by proposing three types of labels: Type-I labels (as defined by ISO 14024) present the results of environmental studies conducted by a third party (for example, the laboratory of an independent institution), according to a number of preset agreed criteria; Type-II labels (as defined by ISO 14021) give manufacturers the greatest level of freedom, as they provide self-declared environmental claims; finally, Type-III labels (ISO 14025) are also called Environmental Product Declarations (EPDs) and are reserved for results arising from an LCA approach. EPDs are particularly important for LCAs carried out at the whole-building level, because they provide the standard environmental-impact information required for the building components used in a project, according to ISO 21930 and BS EN 15804. A particular advantage of EPDs lies in the fact that these assessments are conducted by an independent third party, known as an EPD programme operator.

Structure of environmental product declarations

ISO 21930 and BS EN 15804 harmonize the layout of, and the information to be included in, EPDs within the building industry. Firstly, they set out the product category rules to which an EPD must adhere, with the following parameters:

- definition and description of the product;
- goal and scope (functional unit, system boundaries, description of data, criteria for inclusion of inputs/outputs, data-quality checks and units);
- inventory analysis (data collection, calculation procedures and allocation of materials and energy flows);
- environmental impact categories to be included;

Assessment boundary				Information module	Life-cycle stage
cradle to cradle	cradle to grave	cradle to site	cradle to gate	A1: raw-material supply	product
				A2: transport	
				A3: manufacturing	
				A4: transport to site gate	construction process
				A5: assembly	
				B1: use	use
				B2: maintenance	
				B3: repair	
				B4: replacement	
				B5: refurbishment	
				B6: energy use	
				B7: water use	
				C1: deconstruction, demolition	end-of-life
				C2: transport	
				C3: waste processing	
				C4: disposal	
				D1: reuse, recovery and recycling	outside system boundaries

Table 3.2 Information modules (A1 to D1) considered in an Environmental Product Declaration, according to BS EN 15804. Information modules are grouped into life-cycle stages. Different EPDs might cover different stages, depending on their assessment boundaries, which must be clearly stated in the documentation.

- life-cycle stages to be included in the environmental declaration;
- period of validity.

EPDs might use a declared unit or a functional unit. With declared units, only the physical properties of a product are taken into account (for example, 1kg of thermal insulant), whereas with functional units, the level of service of a product is considered (for example, the amount of insulant needed to offer a thermal resistance of $1.5m^2/(W \cdot K)$). An EPD must clearly state all these components and provide an analysis of results, as required by current LCA standards[5].

Table 3.2 shows the grouping of the individual stages of a product life-cycle. Depending on what stages are considered, EPDs might take the following assessment boundaries: cradle to gate (covering the impacts arising from the manufacturing stages of a product), cradle to site (covering impacts from manufacturing to transportation to construction site), cradle to gate with options (covering the product stage, plus any additional stages) and cradle to grave (covering all stages of a product until it reaches the end of its functional life). An EPD must clearly state what stages have been included in the assessment.

EPD programmes

The demand for EPDs in the construction industry has increased in the last decade. This phenomenon has resulted in the proliferation of programme operators that provide EPDs, triggering the need for regulation and guidelines to improve the comparability and transparency of EPDs. This concern has partially been addressed by the publication of BS EN 15804, but further efforts towards the harmonization of EPDs have recently been achieved with the foundation of ECO Platform in 2013, with the aim of 'coordinating the development of consistent EPD [...]

System Boundary															
Product: particleboard															
Declared unit: m^3															
Stages included	Product stage			Construction stage		Use stage							End-of-life stage			
	A1	A2	A3	A4	A5	B1	B2	B3	B4	B5	B6	B7	C1	C2	C3	C4
	YES	YES	YES	YES	YES	NO	NO	NO	NO	NO	NO	NO	NO	YES	NO	

LCA Results – Environmental Impacts				
Impact category	Unit	A1-A3	A4-A5	C3
Global Warming Potential	kg CO_2-eq.	−707.34	24.74	1,027.25
Ozone Depletion Potential	kg CFC11-eq.	1.84×10^{-5}	3.35×10^{-8}	2.93×10^{-7}
Acidification Potential	kg SO_2-eq.	1.47	6.14×10^{-3}	2.72×10^{-2}
Eutrophication Potential	kg PO_4-eq.	2.38×10^{-1}	1.43×10^{-3}	3.57×10^{-3}
Photochemical Ozone Creation Potential	kg ethene-eq.	1.14×10^{-1}	2.44×10^{-4}	1.23×10^{-3}
Abiotic Depletion Potential	kg Sb-eq.	1.39×10^{-3}	1.04×10^{-6}	4.19×10^{-6}

LCA Results – Energy Use				
Type of energy	Unit	A1-A3	A4-A5	C3
Renewable primary energy resources used as energy carrier	MJ	3,410.75	0.16	14.54
Renewable primary energy resources used as raw materials	MJ	10,896.00	0.00	0.00
Total renewable primary energy	MJ	14,306.75	0.16	14.54
Non-renewable primary energy resources used as energy carrier	MJ	4,939.44	11.50	138.51
Non-renewable primary energy resources used as raw materials	MJ	1,163.74	0.00	0.00
Total non-renewable primary energy	MJ	6,103.18	11.50	138.51

LCA Results – Waste Disposed				
Type of waste	Unit	A1-A3	A4-A5	C3
Hazardous waste	kg	5.00×10^{-3}	8.83×10^{-6}	1.61×10^{-4}
Non-hazardous waste	kg	27.06	0.00	0.00
Radioactive waste	Kg	1.15×10^{-2}	1.24×10^{-5}	1.20×10^{-3}

Table 3.3 Example of the results section of an EPD for particleboard. This document is based on an LCA study whose system boundary is cradle to gate (A1 to A4) with options (assembly, A5; and waste processing, C3).

programmes in Europe and stimulating the use of common implementation of the EPD methodology'[6]. Several EPD programmes adhere to the recommendations from ECO Platform, such as BRE (United Kingdom), EPD Danmark (Denmark), EPD Norge (Norway), Institut Bauen und Umwelt (Germany), EPD International (Sweden), FDES INIES (France), EPDitaly (Italy), Bau EPD (Austria), DAPconstrucción (Spain), DAPHabitat System (Portugal), EPD Ireland (Ireland), Aenor (Spain), ITB (Poland) and MRBI (Netherlands).

In North America, the following companies and associations offer an EPD programme: FP Innovations (Canada), NSF International (United States), Earth Sure EPD (United States), UL Environment (United States), ASTM International (United States), Carbon Leadership Forum (United States), ICC Evaluation Services (United States) and SGS Global Services (United States), among others.

Many manufacturers will add EPDs to the specifications and marketing materials of their products, but it is worth consulting the EPD libraries from the companies mentioned above for comparison of environmental credentials.

EPDs, unlike other environmental labels, ought to be read in the spirit of Life-Cycle Thinking, that is, without expectations for a final overall mark; rather, the environmental suitability of a product is informed by different stages and impact categories. It is also worth remembering the concept of burden trade-off, whereby a product might perform well in a specific environmental category but poorly in another; for example, a product might cause low greenhouse emissions but high hazardous waste.

Global Warming Potential (GWP)

Definition: This is the characterization factor for climate change using the CML method. Greenhouse gas emissions (such as carbon dioxide, methane or nitrous oxide) are measured by their potential to contribute to global warming. Timber products are usually given a negative GWP result for the production stage, due to carbon sequestration.

GWP in the construction industry: The main origin of greenhouse emissions in the construction industry is the fossil fuels consumed during fabrication processes, especially for cement calcination.

Measurement: The baseline substance is carbon dioxide (CO_2): for example, 1kg of dinitrogen oxide is equivalent to 265kg of carbon dioxide. EPDs express this quantity as kg CO_2-eq.

Acidification Potential (AP)

Definition: Acidification is the pH decrease in freshwater, oceans and soil. The main substances that cause acidification are sulphur oxides, nitrogen oxides, ammonia and phosphoric acid. EPDs normally measure AP in freshwater.

AP in the construction industry: The production of clinker for cement contributes considerably to the emissions of sulphur dioxide and nitrogen oxides. Another cause of acidification is the production of plastic-based materials used for membranes, adhesives and thermal-insulation boards.

Measurement: The baseline substance is sulphur dioxide (SO_2): for example, 1kg of nitrogen monoxide is equivalent to 0.07kg of sulphur dioxide. EPDs express this quantity as kg SO_2-eq.

Ozone Depletion Potential (ODP)

Definition: Chlorofluorocarbons (CFCs) and other halocarbon emissions have been found to cause the thinning of the stratospheric ozone, which plays a vital part in protecting the Earth from harmful ultraviolet radiation. ODP is the potential of a material to emit these types of substances.

ODP in the construction industry: Chlorofluorocarbons are emitted during the production of polyurethane foam (which can, for instance, make the core of structural insulated panels).

Measurement: The baseline substance is trichlorofluoromethane (CFC11): for example, 1kg of dichlorodifluoromethane is equivalent to 0.04kg of CFC11. EPDs express this quantity as kg CFC11-eq.

Eutrophication Potential (EP)

Definition: Eutrophication (also known as nutrification, hypertrophication and nutrient enrichment) is the over-fertilization of a body of water or soil, which causes uncontrolled growth of plant matter. It is caused by phosphate, nitrogen, nitrogen oxides and ammonium.

EP in the construction industry: Sources of substances that cause eutrophication include the processing of coarse aggregate for concrete and the production of plastic-based products and insulants.

Measurement: The baseline substance is phosphate (PO_4): for example, 1kg of ammonia monoxide is equivalent to 0.35kg of phosphate. EPDs express this quantity as kg PO_4-eq.

Fig. 3.2. Algal bloom in a river, near a mountainous village in the Chengdu area of Sichuan (China). Eutrophication consists in excessive plant and algal growth in a body of water, due to high concentration of nutrients. This phenomenon depletes the oxygen in the water, thus reducing biodiversity. (Photo: Felix Andrews, CC BY-SA 3.0)

Fig. 3.3. Low smog over Almaty, Kazakhstan's largest city. This is a photochemical phenomenon: air pollutants, such as carbon monoxide, react with solar radiation creating low banks of ozone. (Photo: Igors Jefimovs, CC BY 3.0)

Photochemical Ozone Creation Potential (POCP)

Definition: Tropospheric ozone is created by an imbalance in the level of nitrogen oxide in the lower atmosphere, caused by photochemical reactions, aided by sun rays, with airborne emissions of carbon monoxide (CO) and volatile organic compounds. This phenomenon is popularly known as summer smog. The main substances that cause it are ethene, methane, propane, propene and acetylene. This performance indicator might also be termed photochemical oxidant formation potential.

POCP in the construction industry: Sources of substances that contribute to photochemical ozone formation include the production of, and the waste associated with, concrete, and the manufacture of adhesives and plastics.

Measurement: The baseline substance is ethene: for example, 1kg of propene is equivalent to 0.97kg of ethene. EPDs express this quantity as kg ethene-eq.

Abiotic Depletion Potential (ADP)

Definition: This indicator refers to the amount of non-renewable sources used for energy production.

ADP in the construction industry: Some non-renewable elements used in the construction industry include antimony and aluminium. The production of insulating materials and concrete is a major contributor to this impact.

Measurement: The baseline substance is antimony (Sb). EPDs express this quantity as kg Sb-eq.

Energy Consumption

Definition: EPDs divide energy consumption into renewable and non-renewable energy sources. Renewable energy is further subdivided into raw materials (for example, biomass) and energy carriers (for example, hydropower, geothermal energy, wind energy and solar energy). Some EPDs might use the labels 'renewable primary energy resources used as energy carrier' and 'renewable primary energy resources used as raw materials' to refer to these categories. Non-renewable energy is also subdivided into raw materials (for example, mineral resources, metal ores and fossil fuels) and energy carriers (for example, nuclear energy and fossil energy). Some EPDs might use the labels 'non-renewable primary energy resources used as energy carrier' and 'non-renewable primary energy resources used as raw materials' to refer to these categories.

Energy consumption in the construction industry: Cement demands the largest share of energy in the building sector for two reasons: the high energy-usage needed to produce each unit mass and the sheer quantity of cement required by building projects across the globe. The production of insulants also carries a high energy-demand.

Measurement: Megajoule (MJ)

Waste

Definition: EPDs consider the following types of waste: hazardous waste (such as treated timber, concrete additives, asbestos, adhesives, paint), non-hazardous waste (such as timber, packaging, plastic, carpets, tantalized timber) and radioactive waste (for example, uranium). In Europe, waste is classified according to the European Waste Catalogue (European Commission Decision 2000/532/EC).

Measurement: EPDs present the quantities of disposed waste in kg.

Other Eco-Labels

BREEAM certification

The Building Research Establishment Environmental Assessment Method (BREEAM) [7] from the Building Research Establishment (BRE) assesses the following categories: energy, health and wellbeing, innovation, land use, materials, management, pollution, transport, waste and water. Unlike EPDs, this certification does provide an overall rating (outstanding, excellent, very good, good, pass or unclassified).

An important aspect of BREEAM is that it assesses the timber used in a building project based on the UK's Timber Procurement Policy, which stipulates that all wood must originate from legal and sustainable sources or follow the Forest Law Enforcement, Governance and Trade scheme (which bans products originating from unlawful logging).

Forest certification

Programme for the Endorsement of Forest Certification (PEFC)

Proper forest management, explored in Chapter 1, is a key element in ensuring that timber is truly sustainable. PEFC[8] uses a third-party certification scheme. Companies and products that obtain this certificate must achieve the following targets: ecologically important forests are identified, protected and conserved; the spirit of the Declaration on Fundamental Principles and Rights at Work (1998) and the United Nations Declaration on the Rights of Indigenous Peoples (2007) are met; forest conversions (the clearing of natural forests) are avoided; they contribute to the biodiversity of landscape, ecosystem and species; the capability of forests to produce a range of wood and non-wood forest products and services on a sustainable basis is maintained; and harvesting levels do not exceed a rate that can be sustained in the long term. Additionally, genetically modified trees are not allowed.

Forest Stewardship Council (FSC)

The FSC[9] label offers assurances that a timber product originates from a certified forest where activities are lawful, workers' rights are respected, communities and indigenous peoples' rights are safeguarded, the environment is protected, there is a vision for long-term management, actions are adjusted in response to changes in the woodland, and historical and natural features are protected.

Notes

[1] British Standards Institution, 2014, BS EN 16485
[2] Klöpffer and Grahl, 2014; Lessaveur, 2015
[3] Boustead, 1996; Lundholm and Sundströn, 1985
[4] Guinée et al., 2001
[5] International Organization for Standardization, 2006, ISO 14040 and ISO 14044
[6] ECO Platform, 2013, p.1
[7] BRE, 2021
[8] PEFC, 2021
[9] FSC, ca.2021

Chapter Four

Designing with Timber-Framed Panels

Overview

Timber-frame (TF) panel construction comprises two main systems: platform frame and balloon frame (*see* Figs 4.2 and 4.3). The former derives its name from the fact that, at each level, the wall panels sit on the floor underneath, which acts as a supporting platform. In balloon frame, studs span more than one storey and provide support for the joists of the intermediate floors. This chapter focuses

Fig. 4.2. In platform frame construction, the walls of each storey sit on the platform (the intermediate floor) supported by the walls underneath. (Drawing: *Kit and Modern Timber Frame Homes*, Crowood, 2007)

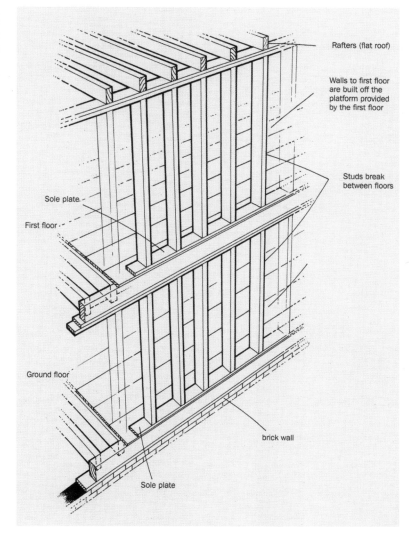

Rafters (flat roof)

Walls to first floor are built off the platform provided by the first floor

Studs break between floors

Sole plate

First floor

Ground floor

brick wall

Sole plate

OPPOSITE: **Fig. 4.1.** Maggie's Centre in Cardiff, designed by Dow Jones Architects. The intimate space (*cwtch*) is separated from the rest of the building by a curtain made from Welsh fabric. (Photo: Anthony Coleman)

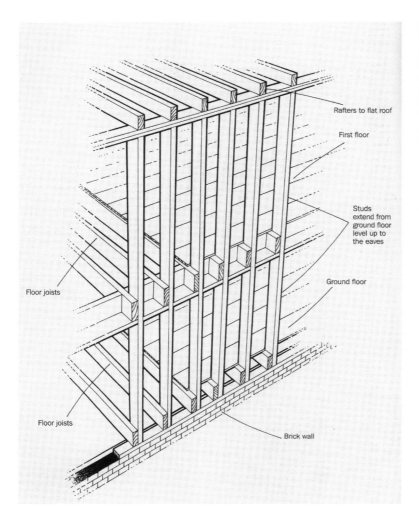

Fig. 4.3. In balloon frame construction, the double-height timber studs support the flexural members that make up the intermediate floor. This system, which dates back to the turn of the nineteenth century, derives its name from the fact that it was deemed as easy to construct 'as blowing up a balloon'. (Drawing: *Kit and Modern Timber Frame Homes*, Crowood, 2007)

Rafters to flat roof

First floor

Studs extend from ground floor level up to the eaves

Floor joists

Ground floor

Floor joists

Brick wall

on the platform-frame system. In most European countries, including the UK, all structural calculations for timber buildings need to adhere to harmonized standard EN 1995, Eurocode 5: Design of timber structures.

External Walls

The framed panel

The techniques that we are going to discuss illustrate walls in which the loadbearing role is fulfilled by the TF panels placed on the inside, complemented by an external cladding system. The outer cladding can be heavyweight (a masonry leaf resting on the foundations) or lightweight (for example timber or metal systems connected to, and supported by, the TF panels).

In a TF panel, the timber studs are typically placed at 600mm centres, or at 400mm centres especially when this is needed for structural reasons. The studs run between two important timbers that define the horizontal sides of the panels: the bottom rail and the top rail. The studs have two fundamental roles:

- they withstand all the forces (vertical and horizontal) to which the TF panels are subjected and transfer them to the bottom rail and thus to the substrate;
- they provide fixing points for the other structural and non-structural components of the panels: for example inner lining, outer sheathing, wall ties (where applicable), insulation quilts or boards.

Where the wall panels are subjected to higher concentrated loads, the studs can be doubled or tripled. The bottom rail and top rail generally employ the same timber section as the studs, which are nailed to the rails. Like the studs, the rails offer fixing support for the sheathing and lining of the panels.

The studs are horizontally connected by timbers called noggings (or 'dwangs', in Scotland), whose functions are:

- to stabilize the pair of studs that they connect, and, as an overall effect, the whole TF panel. Noggings prevent the studs from deflecting or coming out of their plane under the forces exerted on the panels;
- to offer fixing points for lining sheets or a variety of fixtures and fittings (for example switch boxes, radiators, cabinets and wall units).

If a TF panel is subjected to a concentrated vertical load of significant magnitude, then the frame can be locally reinforced with an additional compressive member. This can be achieved by doubling or tripling the standard stud, or by resorting to a stud with a larger cross-section, made from solid timber or engineered timber (for example glulam or LVL). In multi-storey buildings, if the fenestration is not regular and the openings are not vertically aligned, then the studs supporting the lintel of an upper storey will exert concentrated actions on the TF panels of the lower storey. Other concentrated loads might be transferred to the TF panels by beams or trimming joists (which support a larger floor area than ordinary joists), or – on the top floor – by roof beams, trusses, purlins and so on. Where needed, additional posts can also be inserted between adjacent panels to withstand concentrated loads.

The external sheathing is an important layer of TF panels: these are typically covered with OSB sheets or, less frequently, with plywood sheets (with significant economic repercussions). OSB/3 is generally the preferred type of OSB used, in 9mm-thick sheets (or less commonly 11, 15 or 18mm). If plywood is chosen, this should be adequate for humid or exterior conditions, and specified in sheets of at least 9.5mm. Alternatives to these materials are fibreboard, gypsum board or particleboard adequately reinforced or manufactured for this type of application (*see* Chapter 2 for a description of these products). The external sheathing fulfils numerous functions:

- it encloses and protects the framework of the panel and the insulation layer with a continuous surface on its outer side;
- it provides support for the breather membrane and other components (for example cavity barriers installed for fire safety, or flashings);
- it provides the panels with resistance to horizontal forces, such as the in-plane forces exerted by the wind (this is referred to as 'racking resistance');
- it makes the panels more airtight (airtightness can be further increased by taping the joints of adjacent sheets);
- in prefabricated panels awaiting installation, it prevents their distortion.

Each sheathing sheet is fixed all around its perimeter to the substrate (studs, top rail and bottom rail). Such connection can be obtained with nails or staples. The overall racking resistance offered by the external sheathing will depend on the sheet material specified and will increase with increased thickness and reduced nailing or stapling centres.

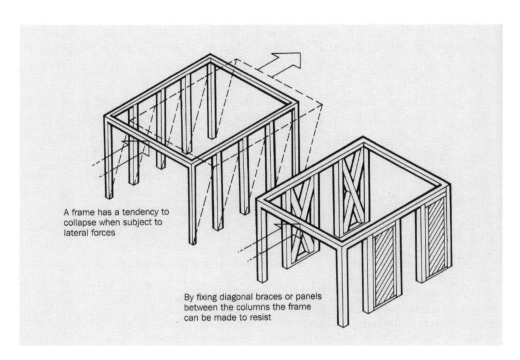

A frame has a tendency to collapse when subject to lateral forces

By fixing diagonal braces or panels between the columns the frame can be made to resist

Fig. 4.4. The columns of a structural frame are mainly designed to resist vertical loads and might need to be complemented by braces or diaphragms in order that horizontal forces, if any, be withstood. (Drawing: *Kit and Modern Timber Frame Homes*, Crowood, 2007)

The TF panels are generally, and advisably, connected to their support not directly, but with the interposition of a sole plate. More specifically, the sole plate serves the following functions:

- during the construction process:
  - it offers a level base for the TF panels. The plate can be levelled with adequate use of spacers and structural grout underneath it;
  - it acts as a nailing plate to which the TF panels can subsequently be fixed with relative ease;
- during use of the building, it transfers the loads from the TF panels to the foundation system or to the intermediate floor.

The sole plate can be fixed to the foundations using various methods; for instance, by shooting ballistic nails through the plate itself and penetrating the damp-proof course (DPC) and the foundations, or by using mechanical anchors (for example metal angles) fixed to the sole plate with carpentry nails and to the foundations with ballistic or masonry nails. In most cases, the portion of the sole plate under a door is cut out after the full installation of the wall panels.

A breather membrane is usually applied on the outer side of the external sheathing, with multiple aims. During the construction phase, the membrane role is:

- to protect the TF panels from the weather elements before such protection is provided by the outer cladding;
- to protect the panels while they are transported from the factory to the construction site and during the subsequent phases (if the membrane has been applied in the factory).

During the operational phase (when the cladding has been installed), the membrane role is:

- to provide extra protection from the weather, especially in the case of wind-driven rainwater penetration through the cladding;
- to contribute to the overall airtightness of the external walls;
- to contribute to the thermal performance of the walls (by reducing their transmittance, especially if reflective membranes are specified).

The breather membrane can be fixed to the TF panels in the factory (which is the advisable option) or on site. Breather membranes are available in different materials. Widely utilized products are obtained from non-woven, polymer-based membranes – for example polypropylene (PP) – less than 1mm thick. The material used must simultaneously offer high resistance to water penetration and low resistance to water-vapour transmission (hence the breathability). The former allows the membrane to guarantee protection from the weather and the latter to allow any vapour trapped inside the panels to pass through it, thus preventing damage to the timbers (especially rotting) and to the thermal-insulation layer. The fabric used for breather membranes can additionally be treated with a low-emissivity reflective coating (which is installed facing the cavity between the panels and the cladding system). The membrane is fixed to the panels, with upper layers overlapping lower layers. Vertical overlapping is also very important, with a typically recommended overlap of 150mm. The membrane can be attached to the sheathing with steel fixings such as stainless staples (most common option) or galvanized nails, applied at stud positions and at suitable intervals. To locate the studs (which are concealed by the sheathing layer), reinforcing tape is often used, which is made of plastic (for example PVC) and offers the additional benefit of strengthening the fixing (especially by increasing tear resistance).

A head binder is often added to the construction, so as to tie adjacent panels and provide the wall with greater stability. The head binder is placed on the top rails of the panels and runs over their joints, thus connecting two or more panels (either aligned or at 90-degree angles). The head binder also improves the path of the loads transferred by joists, beams or rafters to the wall, by distributing them more evenly between adjacent panels.

Thermal insulation is generally achieved by inserting appropriate products between the studs, which can be chosen from a very broad range:

- soft/flexible products; the most common are quilts or batts made of mineral- or glass-wool. Sheep wool can also be used;
- rigid or semi-rigid boards (for example expanded or extruded polystyrene, polyurethane, polyisocyanurate or wood fibre);
- blown cellulose fibre, which can be obtained from recycled newspapers.

The choice of insulant has important repercussions on the dimensions of the studs and, consequently, on the overall thickness of the TF panels. The depth of the studs depends not only on structural aspects (such as mechanical properties of the timber used or loading conditions), but also on the thermal performance of the products fitted between the studs. In low-rise construction, the depth needed for structural purposes is often exceeded by that needed to achieve thermal-insulation targets. As a consequence, the thermal conductivity of the specified product plays an important role in the design and detailing process: if products (such as rigid-foam boards) with very low conductivity are used, then the depth of the studs can be minimized. Irrespective of the type of insulant used, it is important to insulate the TF panels as homogeneously as possible, thus avoiding areas with less insulant (or no insulant at all), especially in parts of the panels that are more difficult to reach for the operatives. It is worth noticing that the thermal-insulation layer also affects other properties of the panels, such as their acoustic insulation and fire resistance.

A vapour-control layer (VCL) is installed on the warm side of the thermal insulant, in order to prevent any water vapour produced inside the building from reaching dewpoint temperature as it passes through the wall make-up and condensing (this phenomenon is referred to as interstitial condensation). The materials on the warm side of the insulant need to be specified attentively, ensuring that their vapour resistivity is significantly higher than that of the materials on the cold side. The VCL is usually a thin (<0.2mm) layer of polythene (PE) stapled to the timber studs or the internal sheathing of the panels. Similar to the breather membrane, adjacent polythene sheets need to be installed with overlaps (of around 100mm), both vertically and horizontally. The joints between sheets can be taped to avoid discontinuity in the VCL. Alternatively, plasterboard can be specified that incorporates the VCL function (the gypsum board is backed with an additional polyester film). The presence of a VCL also reduces the wall's air permeability, hence it is sometimes referred to as the air- and vapour-control layer (AVCL).

The wall construction is completed on one side with an internal lining. A very common product used for this layer is gypsum plasterboard, with a typical thickness of 12.5mm. Other thicknesses are also available (for example 15mm) or can be obtained by installing two boards, preferably with staggered joints. A great advantage of plasterboard is not only its suitability as an internal finish that can easily be painted, but also the fact that it contributes to the overall fire resistance of a wall. Plasterboard is a material of limited combustibility. A 12.5mm-thick layer of plasterboard (with mass per unit area $\geq 10\text{kg/m}^2$)

Fig. 4.6. Strip foundations and suspended ground floor have been completed. A timber sole plate has been placed along the perimeter of the external walls. The TF wall panels will now be installed on top of the sole plate. A damp-proof course (DPC) separates the foundations from the sole plate, to protect the plate itself and the whole TF wall from moisture.

Fig. 4.5. Construction of a detached TF house. The foundation walls have been erected on strip foundations under all perimeter and loadbearing walls, both internal and external. The suspended ground floor will be built using a beam-and-block system. The external walls will be composed of an inner TF leaf and an outer masonry leaf.

Fig. 4.7. A large manufacturing facility for TF components. On the assembly line shown, TF wall panels are being fabricated.

Fig. 4.8. Assembly of closed TF wall panels. In the panel in the background, the mineral-wool quilt has been fitted between the studs. In the panel in the foreground, the VCL has been stapled on the inner side of the quilts and is ready to be further processed with the addition of other layers.

Fig. 4.10. An operative is fixing the OSB sheathing layer to the timber framework of an external-wall panel, by means of a pneumatic nailgun.

Fig. 4.11. An operative is manually fitting a mineral-wool quilt between the studs of a wall panel.

Fig. 4.9. The outside of a closed TF panel, complete with breather membrane (yellow) and windows.

Fig. 4.12. An operative is fixing the vapour-control layer on the inside of the wool quilt, with a pneumatic stapler. He is adding reinforcing tape along the fixing points, to strengthen them and to mark the position of the studs behind the VCL.

Fig. 4.13. Courtyard of the same manufacturing facility shown in Fig. 4.12. The timber components have been grouped and wrapped in a protective plastic layer, while they wait to be loaded onto trucks and transported to the construction site.

Fig. 4.14. Interior side of a house's external wall made of closed TF panels. Technical installations (electric cables and water-supply pipes) run through the floor's metal-web joists and within the service void (the timber battens of which can be seen). The discharge stack will be boxed off.

Fig. 4.15. Service void in a bathroom, with discharge stack, and piping for a washbasin (water supply and drainage pipes). Gypsum plasterboard will be fixed to the timber battens to close the void.

offers a fire resistance of thirty minutes; therefore, if doubled, it will offer a resistance of sixty minutes. The plasterboard can be finished by taping and filling (dry process), or by skim-coating (wet process). Other lining products include timber boards or timber-based materials such as plywood, OSB, MDF and particleboard, including the cement-bonded type (*see* Chapter 2). The internal lining is either nailed or screwed to the timber studs.

Openings

Openings need to be studied carefully and require the addition of special members to the frame, especially if the wall has a loadbearing role. In loadbearing walls, a lintel is necessary and needs to be placed immediately underneath the top rail. The depth of the lintel will depend upon structural factors such as its span, the magnitude of the loads transferred to the lintel itself by the structure above, the mechanical properties of the timber specified and the desired deflection limit. The necessary width of the lintel can be obtained either with a single section or by doubling (and connecting) two sections. It is important to remember that the lintel's maximum deflection will have an effect on the integrity and functioning of the windows or doors installed: if deflection is excessive, it will damage the frame or the glazing of these components.

Lintels need to be supported by *ad hoc* members, called cripple studs, since they are shorter than the ordinary studs running between the bottom and the top rails. Depending on the structural factors

Fig. 4.16. A PVC window inserted into a closed TF wall panel. Various membranes are overlapped around the opening: VCL (foil), breather membrane (yellow) and DPC (black) near the sill.

mentioned above for the depth of the lintel, vertical support to a lintel can be offered by a single or a double cripple stud. The horizontal member defining the sill of a window also requires its own cripple stud(s) at both ends. Therefore, where there is a window, the foot of the panel presents at least three studs on each side of the opening. Forming doors within a loadbearing wall follows a very similar pattern but does not require the members described for the sill.

In non-loadbearing walls (and, in general, if there are no vertical loads acting on the head of a panel where an opening is needed), lintels are not necessary and the top edge of the opening is defined by a more slender horizontal member.

The construction of the frame around an opening is easier and requires less material usage if its position coincides with the framing grid (which results in the opening's width being a multiple of the stud centres).

External cladding

Two categories of external cladding can be identified in terms of their weight and support method: lightweight and heavyweight. Lightweight cladding is attached to the TF panels and transfers all the actions (including its weight) to them. Heavyweight cladding rests directly on the foundations and is not meant to transfer any vertical loads to the TF panels. The only actions exerted by heavy cladding onto the TF leaf are horizontal and occur through the fixings added to restrain the outer wall, as will be explained in more detail in the 'Heavyweight cladding' section.

When detailing the external cladding, it is important to take into careful consideration the problem of differential movement between the cladding itself and the TF panels and – where applicable – between different types of external cladding. Differential movement can occur throughout the lifespan of a building, since different materials will expand or contract at

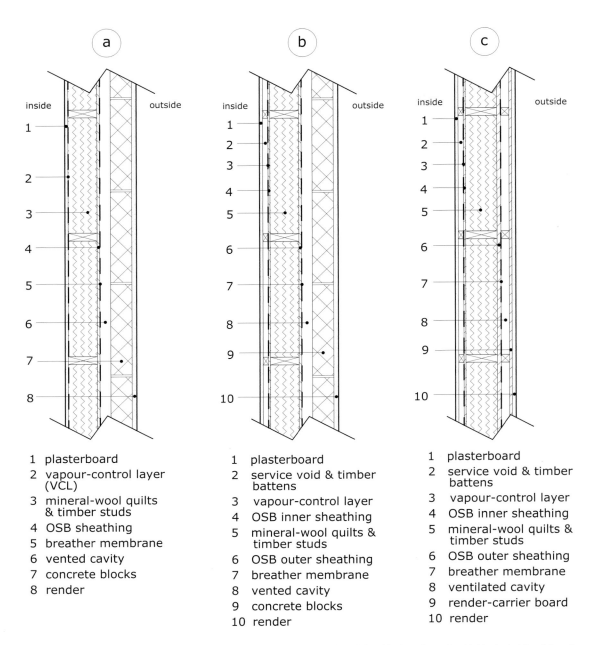

Fig. 4.17. Construction of timber-frame external walls: open panels with block cladding (a), closed panels with block cladding (b), and closed panels with render on carrier board (c). (Drawing: after Sanna, 2018)

a
1 plasterboard
2 vapour-control layer (VCL)
3 mineral-wool quilts & timber studs
4 OSB sheathing
5 breather membrane
6 vented cavity
7 concrete blocks
8 render

b
1 plasterboard
2 service void & timber battens
3 vapour-control layer
4 OSB inner sheathing
5 mineral-wool quilts & timber studs
6 OSB outer sheathing
7 breather membrane
8 vented cavity
9 concrete blocks
10 render

c
1 plasterboard
2 service void & timber battens
3 vapour-control layer
4 OSB inner sheathing
5 mineral-wool quilts & timber studs
6 OSB outer sheathing
7 breather membrane
8 ventilated cavity
9 render-carrier board
10 render

a different rate as a consequence of fluctuations in temperature and humidity. In addition to this, the TF panels are likely to contract during the first months after construction, as they gradually lose moisture content. Finally, settlement can be a further cause for differential movement. For these reasons, the cladding must be constructed in a way that allows the different leaves or components of the external walls to undergo changes in volume without these resulting in any damage (for example, cracking).

Fig. 4.18. Special wall ties need to be utilized to connect a masonry leaf to a timber-framed loadbearing panel. In these fasteners, the horizontal component (inserted into the mortar beds) can move vertically within the component fixed to the timber-frame panel. Thanks to this device, any differential movement between the outer leaf and the timber panels will not result in damage to the wall. (Drawing: Leviat)

Lightweight cladding

Components available for this type of cladding are numerous and include:

- timber boards, which can be arranged according to different patterns: vertically, horizontally and diagonally (timber boarding will be dealt with further down in this section);
- timber shingles;
- tiles made of clay, stone (for example slate), cement, polymers or other synthetic materials (for example artificial slate). Tiles are generally nailed to horizontal battens, which are fixed to vertical counterbattens in turn attached to the studs of the TF panels. The installation of vertical counterbattens is not always executed

but is recommended, as it facilitates drainage of any rainwater that might have penetrated the cladding and thus acts as a protective measure for the TF panels (along with the breather membrane);
- brick slips, which require a supporting substrate (generally a proprietary system) fixed to the timber panels;
- metal screens, which require a rail system to be connected to the TF panels;
- metal sheets (such as copper, aluminium, zinc, or alloys);
- render on *ad hoc* stainless-steel laths or on carrier boards, which can be wood-based or cement-based (such as fibre-cement, cement-bonded particleboard). Carrier boards are generally fixed to vertical timber battens connected to the studs through the external sheathing and the breather membrane. It is good practice to interpose a DPC layer between the timber battens and the carrier board in order to prevent the former from absorbing any moisture from the latter. Various types of render are currently available, from cement-based renders to acrylic ones.

All these cladding systems require a slender cavity (of at least 20mm) between the TF panels and the cladding for drainage and ventilation. Thus, the cavity contributes to the protection and durability of the TF panels.

In all of the cladding systems outlined above, durability of the battens and counterbattens is significantly increased if they have been pre-treated with preservatives. When battens are cut on site, it is advisable to paint the newly formed surfaces with preservatives, so as to avoid weaker areas where the timbers are more vulnerable to biological attack and consequent deterioration (due to fungi or insects, *see* Chapters 1 and 2).

Timber cladding can be constructed with many variations, depending on the geometry of the boards and the patterns in which they are fixed. An important measure to make this type of cladding successful in the long term is to install it in such a way that the boards can shrink and swell following variations in moisture content (associated with their hygroscopicity and exposure to the elements) without undergoing distortion or causing damage. This affects various aspects of the cladding system: the dimension of the boards, the profile of their longitudinal edges, the gaps left between the boards and the anchoring system. The cavity between the TF panels and the boards should be adequately ventilated, with openings both at its top and bottom. Wood species commonly utilized for cladding include spruce, pine, larch and cedar among softwoods, and sweet chestnut and oak among hardwoods. Depending on the natural durability of the selected species, preservative treatment will be more or less important for the long-term performance of the cladding layer. When the selected species is classed as durable (for example Western red cedar) or as moderately durable (for example Douglas fir or European larch), treatment

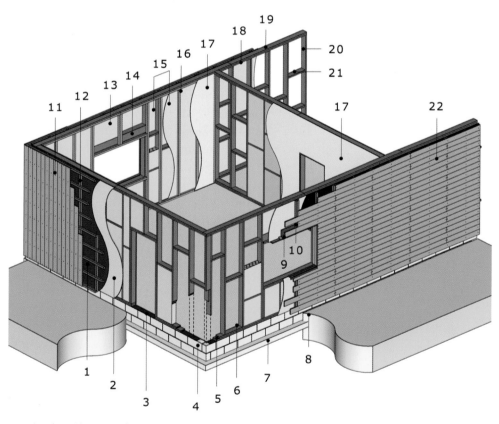

Fig. 4.19. Construction of a timber-frame house clad in timber boards arranged vertically (left) or horizontally (right). The inner, loadbearing leaf of the external walls is constructed of closed panels.

1	breather membrane	12	vertical counterbatten
2	outer sheathing	13	mineral-wool quilt
3	damp-proof course (DPC)	14	timber lintel
4	foundation wall	15	inner & outer sheathing
5	sole plate	16	timber batten (service void)
6	bottom rail	17	plasterboard
7	foundation footing	18	top rail
8	finished ground level	19	head binder
9	metal flashing	20	timber stud
10	vertical batten	21	nogging
11	external cladding: vertical timber boards on horizontal battens	22	external cladding: horizontal timber boards on vertical battens

is often avoided, which means that the boards will gradually weather and acquire a grey tint. The boards should be secured to the timber battens by means of stainless-steel fixings, especially if species are specified that are rich in tannin (such as Western red cedar), which causes rusting. Either nails or screws can be used.

In horizontal boarding, a variety of cross-sections are available for the timber boards. When the longitudinal edges overlap, possible options are: square edge, feather edge (also available rebated), shiplap and tongue and groove. An open-joint system is also possible, whereby boards do not overlap along their longitudinal edges. In all cases, the abutting ends of the boards should not overlap and gaps of at least 5mm are needed, not only to allow the boards to expand without exerting pressure on one another, but also to prevent rainwater from being trapped between boards and being eventually absorbed by the end-grain, where wood is particularly hygroscopic. Fixing horizontal boards to the TF panels is rather straightforward, as it only requires vertical battens, which should be aligned with the studs and fixed to them. Board-to-batten fixing is generally performed with nails.

In vertical boarding, the way in which the boards are mounted onto the TF panels preferably requires one more layer. The boards are fixed to horizontal battens, and these, in turn, should be fixed to vertical counterbattens, to provide sufficient ventilation and drainage in the cavity, and thus preserve the cladding itself and especially the TF panels. This results in a thicker cavity than is needed for horizontal boarding. Both overlapping and open-jointed systems are available in vertical boarding, the former including shiplap, tongue-and-grove and board-on-board profiles[1].

Heavyweight cladding

Common types of heavyweight cladding include:

- bricks, rendered or exposed. Popular types are clay or calcium-silicate bricks;
- concrete or clay blocks (the former being a far more conventional choice than the latter);
- natural stone.

The outer leaf is slender and thus needs to be stabilized by means of wall ties that connect it to the loadbearing TF panels. These ties, however, also need to accommodate differential movement between the two wall leaves and thus need to be specified appropriately. Ties for timber frames are indeed more flexible than those used to connect two masonry skins (for example in brick-and-block cavity walls). Special types of ties exist that can accommodate vertical movement of up to about 7mm. Wall ties are made mostly of stainless steel, and thus cause some degree of thermal bridging between the outer and inner leaves. In order to reduce this undesired phenomenon, optimized types of ties are available that consist of two parts: the part connected to the TF panels is of stainless steel and the part inserted into the masonry is made of a low-conductivity material (for example fibre-reinforced resin). The fixing schedule for the ties depends on the building's level of exposure to the wind. Wall ties need to be fixed to the timber studs, through the sheathing.

The junction between the head of the masonry leaf and a pitched or flat roof must include a gap to accommodate differential movement in the vertical direction. A movement joint (or expansion joint) might be needed depending on the size of the walls, and on the type of cladding specified; for instance, clay bricks have a higher coefficient of expansion than calcium-silicate bricks and concrete blocks. Movement joints can be both vertical and horizontal. It is common practice to seal the gaps between different masonry 'panels' with compressible fillers such as mastic.

The cavity between the TF panels and the masonry skin needs to be at least 40mm thick, and allow drainage and ventilation (typically, at lower rates than is necessary when lightweight cladding is chosen). Air flow through the cavity is facilitated by *ad hoc* perforations in the masonry skin. This can be achieved by not filling some perpends with mortar, or by inserting ventilators between bricks or blocks. Proprietary metal or plastic

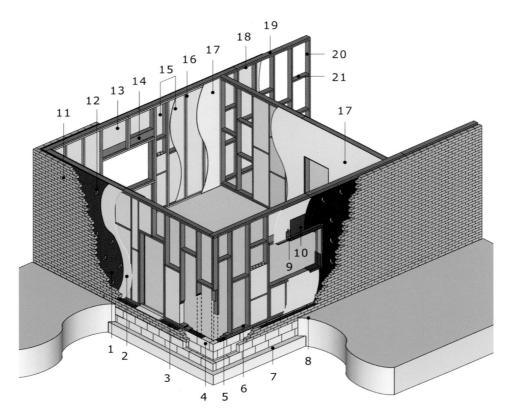

Fig. 4.20.
Construction of a timber-frame house clad in exposed bricks. The inner, loadbearing leaf of the external walls is constructed of closed panels.

1	breather membrane	12	wall tie
2	outer sheathing	13	mineral-wool quilt
3	damp-proof course (DPC)	14	timber lintel
4	inner leaf of foundation wall	15	inner & outer sheathing
5	sole plate	16	timber batten (service void)
6	bottom rail	17	plasterboard
7	foundation footing	18	top rail
8	finished ground level	19	head binder
9	metal lintel	20	timber stud
10	cavity tray	21	nogging
11	external cladding: bricks		

ventilators are usually complete with a grille to impede insect access. When placed at the bottom of the cavity, ventilators also fulfil the role of weep holes, in that they allow any incidental water present in the cavity to drain out. Ventilators should also be inserted where there are cavity trays (for instance, above windows and doors).

Internal Walls

Internal walls may or may not have a loadbearing function: the sizing of the frame members will depend mostly on this parameter. Typically, internal walls do not need to provide thermal insulation, as they generally separate spaces that are all heated. However, these walls do need to provide sufficient acoustic insulation, particularly when – for programmatic reasons – they enclose rooms where high noise can be produced and/or lack of noise is strongly desirable. In residential buildings, it is good practice to provide high acoustic insulation in bedrooms and between toilets/bathrooms and other rooms. In the UK, national building regulations set out different acoustic requirements for internal walls.

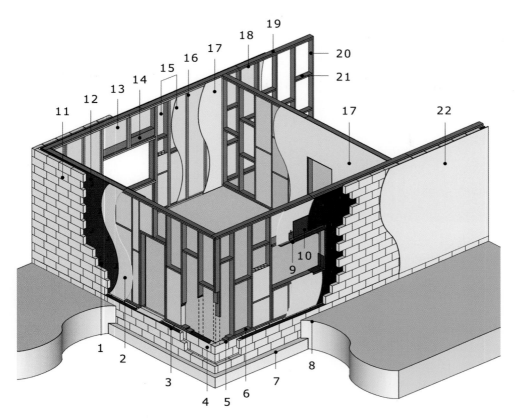

Fig. 4.21.
Construction of
a timber-frame
house clad in
rendered concrete
blocks. The inner,
loadbearing leaf of
the external walls
is constructed of
closed panels.

1	breather membrane	12	wall tie
2	outer sheathing	13	mineral-wool quilt
3	damp-proof course (DPC)	14	timber lintel
4	inner leaf of foundation wall	15	inner & outer sheathing
5	sole plate	16	timber batten (service void)
6	bottom rail	17	plasterboard
7	foundation footing	18	top rail
8	finished ground level	19	head binder
9	metal lintel	20	timber stud
10	cavity tray	21	nogging
11	external cladding: concrete blocks	22	render

The construction of the timber frame follows the principles illustrated in the external walls section. It is common practice, where this is adequate from a structural point of view, to use 38 × 89mm sections for the studs. The studs are positioned at 600, 400 or 300mm centres, depending on the vertical loads that need to be resisted by the TF panel. The panel is delimited horizontally by the bottom rail and top rail; it is advisable to install it on a sole plate and to add a head binder, as was seen for external walls.

Party Walls

Beside structural criteria, party walls need to fulfil two important functions: to acoustically insulate two adjacent residential units and to provide them with a sufficient level of safety in case a fire occurs in either of them. In low-rise dwellings, the construction must offer at least sixty-minute fire resistance from either side. Details of fire-safety requirements vary across the four regions of the UK.

Fig. 4.22. Internal walls with TF panels sheathed on one side with OSB and awaiting insertion of acoustic insulant and lining.

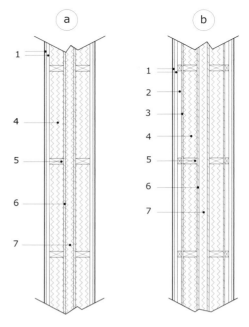

1	plasterboard (double layer)	4	mineral-wool quilt
2	timber battens & service void	5	timber stud
3	inner OSB sheathing	6	outer OSB sheathing
		7	sound-absorbing layer: unfaced, wire-reinforced mineral-wool quilt (fixed to one leaf only)

Fig. 4.23. Build-up of timber-frame separating walls: open panels (a), and closed panels (b). Flanking sound transmission needs to be considered at junctions. (Drawing: after Sanna, 2018)

For the purposes of acoustic insulation, if a TF party wall consists of two leaves, these should be constructed as independently as possible of each other and without any hard connections. However, this might clash with structural safety considerations and the need to connect the two leaves with metal ties (whose typical cross-section is around 40mm × 3mm). Cross-bracing of each individual leaf might also be required and, if so, can be achieved by installing diagonal members.

Within each leaf, the spaces between the studs are typically filled with unfaced mineral-wool quilts, whose density should be high enough to provide good acoustic insulation (density ≥ 12kg/m³ in Scotland and ≥ 10kg/m³ elsewhere in the UK). Internally, the TF panels are lined with sheet materials, generally plasterboard in two or more layers (with staggered joints) to achieve the target sixty-minute resistance. The properties (dimension and thickness) of the plasterboard also play an important role in the achievement of the desired acoustic insulation level, by forming a barrier to airborne sound. The overall thickness of the plasterboard layers is generally no less than 30mm.

Depending on structural calculations, the external side of each leaf might need to be sheathed with OSB, plywood or similar, especially to increase the wall's racking resistance. Even where sheathing is not necessary for structural purposes, it is good practice to install it, so as to make the two leaves as complete as possible and augment the level of separation between the residential units. The cavity between the two leaves does not have to be insulated in all UK nations; where this is a requirement, it is filled with similar quilts to those used between the studs.

Ground Floors

The timber joists can span between loadbearing walls either uninterruptedly or with intermediate supports, typically built as perforated walls made of bricks or blocks that rest on a concrete oversite slab. The cross-sectional dimension of the joists will depend mostly on this decision. Uninterrupted spans will entail larger timber cross-sections but at the same time will allow saving materials for the sleeper walls.

Different types of joists are available:

- solid joists;
- open-web joists;
- I-joists.

The thermal insulant is generally inserted into the spaces between the joists. If solid timber joists are used, then the insulant can be laid on different types of *ad hoc* supports fixed (for example stapled) to the joists:

- galvanized steel mesh, plastic mesh or breather membrane stapled to the joists (either to the sides or to the underside);
- particleboard sheets (or similar products) fixed to the underside of the joists. In this case, the sheets might have higher vapour resistivity than the deck; therefore, a check needs to be carried out to assess condensation risk;
- timber battens fixed to the lower edges of the joists. In this case, rigid insulation boards will be necessary.

In the first two configurations, flexible, semi-rigid or rigid insulant types can be used (mineral-wool quilts are generally specified); in the third case, only rigid boards can be employed.

A deck is laid on top of the joists. This creates a continuous layer that transfers the floor loads to the joists and offers a substrate for the upper layers of the build-up. Materials that can be used for the deck are:

- particleboard;
- plywood;
- fibreboard.

These sheets are nailed or screwed to the joists.

A vapour-control layer (VCL) can be installed on top of the insulant (in this case, the top side of the insulant is the warm side). Flooring can be laid directly on top of the deck or with the interposition of an underlay.

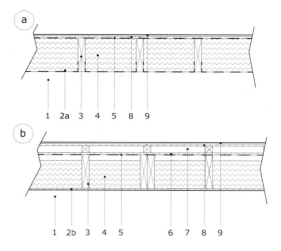

1 ventilated air space	6 OSB sheathing
2a metal or plastic mesh	7 timber battens & service void
2b OSB sheet	
3 solid timber joist	8 particleboard deck
4 mineral-wool quilt	9 flooring
5 vapour-control layer (VCL)	

Fig. 4.24. Examples of common constructions for timber-frame ground floors, with joists installed individually (a), and with floor cassettes (b). (Drawing: after Sanna, 2018)

Fig. 4.25. Ground floor of a TF house. The external walls are closed panels with an aluminium VCL. The timber battens visible on the inside of the walls create a service void. The floor employs metal-web joists. One of the joists (1) is doubled due to increased loads; hence, the studs underneath it in the internal wall (2) are quintuplicated.

Fig. 4.26. Fabrication of a cassette in a factory.
(Photo: Woodknowledge Wales & Rosie Anthony)

Fig. 4.27. Close-up of the cassette shown in Fig. 4.26. Engineered I-joists are used, with solid flanges and OSB webs. The intermediate joists are connected to the edge joists by means of steel hangers. OSB packing will be inserted at the joist-to-joist junctions, in order to thicken the webs and allow mechanical fixing. (Photo: Woodknowledge Wales & Rosie Anthony)

Intermediate Floors

The construction of intermediate floors will depend mostly on one factor: whether they have a separating function or not (separation can be between two different properties or between two different fire compartments). It is worth keeping in mind that, in platform frame construction, intermediate floors are structurally supported by the external/internal walls beneath and, in turn, support the walls of the upper storey.

Non-separating intermediate floors

This section deals with floors without a separating function. The framing of an intermediate floor is not too different from that of a suspended ground floor. Timber joists are placed at 400 or 600mm centres. The centres and the cross-sectional properties will mostly

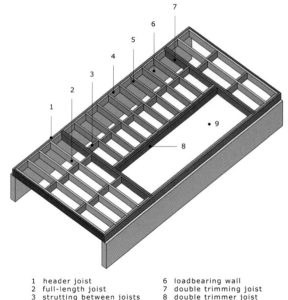

1 header joist	6 loadbearing wall
2 full-length joist	7 double trimming joist
3 strutting between joists	8 double trimmer joist
4 blocking between joists	9 opening for staircase
5 trimmed joist	

Fig. 4.28. Construction of a timber-framed intermediate floor. The opening for the staircase requires the use of trimmer and trimming joists, which can be built by doubling or tripling standard timber sections, so as to achieve the necessary structural capacity.

Fig. 4.29. An opening within a house's intermediate floor, for a staircase. We can observe the trimmer joist (1) and the trimmed joists (2) that it supports, via metal hangers. All joists utilize I-sections of engineered timber. Packing is added to the webs of the trimmer and trimmed joists to create solid sections where the joist hangers are located. The metal staircase is provisional and will be replaced by a permanent timber staircase.

Fig. 4.32. Intermediate floor with I-joists consisting of LVL flanges and fibreboard webs. The trimmed joists sit on metal hangers fixed to the trimmer joist (whose web is packed with OSB sheets to achieve the same thickness as the flanges, where needed for structural connections).

Fig. 4.30. Construction of an intermediate floor resting on closed TF panels. I-sections are used for the joists and for the strutting between them. OSB sheets are used for the deck.

Fig. 4.33. Floor constructed of open-web joists. The metal webs that connect the solid-timber flanges allow running services perpendicular to the direction of span. (Photo: Scotts Timber Engineering)

Fig. 4.31. An intermediate floor with timber I-joists and OSB decking. Strutting is obtained by interposing solid sections between the bottom flanges of the joists, at midspan. The joists rest on an internal TF wall, of which the studs, top rail and head binder can be seen.

Fig. 4.34. The external walls (1) are made in SIPs (by Hemsec Manufacturing Ltd). The first floor is constructed with metal-web joists (2), which are supported by a timber member (3) inserted into the web of a steel I-beam (4): this is done because timber-to-timber connections can easily be obtained, with the use of metal joist hangers. A solid section (5) is used to stabilize the joists laterally. The internal walls are timber-frame panels (6), separated from the concrete sub-structure by a damp-proof course. (Photo: annotated and adapted from Hemsec Manufacturing Ltd)

depend on the permanent and variable loads applied on the joists. Imposed loads on residential buildings' floors typically vary between 1.5 and 2.0 kN/m². Permanent loads will vary mostly on the finishes chosen for the floor. If solid joists are used, then they are typically aligned with the timber studs of the walls underneath. There are cases in which the framing of the floor can be designed more independently of the stud positions and thus reach a more economical configuration; for example, when loadbearing wall panels have both a top rail and a head binder, or when the joists are supported by metal hangers.

Depending on the span of the joists, and on their tendency to lateral-torsional instability, strutting might need to be provided between them, so as to make them stable. Strutting can be executed by inserting different types of components to connect every joist with the one on either side:

- a solid timber (nogging) at 90-degree angles to the joists;
- two timber diagonals (herringbone struts);
- two metal diagonals (galvanized-steel straps nailed or screwed to both the underside and top side of the joists).

Where openings need to be formed within the frame (for instance, to accommodate a staircase), trimmer joists and trimming joists will need to be inserted. As these members generally carry a greater load, they can be formed either by using beams with a larger cross-section, or by joining two (or more) standard sections. Trimmer joists offer support to trimmed joists, which, because of the opening, cannot reach one supporting wall. Trimming joists, in turn, transfer the loads from the trimmer joists to the loadbearing walls. Where trimming joists or beams meet the walls and transfer high concentrated loads, extra or increased vertical supports might need to be introduced into the wall panels, to enable them to withstand these forces. These supports can be made either by joining two or more studs of standard section within a wall panel, or by inserting a post of solid wood or engineered wood (for example LVL, glulam, and so on) between two adjacent wall panels.

A continuous deck is added on top of the joists, using particleboard or, less often, OSB or plywood. Continuous decks act as structural diaphragms and, as such, can transfer horizontal forces to loadbearing walls.

In most cases, intermediate floors are between heated spaces, and thus do not require thermal insulation. However, there are instances in which they are part of the thermal envelope and therefore need appropriate insulation: for example, when they are above an unheated space (for example a garage or storeroom) or when they project from the external walls of the lower storey. When insulation needs to be provided, products ranging from quilts to rigid foam boards can be fitted between the joists, as has been illustrated in the section on ground floors. When thermal insulant is added, a vapour-control layer will need to be installed on top of it, in order to prevent interstitial condensation.

A timber deck can also function as flooring (for instance, when it utilizes tongue-and-groove boards); otherwise, an *ad hoc* layer needs to be installed on top of it. In order to avoid damage to the chosen finish, this must be compatible with the maximum deflection foreseen for the floor. Therefore, characteristics such as brittleness and thickness of the specified flooring products need to be accounted for to ensure compatibility.

For ceiling lining, sheet materials or boards are largely used. Plasterboard is very often the preferred choice and contributes to both acoustic and fire requirements (*see* the 'Separating Floors' section). Ceiling products can be nailed or screwed to the underside of the joists, following the fixing pattern recommended by their respective manufacturers.

Intermediate floors must meet acoustic and fire-safety requirements that are distinct in each UK national code. The level of acoustic requirement will have immediate repercussions on the amount of insulant to be inserted into the build-up, to stop airborne noise. Fire-safety requirements regulate both reaction to fire and resistance to fire, the former being about how fire spreads over surfaces. An intermediate floor is expected to offer resistance to fire from below for a given amount of time; this is achieved with contributions from all the layers of the make-up. The combined thickness of the structural deck and the ceiling will provide a certain level of safety.

Separating floors

In separating floors, requirements relating to fire safety and acoustic insulation become more stringent. Threshold limits are dictated by national regulations. Most intermediate floors will need to provide good insulation from both airborne and impact sound, which can be achieved via different combinations[2] of measures, such as:

- inserting high-density, mineral-wool quilts into the build-up, for instance by placing them between the structural deck and the ceiling lining;
- separating the floor finish from the structural deck, by creating a floating floor;
- separating the ceiling from the timber joists. This can be done by running metal battens

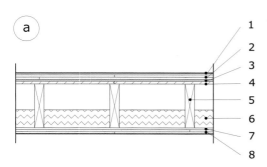

1 floor finish
2 floating floor: double layer of board (e.g., wood- or gypsum-based)
3 resilient layer
4 structural deck (e.g., particleboard)
5 timber joist
6 mineral-wool quilt
7 resilient ceiling bars (perpendicular to joists)
8 double layer of plasterboard

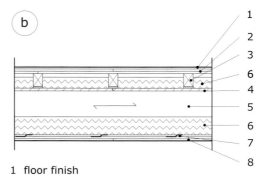

1 floor finish
2 floating floor: double layer of board (e.g., wood- or gypsum-based)
3 resilient batten (i.e., timber batten on resilient strip)
4 structural deck (e.g., particleboard)
5 timber joist
6 mineral-wool quilt fitted between joists
7 resilient ceiling bar (perpendicular to joists)
8 double layer of plasterboard

Fig. 4.35. Examples of timber-framed intermediate floors. Different techniques can be used to build a floating floor: for instance, with a continuous resilient layer laid over the whole area of the deck (a), or with timber battens on resilient strips (b).

perpendicular to the timber joists. The battens are fixed to the underside of the joists in as few points as possible, so as to minimize contact. In order to further reduce sound transmission, special proprietary clips with rubber parts can be used at the interface between the timber joists and the metal battens.

There are also various ways in which a floating floor can be constructed. One way is to interpose a resilient layer between the structural deck and the layers above, which can be for instance gypsum board overlaid with particleboard. Another way to construct a floating floor is to lay timber battens on the structural deck and then gypsum board and particleboard on top of them. The underside of the battens must be completed with a resilient strip. Resilient layers must exhibit sufficient compressive strength, as they are subjected to the loads applied onto the floors. Examples of resilient materials are polyurethane foam, polyethylene foam and rubber. These components are typically fabricated from recycled products (for example tyres). Foams can be open- or closed-cell, depending on the chosen product. In battens, the resilient strip is about 10mm thick and can be pre-bonded to the timber surface or bonded on site, if it has a self-adhesive face. Among other products readily available on the market are particleboard, MDF or other wood-based sheets with a 10-mm pre-bonded, resilient layer, made for instance from foam: as these products incorporate two layers, they speed up the construction process. Care must be taken to isolate a floating floor not only from the substrate, but also from the walls and skirting boards around it: to this end, a resilient strip is used around the perimeter of the floor.

If the ceiling uses 30mm thick plasterboard for acoustic purposes, this will be sufficient to provide the floor with sixty-minute fire resistance from below (an overall thickness of 30mm can be obtained by installing two layers of plasterboard). In order to achieve fire safety within the building as a whole, it is important to ensure that the walls that support the separating floors possess the same fire resistance as the floors.

Flat Roofs

Different types of materials and sections can be used for the joists of a flat roof: solid sections, I-sections or metal-web joists. Typical joist centres are 400 or 600mm, depending on design loads and spans. Adequate falls are obtained by laying tapered timbers (furrings) on top of the joists (which, instead, have a constant cross-section). The deck is generally created with particleboard or plywood.

The waterproofing layer can be created in several ways, the most common ones being:

- bituminous membranes, in double layer (triple in critical areas, where wear-out and damage are most likely to occur). Every layer is about 4mm thick. The top membrane can be enriched by the application of slate chips on the top surface, which protect the layer(s) beneath. Continuity between the membranes is obtained by using a gas-fuelled torch, which rapidly softens the bitumen and makes adherence between overlapping membranes very easy;
- single-ply systems, based on PVC membranes laid in one layer. Continuity between different membranes is obtained by heating them on site (generally with hot-air welding machines).

Cold-deck roofs

In cold-deck roofs, the thermal layer is placed under the deck, generally between the joists. The insulant however should not occupy the whole space between the joists, but leave an unobstructed, ventilated cavity (50mm deep or more, depending on the span) immediately under the decking. In

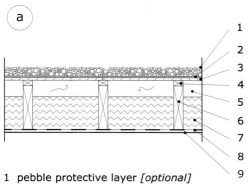

a

1 pebble protective layer *[optional]*
2 waterproofing layer
3 structural deck laid to falls
4 timber furring (i.e., tapered batten)
5 cross-ventilated cavity
6 timber joist
7 thermal-insulation layer (e.g., quilt or board)
8 vapour-control layer (VCL)
9 internal lining (e.g., plasterboard)

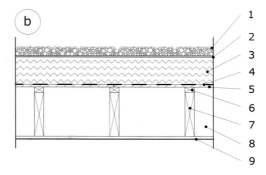

b

1 pebble protective layer *[optional]*
2 waterproofing layer
3 rigid thermal-insulation board
4 vapour-control layer (VCL)
5 structural deck laid to falls
6 timber furring (i.e., tapered batten)
7 timber joist
8 unventilated cavity
9 internal lining (e.g., plasterboard)

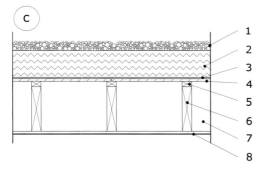

c

1 pebble ballast
2 rigid thermal-insulation board (closed-cell foam)
3 waterproofing layer
4 structural deck laid to falls
5 timber furring (i.e., tapered batten)
6 timber joist
7 unventilated cavity
8 internal lining (e.g., plasterboard)

Fig. 4.36. Construction of timber-framed flat roofs: cold-deck roof (a), warm-deck roof (b), and inverted roof (c). (Drawing: after Sanna, 2018)

order to achieve a satisfactory level of ventilation within such cavity, openings of sufficient dimensions should be formed at the opposite ends of the roof and protected from insects with appropriate mesh. However, this is not always possible (for instance, if the flat roof abuts a wall), therefore ventilators need to be inserted on the top surface of the roof penetrating the waterproofing layer; this arrangement, though, poses a risk of water leakage. A vapour-control layer is placed under the insulant. The VCL and the ventilation cavity jointly contribute to minimizing the risk of condensation near the uppermost layers of the build-up, which are uninsulated.

Different types of insulant can be chosen, from soft to rigid products. The waterproofing layer is laid directly on top of the decking, therefore it is easily accessible for inspection and maintenance, and ceiling lining is fixed to the underside of the joists. If the insulant is exclusively placed between the joists, then thermal bridging through these timbers is likely to occur when there is a significant difference in temperature between the interior and the exterior of the building. These issues of thermal bridging and condensation risk often make warm roofs the preferred choice (which is also encouraged in some national regulations, such as Scotland's).

Warm-deck roofs

In warm-deck roofs, the thermal insulant (rigid boards) is continuous and placed above the deck. This means that the deck itself and all the loadbearing members beneath it are warm, that is, they have a temperature close to that of the interior space. A vapour-control layer is interposed between the deck and the thermal insulant. A lining finish (for example plasterboard or timber boards) is placed on the underside of the joists.

In a warm-deck configuration, the thermal layer is protected by the waterproofing membranes, but can experience wide variations in temperature, to the detriment of its durability in the long term. This poses the need for adequate surface treatment: it is recommendable to make the top surface as reflective as possible. Another disadvantage associated with warm roofs lies in the risk of moisture being trapped within the insulation layer (sandwiched between the VCL and the waterproof membranes), causing it to lose part of its intended performance and possibly to deteriorate over time. This moisture could have penetrated the insulation layer either during the construction phase, or during the operational phase if the membranes and/or the VCL are damaged.

Inverted roofs

Inverted roofs are a type of warm roof in which the mutual position of the thermal layer and the waterproofing layer is inverted with respect to the arrangement seen for warm-deck roofs. In other words, the waterproofing membrane is laid on top of the decking (and also acts as a vapour-control layer). The thermal-insulation boards are placed above the waterproofing layer and so are exposed to precipitation: this means that the type of product specified needs to be compatible with these conditions. Closed-cell foams are generally used. It is necessary to protect the thermal layer from direct solar radiation and extreme temperature oscillation, which can cause its deterioration over time: possible solutions are pebble, ballast or tiling. If tiles are used, the joints between them are typically left open.

The most valuable advantage of an inverted roof over a warm one is that the waterproofing layer is better protected, since it does not undergo excessive temperature swings (thanks to the thermal insulant above it) and is not directly exposed to maintenance traffic. It is important to notice, however, that the waterproof layer is not easily accessible, due to the layers that lie above it: this makes inspection, maintenance and replacement of the layer itself more difficult than in other roof types. Another disadvantage arises from the pebbles increasing the permanent load of the roof.

In both warm and inverted roofs, the overall thickness of the construction can become noticeable, due to the thickness of the insulation layer needed to meet (or, if desired, exceed) the requirements set out by building regulations.

Pitched Roofs

Many solutions are available today for pitched roofs: each relies on a different level of prefabrication, with implications for the duration and

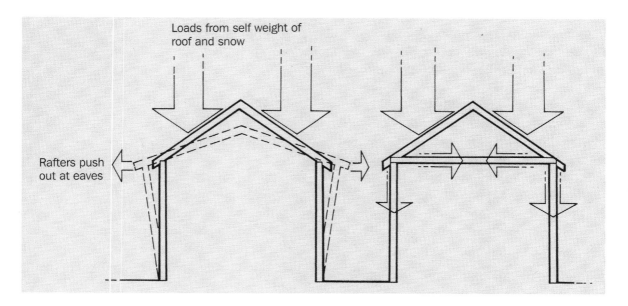

Fig. 4.37. The rafters exert lateral thrust onto the wall heads. Triangulation in the roof structure (right) can efficiently solve this problem: the outward horizontal forces are withstood by a ceiling tie. Conversely, without triangulation (left), the walls must be able to resist the lateral thrust in addition to the vertical loads. (Drawing: *Kit and Modern Timber Frame Homes,* Crowood, 2007)

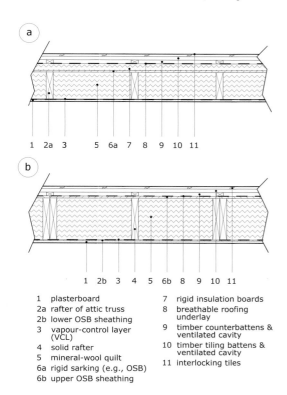

Fig. 4.39. In a pitched roof, the primary structure can consist of a series of parallel timber trusses that, if exposed, become an integral part of the architectural language defining the interior space. (Photo: Scotts Timber Engineering)

1 plasterboard	7 rigid insulation boards
2a rafter of attic truss	8 breathable roofing underlay
2b lower OSB sheathing	
3 vapour-control layer (VCL)	9 timber counterbattens & ventilated cavity
4 solid rafter	10 timber tiling battens & ventilated cavity
5 mineral-wool quilt	11 interlocking tiles
6a rigid sarking (e.g., OSB)	
6b upper OSB sheathing	

Fig. 4.38. Construction of a timber-frame pitched roof (section perpendicular to the plane of slope), using attic trussed rafters (a) or cassettes (b). (Drawing: after Sanna, 2018)

nature of on-site operations. Some fundamental factors that influence the choice of a roof's construction method are:

- whether or not the space under the roof is going to be habitable;
- whether the structural system is going to be concealed or to be expressed, thus becoming an

integral part of the architectural language, with the structural members exposed internally;
- whether the ceiling is going to be pitched or flat;
- the characteristics of the site, and – in particular – whether the site can be accessed by big lorries (for transportation of prefabricated components), whether a large crane can be utilized, and whether there is an area on the ground where the roof can be fabricated and/or assembled before it is lifted into position.

In all the configurations described in the next sections, different types of structural members can be used, alone or in multiple combinations, such as solid rafters, open-web rafters (with either timber or metal webs) or I-sections.

Trussed rafters

Trussed rafters are manufactured in a broad variety of configurations, able to suit different spans, geometrical arrangements (for example monopitch or duopitch) and roof pitches. Trussed rafters are able to cover longer spans than simple rafters, thus making roof construction more economical.

Trussed rafters[3] are manufactured in the factory and then delivered to the site. Here, two processes are possible:

- each trussed rafter is installed individually in its intended position;
- the trussed rafters are assembled on the ground and, when the whole roof (or a portion of it) is complete, it is craned into position. This method is only possible when the site offers sufficient space for these operations to be carried out, and when there is access to cranes of adequate dimension (see Fig. 4.47).

A typical trussed rafter is based on the concept of triangulation and consists of different members arranged to form multiple triangles. In a trussed rafter like the one in Fig. 4.40, the members are:

- two top chords (rafters), which define the profile of the roof and are subjected to combined bending;
- a bottom chord (ceiling tie or ceiling joist), which fulfils the very important role of withstanding the lateral thrust exerted by the rafters where they meet their supports. Consequently, the tie is mostly subjected to tensile forces. If heavy equipment (for example water-storage tanks) is placed on tie beams, then they are subjected to combined tension and bending;
- internal members (webs) – the ones between the rafters and the tie – which are mostly subjected to axial forces, either tension or compression.

The timbers are typically joined (on both sides) by means of galvanized-steel toothed plate connectors (also referred to as punched metal plate fasteners). Trussed rafters rest on a wall plate, the uppermost horizontal member of a TF wall (the headbinder or, if this is not installed, the top rail). The connection between trusses and TF walls can be performed by means of proprietary metal connectors (truss clips), which typically consist of different folded plates that adapt to the geometry of the trussed rafter and of the headbinder, and are perforated to allow screwing or nailing into the timbers. Trussed rafters are generally placed at 600mm centres or, less often and where necessary, at 400mm centres.

Permanent bracing between the trusses is necessary to maintain their intended position and to make the roof as a whole sufficiently rigid and stable under its gravitational and wind-induced loads. It includes:

- **longitudinal bracing**, achieved with a series of timber braces (or binders) that all run in the longitudinal direction of the roof, but at various heights and – preferably – at every unsupported node point within the truss. Some binders connect the ceiling ties; others connect the webs near the nodes with the rafters (they are not fixed directly to the rafters so as to allow the diagonal braces to pass through). Longitudinal

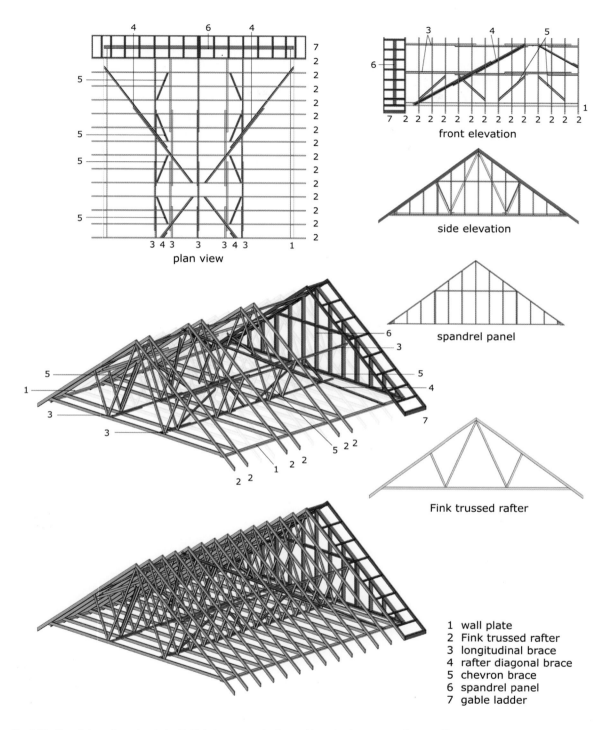

plan view

front elevation

side elevation

spandrel panel

Fink trussed rafter

1 wall plate
2 Fink trussed rafter
3 longitudinal brace
4 rafter diagonal brace
5 chevron brace
6 spandrel panel
7 gable ladder

Fig. 4.40. Duopitch roof constructed with Fink-type trussed rafters, with projecting eaves and verges. The trusses are connected to one another with three types of permanent braces: longitudinal braces, rafter diagonal braces and chevron braces (which connect the webs). This system provides the roof system with a great level of stiffness and stability, including against wind forces.

binders should stretch the whole length of the roof. Tiling battens also contribute to the longitudinal bracing of the trusses;

- **diagonal bracing** involves the rafters being stabilized by members (rafter diagonal braces) that are nailed to their underside and thus lie in the sloping plane of the roof; these braces are positioned at about 45-degree angles to the rafters (in plan) and run from the wall plate up to the ridge. In addition, other binders (chevron braces) might be needed (especially in long-spanning trusses) in the plane of the webs, to connect the webs of multiple trusses.

All bracing members should be fabricated from wood without any significant defects. If a binder consists of two pieces to achieve the necessary length, then the pieces must be lap-jointed over at least two trussed rafters. Binders must be nailed to every trussed rafter that they cross, with galvanized-steel nails.

The trusses can also be connected by means of sheathing (sarking) that creates a continuous layer on top of them: this practice – especially widespread in Scotland – makes the whole roof structure more rigid and provides a substrate for all the non-structural components that are needed to complete the roof.

Fig. 4.42. A T-intersection in the trussed-rafter roof shown in the previous image. There is no discontinuity in the framework of the larger roof. The connection between the smaller roof and the main one is made possible with a valley set, that is, a series of trusses that diminish in size as they approach the larger roof.

Fig. 4.43. Verge of the roof shown in the previous images. The spandrel panel (1) is constructed of timber studs at 600mm centres. The gable ladder (2) has already been installed and fixed to the first trussed rafter (3). Longitudinal binders (4) connect the ceiling ties near the nodes with the web members.

Fig. 4.41. A trussed-rafter roof for a detached house. The trussed rafters have been manufactured in the factory and have now been assembled on the ground. Once the walls have been erected, the roof will be crane-lifted into position.

Fig. 4.44. View of the outer side of the gable end, which has been wrapped in breather membrane. Soffit sheets have been fixed to the gable ladder.

Fig. 4.45. Apex of the gable wall. The spandrel panel consists of two abutting TF panels (1 and 2). We can see the trussed rafter (3) closest to the gable, which supports the gable ladder (4), and the bracing members: longitudinal binders (5) and diagonal braces (6) that connect the top chords of the trusses.

Fig. 4.46. Construction of a terrace of three houses: the roof is composed of trussed rafters that have been fabricated in the factory, assembled on site and crane-lifted into position. We can see the two triangular party walls that separate the residential units (within the roof space), and the gable ladders installed at the verges.

Fig. 4.47. Construction of a residential scheme that employs closed TF panels for the external walls and trussed rafters for the roofs. A telescopic crane is used to place these timber elements into position.

Sarking can be made of OSB, plywood, particleboard or timber boards. Where rigid sarking is in place, some of the bracing members described above might not be necessary, but longitudinal braces at ceiling-tie level are likely to still be needed.

The positioning of the thermal-insulation layer fulfils an important role in the detailing of the roof. Essentially, two main options are available:

- the insulant is placed at ceiling level;
- the insulant is placed at rafter level.

Different solutions are available for the eaves, which can be clipped or projecting. Clipped eaves are generally the preferred option for buildings which aim at a very neat, sleek appearance, although their construction, especially when the gutters are concealed, requires more care in order for the roof to meet all its functional requirements and allow for maintenance or repair work over the building's lifespan. Similarly to the eaves, the verge can also be clipped or projecting from the gable wall. The projecting part of the verge can be realized by means of a gable ladder, which straddles the gable wall and is supported by the trussed rafter closest to the wall itself (*see* Fig. 4.43). A gable ladder has several rungs between the supporting rafter and the barge board.

Hipped roofs

The construction of a trussed-rafter roof becomes more complex when there is a hip slope. Various methods are available to construct this part of the roof; one of the most common is illustrated in Fig. 4.48 and is sometimes referred to as the standard-centres hip system. In such a roof, standard trusses are complemented by special ones, more specifically:

- a series of flat-top hip trusses, set at the same centres as the standard trusses. In each of these trusses, the length of the flying rafters is different and depends on how close they are to the apex of the hipped roof. The flying rafters

are trimmed to meet the hip rafter, to which they are nailed;

- a girder truss, obtained by joining two (or more) flat-top hip trusses and thus achieving increased structural capacity. The girder truss offers support to the trusses that define the hipped surface (the mono-truss rafters). Since the girder truss transfers high concentrated loads to the walls, double studs or larger posts are inserted into the wall lay-up, at the junction with this truss;
- two hip rafters (or hip boards), which define the intersection between two different roof planes;
- a series of monopitch trusses, which span between the wall plate and the girder truss. The girder truss supports these rafters at two levels: at the bottom chord (with a truss shoe) and at the top chord (with a truss clip). These trusses have a portion of rafter (flying jack) that spans between the hip rafter and the girder truss;
- two sets of infill trusses (of variable length), which span between the lower portion of the hip rafters and the wall plates.

T-junctions and valleys

The construction of a T-junction in which a smaller duopitch roof merges with a larger one requires the use of some special members. The ridge of the smaller roof is extended up to the intersection with the sloping surface of the larger roof.

A series of trussed rafters of decreasing size (valley set) is needed to fill the part of the smaller roof delimited by the two valleys: the ridge of these is at constant height, while the tie at the bottom is placed each time at a greater height. Alternatively, simple rafters (as opposed to trussed rafters) of varying length can be used in this portion of the junction (valley jack rafters). In the smaller roof, the full-height trussed rafter that is closest to the larger roof can be doubled to increase its structural capacity.

Battens are necessary to create a connection between the supporting rafters of the main roof

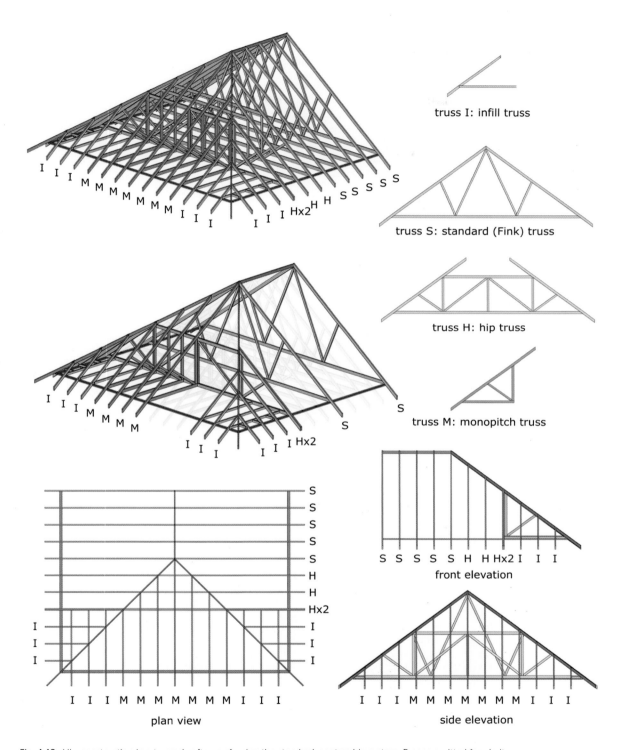

truss I: infill truss

truss S: standard (Fink) truss

truss H: hip truss

truss M: monopitch truss

front elevation

plan view

side elevation

Fig. 4.48. Hip construction in a trussed-rafter roof, using the standard-centres hip system. Braces omitted for clarity.

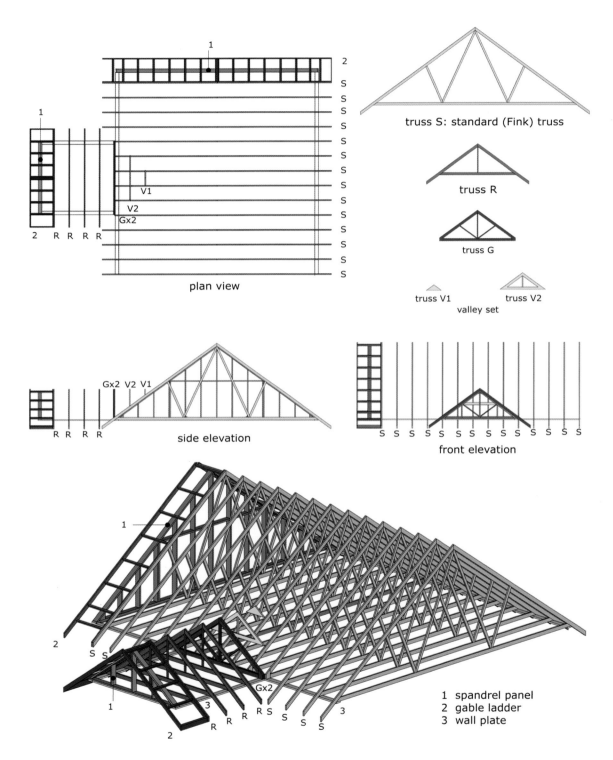

1

2

S
S
S
S
S
S
S
S
S
S
S
S
S
S
S
S

V1

V2

Gx2

2   R   R   R   R

plan view

truss S: standard (Fink) truss

truss R

truss G

truss V1   truss V2

valley set

Gx2 V2 V1

R R R R

side elevation

S S S S S S S S S S S S

front elevation

1

2

S S

Gx2

1

2

R   R   R   R S   S   S   3

1 spandrel panel
2 gable ladder
3 wall plate

Fig. 4.49. T-intersection in a trussed-rafter roof. Braces omitted for clarity.

and the trussed rafters of the smaller roof. Along the valleys, boards can be added to connect the rafters of both roofs and augment the rigidity of the T-junction as a whole. As an alternative, the valley jack rafters or trussed rafters can be connected to *ad hoc* timbers that rest on the rafters of the main roof (valley boards or valley rafters). In both the smaller and larger roofs, longitudinal and – where needed – diagonal bracing is added to connect parallel trussed rafters.

Attic roofs

Attic trussed rafters are shaped to make the central part of the roof habitable. In these trusses, the tie beam acts, in effect, as a floor joist, and provides support for the loads coming from the attic space.

These trusses are typically spaced at 400 or 600mm, depending on their span and loading conditions. Two short verticals (dwarf studs) define the extension of the habitable space and, along with a ceiling strut, limit the bending of the rafters; consequently, the dwarf studs and the ceiling strut are subjected to compressive axial forces. The position of the ceiling strut also affects the ceiling height. The intermediate section of the rafters (between the dwarf stud and the collar) can be increased in depth, so as to accommodate a larger amount of thermal insulant, if necessary.

Two options are available for the positioning of the thermal-insulation layer:

- the insulant is placed at rafter level;
- the insulant follows the profile of the attic space. As a consequence, the unused spaces

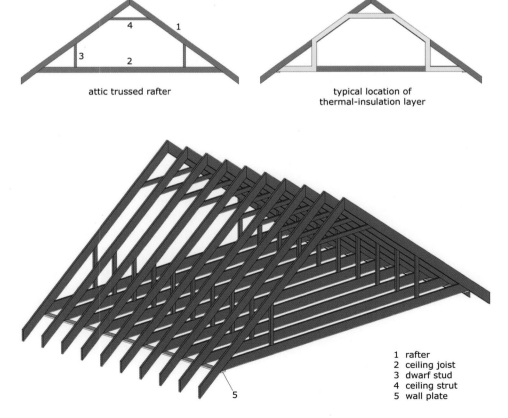

attic trussed rafter

typical location of thermal-insulation layer

1 rafter
2 ceiling joist
3 dwarf stud
4 ceiling strut
5 wall plate

Fig. 4.50. Attic constructed with trussed rafters. Braces omitted for clarity.

Fig. 4.51. Attic of a mid-rise, residential building that employs closed TF panels. The upper section of the roof (above ceiling level) is realized with trussed rafters that span between a ridge beam and a purlin, both made of glulam. The purlin-to-rafter connection uses metal hangers. Where the purlins meet the gable wall, the studs are doubled to achieve sufficient compressive strength.

under the ridge and at the foot of the trusses remain uninsulated.

As was seen in one of the previous sections for ordinary trussed rafters, attic trusses also need adequate bracing, with sarking and/or binders running perpendicular to the trusses themselves. Sometimes, a bracing diaphragm is created by fixing plywood sheets between the rafters (more precisely, in the portion of the rafters over the attic room). The floor, walls and roof of the attic must possess the same resistance to fire as those of the lower storeys.

Panelized roofs

There are many generic and proprietary panelized systems available to designers for pitched roofs with an attic space. Depending on how the panels are constructed, the insulant can be placed at different locations, thus creating arrangements that fall within the categories of cold roofs or warm roofs.

The lateral thrust in panelized systems is generally withstood by the joists of the top floor.

Consequently, these joists are subjected not only to bending (due to the gravitational loads exerted onto the floor), but also to tensile forces. In duopitch roofs, ceiling struts might be installed, in order to minimize the deflection of the panels. Ceiling struts are compression members: they must be able to resist compressive forces and remain stable under these.

Depending on the position of the thermal insulant, different types of roofs can be achieved:

- **warm roofs**, with the insulation layer located above the sheathing (which is, in turn, placed on top of the rafters). There might also be extra insulant fitted between the rafters;
- **cold roofs**, with the insulant fitted between the rafters. There might also be a continuous layer of insulation on the underside of the rafters, which will reduce thermal bridging through these timbers.

At the top, the roof panels are often supported by a ridge beam (for example solid timber, engineered timber or steel section).

Roof cassettes

Roof cassettes are manufactured in the factory and, once delivered to the site, erected by crane. They typically arrive on site complete with:

- **rafters**, whose ends are cut in the factory to suit the pitch of the roof and the connection to the wall. Different options are available: from solid sections to I-sections and open-web members;
- **upper sheathing layer**, made of OSB, plywood or similar wood-based sheet products. The sheathing layer provides racking resistance and overall rigidity to the cassettes, keeping all the rafters in place;
- **thermal insulant** fitted between the rafters (typically, mineral-wool quilts, but rigid foam boards are also possible). Roof cassettes tend to create a cold-roof configuration;

- **lower sheathing layer** (OSB or other timber-based sheets). If this is not installed in the factory, then the thermal insulant is kept in place between the rafters by an *ad hoc* component, such as adhesive tape or similar;

- built-in **lifting straps** (or equivalent devices) for craneage during the transport and erection phases.

Depending on whether or not the insulant and the lower sheathing layer are added in the factory, roof

Project: Galuresa Service Area (*Centro de Servicios Galuresa*)

Location: Teo (A Coruña), Galicia, Spain
Building type: non-residential – commercial
Completion date: 2020
Architectural design: MRM (Miguel Alonso Flamarique, Roberto Erviti Machain, Mamen Escorihuela Vitales) & Anton Varela García, Architects
Key words: timber frame, thermal treatment, plywood, hybrid structures, steel beams, inverted roof

In accordance with the topographical conditions of the plot, this intervention generates two different levels by means of retaining walls made of large granite blocks. The upper level accommodates services such as a car park, a supermarket (which overlooks a wooded slope) and a cafeteria, whose terrace opens up towards the surrounding landscape. The lower level follows the natural slope of the terrain and will accommodate a recreational area. The building consists of a central space with large glazing, which houses a supermarket and a cafeteria, and four windowless timber pods around its perimeter, for the ancillary spaces (toilets, storerooms, office, changing rooms, workshop and plant room). The overall result is a combination of opaque and diaphanous volumes (*see* Figs 4.52 and 4.54).

The design hinges on a straightforward and coherent constructional strategy, which is governed by a square structural grid (2.4 × 2.4m), allowed for rapid on-site erection, and focused on a few well-resolved details. The four pods employ a timber-frame system and contribute to supporting the central canopy (over the supermarket and cafeteria), constructed of steel beams and a profiled deck. In this way, the central space does not need any internal supports and, with its 9.6m span, remains very flexible and versatile. The framing of the walls, roofs and floors employs pine sections. The TF wall panels were constructed on site and insulated with mineral wool (80mm). On both the interior and exterior sides, the panels have been sheathed with 18mm-thick wood-based sheets developed for structural applications in a humid environment, with a particleboard core sandwiched between two thin MDF skins. The outside of the panels has been wrapped in breather membrane and clad with vertical, thermally treated wooden boards, finished with black wax. The pods sit directly on a reinforced-concrete slab; their floors have been insulated with mineral wool fitted between 100mm-deep timber battens; with a birch-plywood deck on top and vinyl flooring. An inverted roof covers the pods, with 50mm-thick extruded-polystyrene boards on top of the waterproof layer and protected with geotextile felt and gravel. Thermal insulation of the roof is also achieved thanks to mineral wool inserted between the ceiling joists. A screed laid to falls is placed between the birch plywood and the waterproof layer.

With the only exception of the concrete slab and the roof's waterproofing membranes, all building components can be disassembled and reused. By virtue of the design measures in the interest of sustainability, the building has achieved good environmental ratings, including 'very good' with BREEAM (*see* Chapter 3).

cassettes will resemble either open or closed TF wall panel systems. The internal finishes and the roof covering with its associated components (breathable membranes, tiling battens and so on) are generally installed on site, although more advanced forms of prefabrication are possible. Some manufacturers are able to deliver roof cassettes complete not only with the components listed above, but also with breathable membrane and tiling battens (arranged horizontally) and counterbattens (in the direction of the slope), if required by the client.

Similarly to closed-panel walls, a service cavity might be required on the underside of the cassettes, if the space underneath them is habitable. This can be achieved by fixing timber battens to the underside of the cassettes and then applying an internal finish (for example plasterboard or timber boarding).

Like all prefabricated systems, roof cassettes become more economical when used within a modular system based on the juxtaposition of standardized units. However, cassettes are also possible where standardization is less easy to achieve. As regards dimensions, cassettes can be up to about 13m long and 2.5m wide (the size of the lorry for factory-to-site transportation will determine the dimensional limits). Depending on the proprietary system employed, the edges of the cassettes can be rebated, so as to facilitate and enhance their juxtaposition on site.

Fig. 4.52. Supermarket of Galuresa Service Area in Teo (Spain), designed by MRM Arquitectos. This one-storey building is based on a hybrid structural system. The main retail area is an open space delimited by large glazed façades and a lightweight steel canopy. Along the perimeter of this space are four timber-framed pods, one of which can be seen in the foreground. (Photo: Héctor Santos-Díez, fotógrafo)

Fig. 4.53. The pods sit on a reinforced-concrete slab alongside the remainder of the building and use timber-framed panels. (Photo: Héctor Santos-Díez, fotógrafo)

Fig. 4.54. The timber pods are clad in thermally treated wooden boards, which contrast with the transparency of the glazed surfaces. (Photo: Héctor Santos-Díez, fotógrafo)

Fig. 4.56. The pod's walls have been protected with breather membrane and now await installation of the external cladding. As can be seen, the pods offer structural support to the steel beams that make the canopy over the supermarket's main space. The roof deck, consisting of steel profiled sheets, will soon be laid on top of these beams. (Photo: Héctor Santos-Díez, fotógrafo)

Fig. 4.55. The timber framework of the walls is sheathed, both internally and externally, with 18mm-thick, multi-layer sheets suitable for structural use (a particleboard core sandwiched between two thin MDF skins). Mineral wool is fitted in the gaps between the wall studs and roof joists. (Photo: Héctor Santos-Díez, fotógrafo)

Case Study 2: Feilden Fowles' Studio

Fausto Sanna & Annalaura Fornasier

Location: Lambeth, London, UK
Building type: offices
Completion date: 2016
Design Team:
    Architects: Feilden Fowles
    Structural engineer: Structure Workshop
    Landscape designer: Dan Pearson Studio
Client: Feilden Fowles
Gross floor internal area: 133m²
Awards:
    Winner – RIBA London Award (Studio), 2017

Winner – Wood Awards (Small Project Winner), 2017
Winner – RIBA London Award (Waterloo City Farm), 2018
Winner – NLA Awards (Waterloo City Farm): Mayor's Prize Commendation, 2018
Nominated – RIBA Journal MacEwen Award – Finalist (Waterloo City Farm), 2018
Keywords: timber-frame panels, plywood, offices, monopitch roof, assembly & disassembly

Fig. 4.57. Feilden Fowles Studio is part of Waterloo City Farm, a collective educational and shared-working space near London's Waterloo Station. The site also includes animal pens, a barn and an outdoor kitchen. The monopitch, timber-framed roof faces north and takes its inspiration from artists' studios. Clerestory windows run along the northern wall to allow the most consistent levels of indoor lighting throughout the day, optimal for a working environment. The internal sheathing is made of Douglas fir ply. (Photo: David Grandorge)

Brief and design process

Feilden Fowles Studios is a self-raised and self-funded studio space by, and for, Feilden Fowles architects in London. The studio is part of a bigger masterplan called Waterloo City Farm, developed on a short-lease site. The farm is the closest urban farm to the city centre and is located in Lambeth, near Waterloo Railway Station. It was established in 2014 on a derelict site owned by Guy's and St Thomas' Hospital. The initiative came from local charity Jamie's Farm, which approached Feilden Fowles to develop the site. The architects suggested transforming the site into a collaborative space where they themselves and Jamie's Farm could co-work. The charity accepted

this proposal and the architects offered architectural services in lieu of rent. This was a unique opportunity for Feilden Fowles, not only to avoid the usually high renting costs of central London, but also to create a space that could embody the practice's low-tech and sustainability ethos.

The neglected site thus became home to Feilden Fowles, Jamie's Farm and another charity called Oasis Waterloo. The three organizations self-funded the entire masterplan (developed in three phases) and shared similar views on developing spaces that could benefit the wider local community, offer educational activities for schools and be sustainable.

The site is a 1,630m^2, narrow rectangular plot of land, at the corner between Royal Street and

Carlisle Lane (*see* Fig. 4.58). The concept behind the programme and organization of the site was to place the barn on the east side and the architects' studio on the opposite side. In this way, the barn becomes the most civic and celebratory element of the farm, while the studio is in a more intimate and secluded setting, delimited by a Victorian wall. The studio's position within the site also allowed the creation of a shared courtyard, designed by local practice Dan Pearson Studio. The barn and the studio are connected by a central pathway with animal pens, an outdoor kitchen and an area for educational activities relating to gardening, carpentry, cooking and animal care.

All the buildings on-site, including the architects' studio, were inspired by vernacular and agricultural structures, with pitched roofs and timber-framed walls. Feilden Fowles' Studio is a single-storey, mono-pitched building, consisting of a workshop and office space, a break-out space for meetings and meals, and a quiet learning space for students visiting the farm. The workspace occupies the central part of the 133m^2 building, while the services (kitchen and toilets) and a meeting room are located at the west end and east end, respectively. The studio's southern wall, which fronts onto the courtyard, is fully glazed; while the northern wall, which borders Royal Street, is only glazed at ceiling level to ensure privacy. Subsequently, an additional overspill space – in the form of an outbuilding – was added for the studio to hold meetings and pin-up presentations, which could not easily be accommodated in the office shared with Jamie's Farm employees. The studio project needed to be realized within budgetary constraints: low costs were achieved through careful optimization and calculation of material usage and prefabricated components. The site was initially envisaged to be occupied and used for a five-year period, therefore Feilden Fowles' Studio was designed in such a way to be easily disassembled and potentially relocated elsewhere.

Fig. 4.58. Overall view of Waterloo City Farm. The eastern end, with a large barn, is the most public part of the site, while the central area accommodates animal pens and growing beds. Feilden Fowles' spaces are at the west end and comprise a studio, a courtyard and a small outbuilding used for meetings and pin-ups. The site is occupied on a short-term lease, so the architects opted for the studio to be a prefabricated structure that could easily be disassembled and re-assembled in a new location, if necessary. (Drawing: Feilden Fowles)

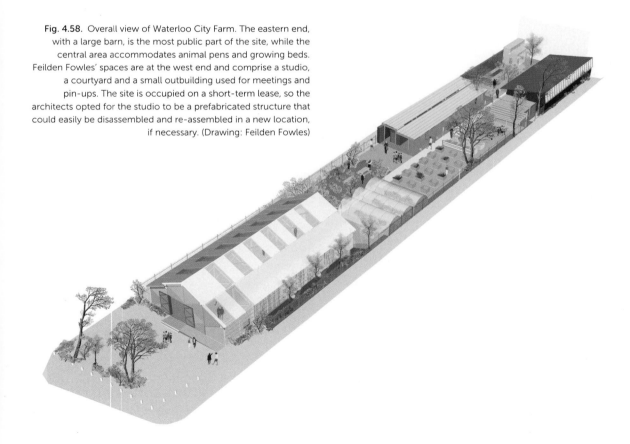

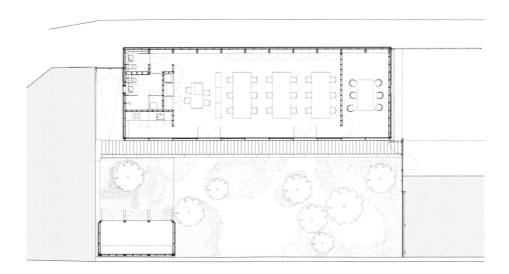

Fig. 4.59. Plan view. The central part of the studio is used as an open-plan space with numerous workstations, sandwiched between a meeting room and a cluster of services (such as toilets and kitchen). Across the garden is a small outbuilding used for meetings. (Drawing: Feilden Fowles)

Fig. 4.60. The studio's southern façade is glazed and fronts onto the garden, which was designed by local landscape designer Dan Pearson Studio. (Photo: David Grandorge)

Construction

Structural system:
   Foundations: concrete raft foundation
   Vertical supports: timber-framed panels and steel sections
   Ground floor: concrete slab
   Roof: timber-framed panels
Thermal insulation: polyisocyanurate (PIR) boards (walls, roof and ground-floor slab)

The whole conception of the studio is based on low-cost materials and low-tech construction methods. The primary structure was fabricated offsite and has a simple, modular configuration, chiefly realized with solid, Douglas fir sections (*see* Fig. 4.61). The vertical supports, which all sit on a concrete raft foundation, are timber studs along the higher (northern) wall and steel T-sections on the opposite side. The rafters and studs of adjacent modules are joined by means of bolts, while the rafters and studs of the same module are connected and stabilized by timber purlins and noggings, respectively.

Both the wall panels and the roof panels are externally covered with corrugated bitumen sheets (*see* Fig. 4.63) and are sheathed in Douglas fir ply, which is left exposed and gives a special warmth to the interior space.

The ground-floor slab is made of power-floated concrete and is thermally insulated on the underside.

Environmental sustainability

Through this project, Feilden Fowles took the opportunity to showcase their values around environmental and social sustainability. It was a personal challenge

Fig. 4.61. View of the primary timber structure, whose modules were partially fabricated offsite and then assembled and completed on site. (Photo: David Grandorge)

Fig. 4.62. The primary structure of the northern wall is divided into three parts by the horizontal noggings. The uppermost part will be glazed, while the other two will be thermally insulated, clad, and finally equipped with built-in, timber shelving on the inside. (Photo: David Grandorge)

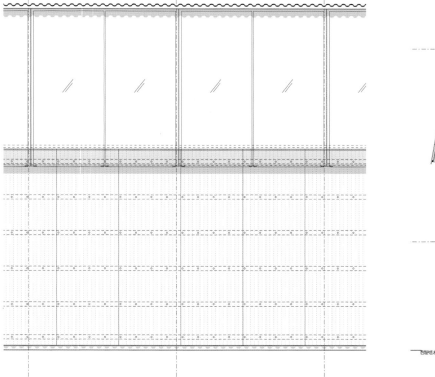

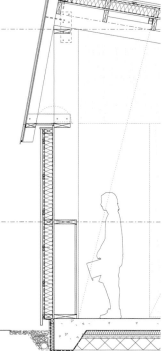

Fig. 4.63. Elevation and cross-section of the northern wall, showing the fixing points of the corrugated bitumen cladding, which is dark-red and thus blends in with the surrounding red-brick buildings. (Drawing: Feilden Fowles)

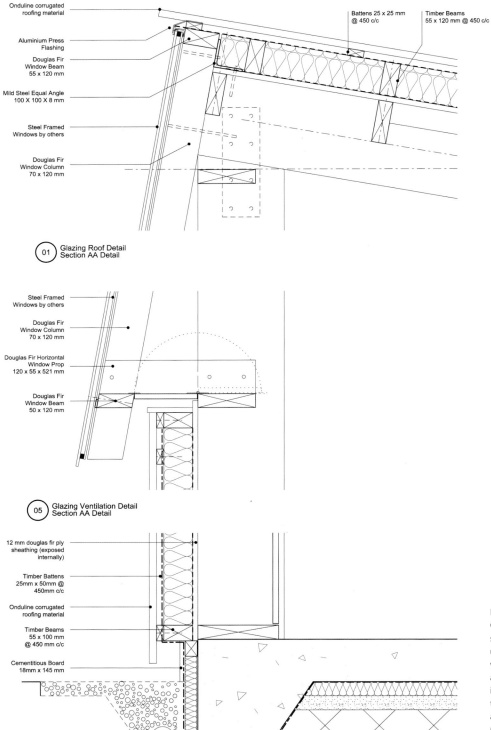

Onduline corrugated
roofing material

Battens 25 x 25 mm
@ 450 c/c

Timber Beams
55 x 120 mm @ 450 c/c

Aluminium Press
Flashing

Douglas Fir
Window Beam
55 x 120 mm

Mild Steel Equal Angle
100 X 100 X 8 mm

Steel Framed
Windows by others

Douglas Fir
Window Column
70 x 120 mm

01 Glazing Roof Detail
Section AA Detail

Steel Framed
Windows by others

Douglas Fir
Window Column
70 x 120 mm

Douglas Fir Horizontal
Window Prop
120 x 55 x 521 mm

Douglas Fir
Window Beam
50 x 120 mm

05 Glazing Ventilation Detail
Section AA Detail

12 mm douglas fir ply
sheathing (exposed
internally)

Timber Battens
25mm x 50mm @
450mm c/c

Onduline corrugated
roofing material

Timber Beams
55 x 100 mm
@ 450 mm c/c

Cementitious Board
18mm x 145 mm

Fig. 4.64.
Construction detail
showing the build-
up of the northern
wall (which abuts
a busy street) and
its junctions with
the foundations
and pitched roof.
(Drawing: adapted
from Feilden
Fowles)

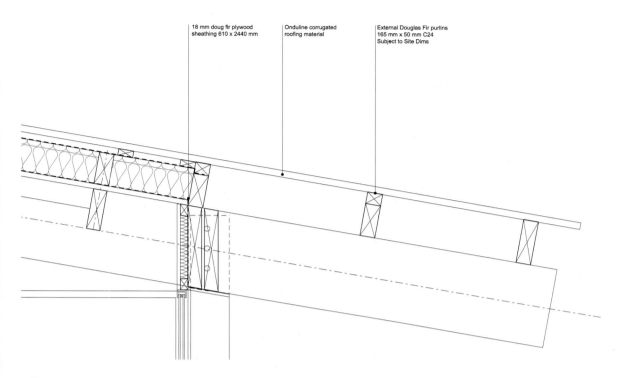

18 mm doug fir plywood
sheathing 610 x 2440 mm

Onduline corrugated
roofing material

External Douglas Fir purlins
165 mm x 50 mm C24
Subject to Site Dims

02 Overhang detail
Section AA Detail

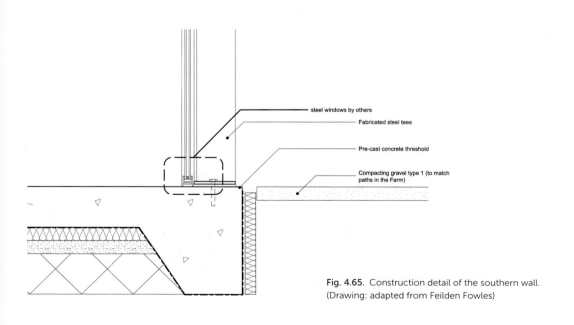

steel windows by others

Fabricated steel tees

Pre-cast concrete threshold

Compacting gravel type 1 (to match
paths in the Farm)

Fig. 4.65. Construction detail of the southern wall.
(Drawing: adapted from Feilden Fowles)

for the architects, as well as a chance to demonstrate their skills to prospective clients visiting the studio. Since the architects had been aware from the outset of the temporality of the project, they decided to design a structure that could quickly be put together and then easily disassembled to be transported and reassembled elsewhere. This project was also a unique opportunity for Feilden Fowles, as a young London-based practice, to build their own studio. Hence, it was essential for them to design a building that could be flexible to potential site changes and expansion.

The building was inspired by artists' studios and, as such, has a monopitched roof combined with windows up high on the north-facing wall, complete with hidden vents for passive ventilation. The fully glazed southern wall has a wide overhang – formed as an extension of the monopitched roof – which provides shade and prevents glare inside.

Fig. 4.66. View of the courtyard and main studio through the windows of the outbuilding. The courtyard is the quietest and most private outdoor area of the whole farm and is used by Feilden Fowles and the other two organizations for meals and events *al fresco*. (Photo: Peter Cook)

Fig. 4.67. View of the main studio and the courtyard at dusk. Waterloo City Farm is located in a high-density and busy area of London, with high- and mid-rise buildings. (Photo: Peter Cook)

Case Study 3: Maggie's Centre Cardiff

Fausto Sanna & Annalaura Fornasier

Location: Velindre Cancer Care Centre, Whitchurch, Cardiff, Wales, UK

Building type: healthcare centre

Completion date: 2019

Design Team:

Architect: Dow Jones Architects, London, UK

Structural engineer: Momentum, London, UK

Building-services engineer: Mott MacDonald

Quantity surveyor: RPA, South Wales, UK

Landscape designer: Cleve West, Kingston upon Thames, UK

Artists and makers: glass fritting and fire-place-tile design: Linda Florence, UK; ceramics: Pat O'Leary, London, UK; bollards: Antony Gormley, UK; art curator: Mike Tooby, UK

Client: Maggie's Cancer Care

Gross floor internal area: 220m²

Awards:

Winner – National Eisteddfod Architecture Plaque of Merit, 2019

Winner – Civic Trust Awards, 2020

Shortlisted – Wood Awards, 2019

Shortlisted – National Eisteddfod Architecture Gold Medal, 2019

Shortlisted – AJ Awards, Health and Wellbeing, 2019

Shortlisted – RICS Awards, 2020

Key words: timber-frame panels, healthcare, steel frame, hybrid structural system

Fig. 4.68. The site of Maggie's Centre Cardiff is located in a corner of a hospital car park. The façade is clad in corrugated Cor-ten steel and the entrance adorned with a ceramic sign by Pat O'Leary. Anthony Gormley's metal bollards are aligned with pre-existing stone bollards. The western and southern elevations (pictured here) overlook the car park and have few openings: this decision was made to ensure patients' privacy and to orientate the fenestration towards the courtyard and the tall trees along the north edge of the site. (Photo: Anthony Coleman)

Brief and design process

Maggie's Centres were founded in 1996, as free walk-in facilities all around the UK, in Hong Kong and, later, in Tokyo and Barcelona, to offer support and guidance to patients with cancer and their families. There are twenty-seven Maggie's Centres in the UK; each of them is located next to a major cancer hospital. They are self-funded and unique in their design: the result of a collaborative effort from architects, landscape designers and artists. Maggie's Board does not provide architects with strict guidelines or briefs, but rather with a series of necessary functions (kitchen, office, library, consultation rooms, retreat space) and desired atmospheres, along with an essay written by founder Maggie Keswick Jencks, *A View from the Front Line*[4]. This piece of writing encourages the architect's empathic and exuberant character while ensuring the centre's domestic and personal environment is the antithesis to that of a hospital. Hospitals and Maggie's Centres complement one another in the type of support they offer to patients.

Dow Jones Architects were selected for the design of a Maggie's Centre in Cardiff, the construction of which was completed in 2019. The centre is located in a corner of Velindre Cancer Care Centre's car park, in north-west Cardiff. It is an interim facility expected to be in use for ten years, as the hospital has plans to relocate to a new site. For this reason, the centre needed to be smaller and able to be constructed more quickly and economically than a typical Maggie's. This is a single-storey building, with a triangular shape and a 240m² footprint (smaller than most Maggie's Centres, which have a footprint of around 350m²). It was built in sixteen months only and used just one-third of the available budget.

Central to Maggie's ethos is the relationship between building and landscape, and the latter's therapeutic effects. Due to the configuration of the site and the hospital car park, it was not possible for the new building to be completely surrounded by vegetation. The architects worked with landscape designer Cleve West to devise a planning strategy based around an inner courtyard and the pre-existing line of twenty leylandii trees on the site's northern boundary. The plan is organized in such a way that visitors can immerse themselves into the greenery offered by the courtyard and the garden, which is

Fig. 4.69. Pencil sketch of the building. (Drawing: Alun Jones)

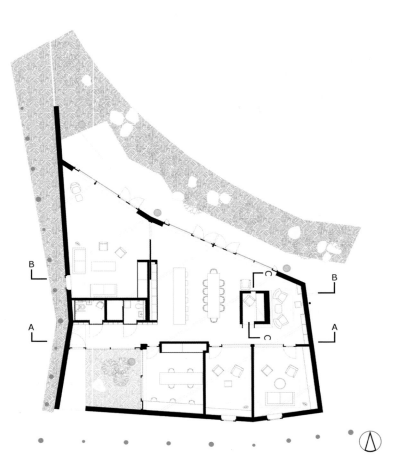

Fig. 4.70. Ground-floor plan. Dow Jones Architects and Cleve West based the landscape strategy on a courtyard, located at the building's entrance, and a line of greenery surrounding the northern boundary of the site. (Drawing: re-annotated from Dow Jones Architects)

A   A

B   B

Fig. 4.71. Dow Jones Architects worked with landscape designer Cleve West, who selected local plant species for the courtyard through which the building is entered. (Photo: Anthony Coleman)

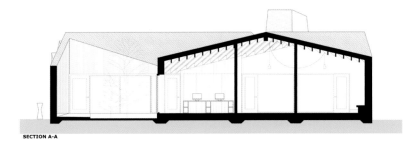

SECTION A-A

Fig. 4.72. Section A-A shows the internal courtyard, which brings light into the building through large glazing on two sides.
Section B-B shows the *cwtch* central space with a skylight inspired by *simnau fawr* chimneys, typical of vernacular Welsh architecture. (Drawing: adapted and annotated from Dow Jones Architects)

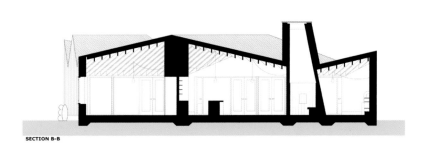

SECTION B-B

also visible through the glazing in the kitchen, a distinctive element in all Maggie's Centres. Cleve West selected indigenous plant species and worked with local volunteers, creating an intimate and immersive organic environment.

Maggie's Cardiff makes a connection with the local topography and industrial past of South Wales, through everyday materials that are often used in Welsh rural buildings. The building's irregular and uneven silhouette echoes that of the Pen-y-Fan mountains, forty miles north of the site, while the orange rusting of the corrugated steel cladding resembles the autumnal colours of the neighbouring bracken-covered hills. The interior is partly clad in timber and filled with natural light coming from the inner courtyard and the *cwtch*, located at the heart of the building. The Welsh word *cwtch* means a small, comforting space or a cuddle. At Maggie's Cardiff, the *cwtch* is a tall, intimate, rooflit space, inspired by the *simnau fawr* ('big chimneys' in Welsh) of vernacular Welsh architecture. In the context of Welsh homes, *cwtch* refers to small cupboards, like those situated under a flight of

stairs, which kids often see as their hidden, intimate space. The *cwtch* at Maggie's Centre becomes the small hide-away room where patients can retreat, meditate and observe the sky through the high rooflight.

The design benefitted from numerous collaborations between architects, artists and makers, whose fruitful results enliven the user experience. Welsh artist Osi Rhys Osmond's last painting, entitled *Self Portrait* (2015), has a permanent home at Maggie's Cardiff. The painting was left unfinished, since Osmond was working on it during the last month of his life, while receiving treatment for cancer.

Maggie's Cardiff's curator Mike Tooby worked closely with the architects to introduce art into the building: he selected several pieces, lent by the National Museum of Wales, which are hung on the internal walls. The artwork was selected in response to Osmond's painting, which stimulates reflection on life, memory and place, and became the most important piece in the centre. Sculptor Anthony Gormley made cast-iron bollards, which are located along the building's perimeter and are similar in colour and texture to the façade cladding. Ceramicist Pat O'Leary designed the entrance sign.

The centre exemplifies Dow Jones Architects' aim to design buildings that are responsive to people and places, that are comfortable and accessible, and that use materials able to connect a project to its own place.

Construction

> **Structural system:** hybrid system; timber-frame panels and steel skeleton
> **Foundations:** concrete raft foundations
> **Vertical supports:** 200 × 50mm prefabricated (and pre-insulated) timber-frame panels; steel sections (square or rectangular hollow sections and I-sections)
> **Ground floor:** ground-bearing, reinforced-concrete slab
> **Roof:** 200 × 50mm timber rafters
> **Thermal insulation:** rigid foam insulation
> **Acoustic insulation:** stone-wool acoustic insulation

Maggie's Cardiff's structural strategy aimed at lightweight and prefabricated building elements, due to the need for inexpensive and fast construction methods posed by the brief. A hybrid loadbearing system was elected: the primary structure is a steel frame and the secondary structure is based on timber framing. The steel skeleton includes different types of members: I-sections and square or rectangular hollow sections for the columns, and I-sections for the beams. The steel columns are fixed to the concrete slab by means of steel base plates and resin-bonded anchors. Bolted connections were used to join the steel members to one another. The steel frame is infilled with the timber wall panels.

The building sits on reinforced-concrete raft foundations constructed on a blinding layer laid, in turn, on well-compacted granular fill. The slab is insulated with rigid-foam boards and finished with a 100mm-thick power-floated concrete screed.

The timber-frame wall panels – prefabricated and installed by a specialist company – are made of softwood components and OSB sheathing on both sides. The studs are manufactured from C16-graded timber and have a 200 × 50mm cross-section; the panels are insulated with 200mm-thick rigid-foam boards fitted between the studs. These wall panels are supported by reinforced-concrete upstands (rising from the slab) and a timber sole plate is interposed between the upstands and the bottom rails (*see* Fig. 4.73). The panels are internally lined with plasterboard and externally clad with corrugated Cor-ten steel sheets.

The chimney-like structure of the *cwtch* space consists of framed panels prefabricated from C16-graded wood (*see* Fig. 4.75), insulated with 125mm-thick rigid boards, and internally lined with Douglas fir panels, also used for built-in seats and door linings. This timber finish delineates the main spaces and contrasts with the sleek, polished-concrete floors.

Within the roof, steel I-beams run along the ridges and valleys and thus define the geometry of the 45-degree-angled planes. The lower flanges of these beams support C24-graded timber rafters (200 × 50mm), which are internally exposed and finished with passive fire protection and a white topcoat. On top of the sarking (marine-plywood sheets) are two layers of rigid-foam insulation boards: these total 210mm in thickness and the upper one has incorporated counterbattens. The covering consists of Cor-ten steel sheets fixed to timber battens. The uneven geometry of the roof and the internally exposed rafters confer character upon the interior, creating an attractive alternation of intimate and open spaces.

Environmental sustainability

Dow Jones Architects specified the materials for Maggie's Centre from a cultural and sustainability

Fig. 4.73. The prefabricated timber-frame panels are assembled on-site, by means of a crane. They sit on a timber bottom rail, which is fixed to a reinforced-concrete upstand. In the middle ground, red metal members can be seen, which are part of the hybrid (timber-steel) structural system. (Photo: Phillip Roberts)

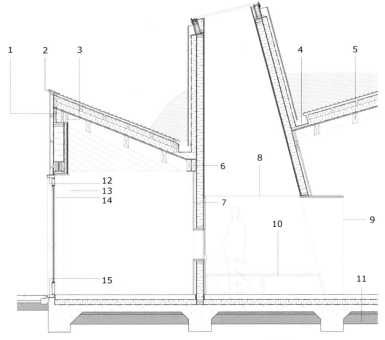

- breather membrane
- 90mm rigid insulation boards + incorporated battens
- 120mm rigid insulation boards
- vapour barrier
- 18mm marine ply
- 200x50mm C24 timber roof joists
- fire protection with white top coat
6 254x146 UB with timber packers
7 *build-up of internal wall:*
  ● Douglas fir cladding
  ● 50mm battens & service void
  ● 9mm OSB sheathing
  ● 125mm C16 timber studs
  ● 125mm rigid insulation boards
  ● 9mm OSB sheathing
  ● 15mm battens
  ● Douglas fir cladding
  ● 62.5mm insulated plasterboard
  ● 12.5mm plasterboard
  ● skim and paint finish
8 Douglas fir wall cladding
9 Douglas fir door
10 Douglas fir built-in seat
11 *floor build-up:*
  ● 10mm power-floated concrete
  ● damp-proof membrane
  ● 100mm rigid insulation boards
  ● damp-proof course
  ● 200mm reinforced-concrete slab
  ● 50mm sand blinding
  ● 750mm granular fill
12 steel flashing
13 Douglas fir lining
14 Douglas fir windows & doors
15 reinforced-concrete upstand

1 rim joist
2 folded steel flashing
3 noggin
4 aluminium gutter on breather membrane

5 *roof build-up:*
  ● 19mm corrugated weathering steel sheet
  ● 50mm battens

Fig. 4.74. Detailed section passing through the *cwtch* space. (Drawing: re-annotated from Dow Jones Architects)

Fig. 4.75. Timber-frame panels (with outer OSB skin) enclosing the upper part of the *cwtch* space, with an opening for the skylight inspired by Wales' vernacular chimneys. (Photo: Phillip Roberts)

Fig. 4.76. Interior view showing the exposed timber rafters of different roof planes, which sit on steel I-beams. (Photo: Anthony Coleman)

perspective. Where possible, they avoided use of materials that entail harmful manufacturing processes or high life-cycle costs. The timber-frame panels achieve a level of thermal insulation that surpasses the requirements set by building regulations. The majority of the materials chosen are self-finishing and can be left in their raw state, minimizing the use of paints and seals, and reducing maintenance. The corrugated steel cladding is recycled and sourced from the UK, while all the windows and doors have been manufactured in Cardiff itself.

The building's form and massing are arranged so that there are only a few small openings on the south façade, which look out onto the hospital's car park. Natural light mostly comes from the courtyard, through the north façade (which fronts onto the existing line of trees at the back of the site), and from the skylight of the *cwtch*. All windows are openable, thus ensuring natural ventilation through the building; the *cwtch*'s skylight, in particular, acts as a passive ventilation chimney.

Fig. 4.77. Interior view showing the *cwtch* space on the left (timber-clad walls). The furniture is made from Douglas fir. (Photo: Anthony Coleman)

Case Study 4: Woodland Classrooms

Fausto Sanna & Annalaura Fornasier

Location: Belvue School, Northolt, London, UK

Building type: school

Completion date: 2017

Design Team:

Architects: Studio Weave

Structural engineer: Timberwright

Building-services engineer: Arup

Environmental consultant: Arup

Client: Belvue School

Gross floor internal area: 91m²

Awards:

Winner – Wood Awards (Education and Public Sector), 2018

Winner – RIBA London Award, 2018

Winner – RIBA London Client of the Year Award, 2018

Winner – AJ Architecture Awards: Project of the Year, 2018

Shortlisted – RIBA Journal MacEwen Award, 2018

Shortlisted – AJ Small Projects, 2018

Shortlisted – British Property Federation's '2018 Tomorrow's Leaders' awards

Keywords: open timber-frame panels, educational, glulam, suspended floors, curved roof, box truss

Fig. 4.78. The façades of the Woodland Classrooms are clad with PEFC-certified cedar boards. The 'Messy Barn', in the centre of the building, has large sliding panels, also clad with cedar boards. (Photo: Jim Stephenson)

Brief and design process

Belvue School offers secondary education to boys and girls with learning difficulties in Northolt, West London. The school was given custody of the adjacent Wulfgar Wood, which had been underutilized and neglected for a long time, with a view to use it as an educational nature reserve. The initial plan was to locate two shipping containers on the boundary between the playground and the woods, and use them chiefly as storage space. However, when the school saw potential for a more permanent solution, it raised funding for a new development and contacted Studio Weave, asking them to formulate a proposal for a building in the same location selected for the container scheme.

Belvue wished to create an improved 150m² flexible space, detached from the rest of the building, to help students engage with the woodland. These unique facilities were built using timber-framed panels for their warmth, natural patina and comfort, as well as to reflect the woodland context. The new classrooms – in contrast to traditional ones – were designed to have a domestic scale, so as to encourage students to learn from the wooded surroundings, and to incite creativity and spatial awareness. Studio Weave's approach to the new learning space revolved around a narrative inspired by the gatehouse building type. The boundary between the school's playground and Wulfgar Wood was imagined as the boundary between the familiar school space and the magical, mysterious world of the woods. For this reason, the new classrooms were meant as a physical threshold between the two worlds. The design process was also informed and enriched by a series of story-writing workshops that the architects had held with the students, to gain their perspective on how the school's 'gatehouse' could interact with the woodland.

Studio Weave were required to provide three learning spaces: a 'Cosy Lounge' for teaching and engaging with the woodland and wildlife; a 'Sociable Kitchen', with a café for preparing food and hosting small dining groups; and a 'Messy Barn', located between the two classrooms and offering a covered outdoor recreational space. The timber-lined classrooms have very wide cedar-clad sliding doors that, when open, offer a view towards the playground, and, when closed, create a more intimate interior atmosphere.

Studio Weave are passionate about design briefs that have a multi-disciplinary approach. They seek to work with a variety of stakeholders, across different socio-economic contexts, to develop architectural proposals that are embedded in their place and community. Public participation and development of a narrative are a recurring element in the Studio's work, as exemplified by this project.

Fig. 4.79. The Woodland Classrooms lie on the boundary between the playground and the woods. (Photo: Jim Stephenson)

Construction

Structural system:
    Foundations: helical-pile foundations
    Vertical supports: hybrid, with posts & open timber-frame panels
    Ground floor: suspended, timber-framed floor
    Roof: curved glulam rafters, glulam box truss, and plywood/OSB sheathing

Small diameter helical piles were chosen for the foundation system, to reduce the building's impact on the existing trees. The floor is raised off the ground on the north side, to adapt to its slope and allow ventilation beneath the timber frame. Thermal insulation was achieved with 200mm-thick polyisocyanurate (PIR) boards. The construction is finished with yellow rubber flooring in the Sociable Kitchen and Cosy Lounge, and with non-slip larch decking in the Messy Barn.

Fig. 4.80. Having been given permission to use Wulfgar Woods, Belvue School initially decided to place some containers at the edge between its playground and the woodland that would provide extra storage and learning space. Once a more substantial budget had become available, however, the school abandoned the idea of the containers to pursue a permanent solution. Studio Weave decided to locate the new scheme (highlighted in red) in the same place as the containers, to avoid disrupting the woodland and having to fell any trees. (Drawing: adapted from Studio Weave)

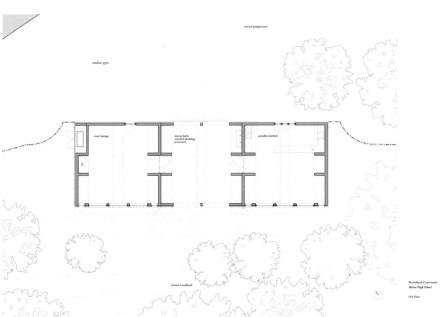

Fig. 4.81. The architects, in liaison with the school, imagined two classrooms connected by a central, covered space, referred to as the 'Messy Barn'. The learning spaces are called 'Cosy Lounge' and 'Sociable Kitchen', the latter offering a space for cooking and hosting group lunches. (Drawing: Studio Weave)

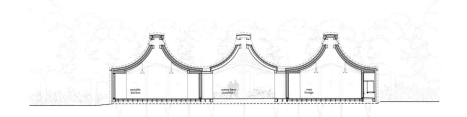

Woodland Classrooms
Balroe High School

Section AA

Fig. 4.83. The 'Messy Barn' has been imagined as a place where students can interact with the woodland. It provides the main access to the woodland and acts as a gate that can be closed and opened thanks to large sliding doors, clad in cedar boards like the façade. The curved rafters (45 × 195mm) are laid at 600mm centres and externally sheathed with weather- and boil-proof (WBP) plywood. This roof differs from the roofs over the other two spaces in that it does not need any thermal insulation and its rafters are not concealed but left exposed. (Photo: Jim Stephenson)

Fig. 4.84. Example of a gatehouse: North Lodge, designed by Victorian architect Alfred Waterhouse, in Brockenhurst Park, New Forest, Hampshire. England's gatehouses provided inspiration for the design of the Woodland Classrooms, which the architects imagined as the gateway between the real world (the school) and the magical world of the woods. (Photo: Ashley Basil, CC BY 2.0)

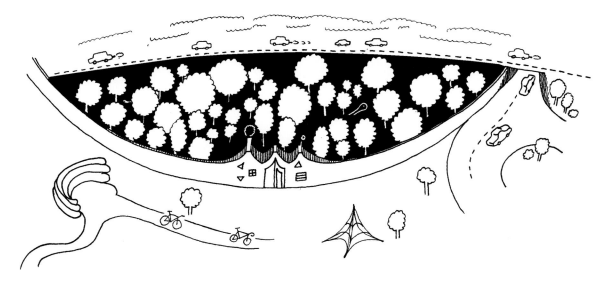

Fig. 4.85. Studio Weave worked closely with Belvue School and organized a series of workshops with its students to involve them in the design process, make the building project a part of their learning and help them develop a sense of ownership of the new Woodland Classrooms. (Drawing: Studio Weave)

This project uses a post-and-beam system combined with timber-frame panels, made from UK-grown Douglas fir. The posts and beams were fabricated by joining four standard members mechanically (the same members used for the studs of the wall panels and floor joists). In each of the three parts of the roof, curved rafters span between the beams of the skeleton (at the foot) and a box-truss at the ridge (*see* Fig. 4.87). The box truss, in turn, spans between opposite gable ends. The lateral thrust exerted by the curved rafters is fully withstood by the structure of the low-ceiling spaces located on either side of each roof; therefore, ceiling ties at the feet of the rafters are not necessary. Glulam fabricated from whitewood was used for the rafters and box trusses. Externally, the rafters of all three spaces are sheathed in plywood, whilst internally the rafters of the Sociable Kitchen and Cosy Lounge are lined with OSB (*see* Fig. 4.88) and with exposed birch-ply sheets. These sheets were bent on site and treated,

Fig. 4.86. The primary beams of the floor rest on stainless-steel feet bolted to the concrete caps of helical-pile foundations. Timber joists span in the direction perpendicular to these beams. Each beam is fabricated by bolting together four timber sections like the ones used for the joists. (Photo: Studio Weave)

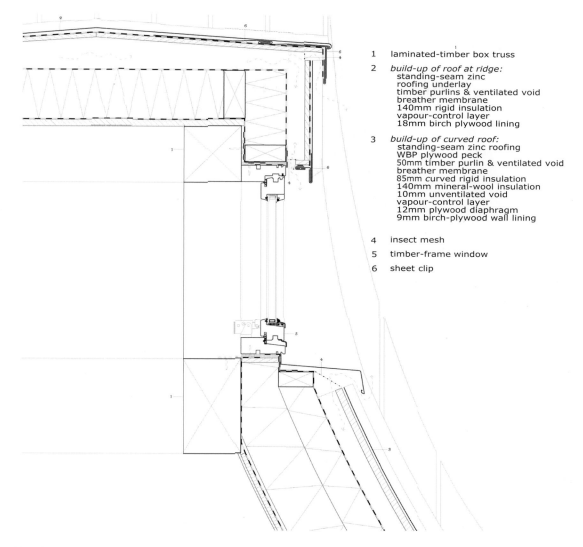

1   laminated-timber box truss

2   *build-up of roof at ridge:*
       standing-seam zinc
       roofing underlay
       timber purlins & ventilated void
       breather membrane
       140mm rigid insulation
       vapour-control layer
       18mm birch plywood lining

3   *build-up of curved roof:*
       standing-seam zinc roofing
       WBP plywood peck
       50mm timber purlin & ventilated void
       breather membrane
       85mm curved rigid insulation
       140mm mineral-wool insulation
       10mm unventilated void
       vapour-control layer
       12mm plywood diaphragm
       9mm birch-plywood wall lining

4   insect mesh

5   timber-frame window

6   sheet clip

Fig. 4.87. Detailed vertical section of the roof showing the ridge (constructed around a glulam box truss) and the curved surface. (Drawing: adapted and re-annotated from Studio Weave)

once installed, with a mix of oils and waxes and with an intumescent coating. The roof is insulated by means of two complementary layers: 70mm-thick curved rigid panels laid over 140mm-thick flexible mineral wool. In the Messy Barn, the roof is uninsulated (like the floor and the walls) and the rafters are not lined, thus remaining exposed. The outer covering of all three roofs consists of zinc sheets with standing seams.

The external walls are constructed with open timber-frame panels with rigid insulation boards fitted on site between the studs. The panels are clad on the outside with vertical boards fabricated from British-grown, PEFC-certified Western red cedar and finished internally with birch plywood, like the ceiling. Both the wall and floor panels are made from treated, standard-size timbers.

Fig. 4.88. Construction of the Sociable Kitchen. The curved glulam rafters (45 × 145mm) are positioned at 400mm centres and supported by timber beams at the lower end and by a glulam box-truss at the upper end. The wall panels match the profile of the roof and are sheathed externally with OSB and insulated with rigid boards. (Photo: Studio Weave)

Fig. 4.89. One of the box-trusses that are placed at the ridge of the roof and offer structural support to the upper ends of the curved rafters. The truss is made of glue-laminated whitewood members. (Photo: Studio Weave)

Fig. 4.90. The external wall fronting onto the woodland awaits its interior lining. In the meantime, the roof's curved rafters have been lined in OSB sheets, which, in turn, will be covered in birch ply. (Photo: Studio Weave)

Fig. 4.91. Cosy Lounge: the convex ceiling reflects the light that permeates through the windows positioned along either side of the box-truss at the ridge. The roof and the walls are internally finished with birch-ply sheets treated with clear products: a mix of natural plant oils and waxes, and an intumescent coating. (Photo: Jim Stephenson)

Case Study 5: Taverny Medical Centre

Fausto Sanna & Annalaura Fornasier

Location: Taverny, Ile de France, France
Building type: healthcare centre
Completion date: 2019
Design Team:
  Architects: MAAJ Architectes
  Structural engineer: Batiserf Ingénierie
  Thermal, electrical & environmental engineering: WOR Ingénierie
  Acoustic engineering: Acoustique Vivié & Associés (AVA)
  Landscape designer: Praxys Paysage
Client: Ville de Taverny
Gross floor internal area: 1,095m²
Keywords: timber frame, CLT, courtyard, skylight, Canadian well, healthcare

Environmental sustainability

While working on the design of the classrooms, Studio Weave collaborated with a forest-management specialist to develop a strategy for the maintenance and upkeep of Wulfgar Wood. Their goal was to bring benefits to the local community by enhancing biodiversity in the area and limiting the effects of the A-road that runs at the back of the woodland. The new classrooms are in the same location as the initial container scheme, because this had been chosen to limit disruption to the woodland and preserve the existing trees.

The classrooms were completely built out of FSC- and PEFC-certified sustainable timber (*see* Chapter 3 for an explanation of FSC and PEFC), and clad with cedar boards on the exterior and plywood on the interior, as seen in the previous section. The clerestory windows can facilitate natural, stack ventilation through the building. The large glazed areas fronted by the woodland face south-west to maximize solar gain.

Fig. 4.92. The Medical Centre is located in the suburban town of Taverny, north-west of Paris, and brings under one roof healthcare professionals that were previously spread across a number of smaller surgeries. Since medical services tend to be scarce in the Parisian suburbs, the establishment of this facility allowed locals to receive high-quality care without having to travel to central Paris. The Centre has on-site parking and is surrounded by outdoor areas curated by Praxys Paysage landscape-designers. (Photo: François-Xavier Da Cunha Leal)

Brief and design process

Taverny is a *commune* in the north-western suburbs of Paris. The Medical Centre was commissioned by Taverny Municipal Council in 2016, to address the lack of healthcare facilities in the area (which is a recurrent problem in the capital's peripheries). The Centre is located in a fragmented townscape and near a motorway. As a response to these site conditions, MAAJ Architectes proposed a square layout with a central patio and different levels of privacy across the building: the fenestration is concentrated in the walls that border the internal patio, while the external elevations (which front onto the neighbourhood) are conceived as a more private shell with fewer openings. The plan layouts have been designed for staff and patients to easily move inside the building and orientate themselves: on both floors, the offices and consulting rooms are around the outer perimeter and have small windows that front onto the surroundings, while corridors and waiting rooms are around the inner perimeter and offer views towards the central patio.

The Centre is mostly timber-constructed, in both its structural and cladding components. The façade is clad in Douglas fir slats arranged vertically, which camouflage the windows and provide further privacy to the consulting rooms. The exterior space around the building was designed by Praxys Paysage (a Paris-based landscape and architectural firm) to create a soft transition between the Medical Centre and the suburban context. As mentioned above, the building is introverted, in that the elevations around the patio are largely glazed – with vertical panes of glass framed by timber studs – and look towards the flowerbeds, in which medicinal plants are grown. Double-height glazing has been used to mark the building's entrance and bring light into the reception hall and circulation space above it, on the upper floor.

The Medical Centre's plan resembles that of a medieval monastery, with its courtyard surrounded by a covered passage (cloister) on all sides: most rooms and monks' cells open inwards (into the cloister), while

Fig. 4.93. Few and small in size are the windows on the elevations of the Medical Centre that face onto the surroundings, so as to ensure a high level of privacy to doctors and patients in the consulting rooms. Further privacy has been achieved through the timber studs that protrude from the external walls and frame the windows. (Photo: François-Xavier Da Cunha Leal)

Fig. 4.94. Trenton Bath House in Ewing, New Jersey (USA), designed by Louis Kahn and Anne Tyng, and completed in 1955. This renowned building has inspired the design of Taverny Medical Centre, especially with its courtyard and four pyramidal roofs at the corners. (Photo: Smallbones, CC0)

Fig. 4.95. The cross-shaped courtyard, where medicinal herbs are grown, resembles a monastery's courtyard. The idea of opening the building inwards onto a central patio was also influenced by two buildings designed by Louis Kahn: Trenton Bath House (1955) and Phillips Exeter Academy (1972). (Photo: François-Xavier Da Cunha Leal)

the external façades have few or no windows. Another source of inspiration for MAAJ Architectes was the geometrical precision of Louis Kahn's work, which influenced their aesthetical choices and approach to the floor plans. Particularly inspiring were two projects developed around a central courtyard: Phillips Exeter Academy (1972) and Trenton Bath House (1955), which has four pyramidal timber roofs with an oculus at the top, to let light in and naturally ventilate the spaces below[5]. Similarly, at each corner of Taverny Medical Centre is a squared pavilion covered by a pyramidal roof, with a skylight at the apex, to allow light and air into the circulation space.

MAAJ Architectes are an emerging firm and aspire to design buildings that create a link between users, site and architecture.

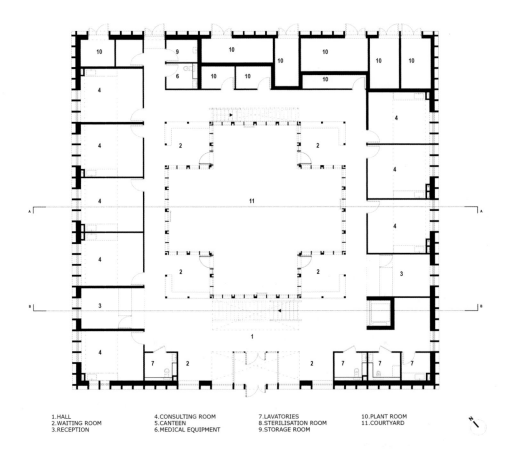

1.HALL
2.WAITING ROOM
3.RECEPTION
4.CONSULTING ROOM
5.CANTEEN
6.MEDICAL EQUIPMENT
7.LAVATORIES
8.STERILISATION ROOM
9.STORAGE ROOM
10.PLANT ROOM
11.COURTYARD

Fig. 4.96. From a programmatic point of view, the circulation space wraps around the central patio, as a cloister runs around a courtyard in a monastery. Monks' cells would usually be accessed through the cloister and would have small windows on the outer-perimeter walls. MAAJ Architectes have taken a similar approach; the consulting rooms are located around the outer perimeter and have fewer and smaller windows than the circulation space around the inner perimeter. (Drawing: translated from MAAJ Architectes)

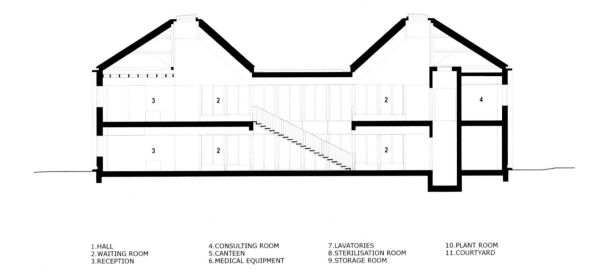

1.HALL	4.CONSULTING ROOM	7.LAVATORIES	10.PLANT ROOM
2.WAITING ROOM	5.CANTEEN	8.STERILISATION ROOM	11.COURTYARD
3.RECEPTION	6.MEDICAL EQUIPMENT	9.STORAGE ROOM	

Fig. 4.97. Vertical section of the building, showing the staircase between the entrance hall on the ground floor and the corridor on the first floor, which runs around the inner perimeter of the facility. Two of the pyramidal roofs can also be seen, with their skylights pouring light into the waiting rooms on the first floor. (Drawing: translated from MAAJ Architectes)

Construction

Structural system:
   Foundations: raft foundations
   Vertical supports: timber-frame panels + external timber studs, timber posts (post-and-beam skeleton), masonry (concrete blocks)
   Ground floor: ground-bearing concrete slab (raft foundation)
   Intermediate floor: CLT panels (spruce)
   Roof: spruce trusses for pyramidal roof
Thermal insulation: glass wool (external walls & roof)
Acoustic insulation: perforated plasterboard (waiting rooms), acoustic fibreboard (corridors), timber suspended ceiling (offices)

The building's loadbearing structure comprises different systems: vertical supports are mostly constructed with timber-frame panels, timber posts and, to a lesser extent, concrete blockwork, especially on the ground floor. The intermediate floors are realized in CLT panels, and the pyramidal roofs in timber frame.

The studs for open timber-frame panels are made of 70 × 140mm sections. However, the studs have an alternate arrangement: every other stud is doubled with the juxtaposition of two sections, thus resulting in a 140 × 140mm support. The studs are placed at about 430mm centres. All the timbers for these panels are made from spruce. Glass-wool quilts fill the gaps between the studs, and the panels are externally sheathed in OSB/3 sheets. On the inside, the panels are completed with an acoustic-insulation layer and two or three layers of plasterboard, depending on the orientation of the walls: two layers for those facing SE and SW, and three for those facing NE and NW. What makes the façade system unconventional is the fact that Douglas fir studs are placed all along the façade and match the position of the double studs inside the panels. Between the external studs and the panels is an additional layer of flexible glass-wool mats, which insulates the wall without any interruptions. The surfaces between the external studs are clad in Douglas fir boards, laid vertically on battens and counterbattens.

The ground floor is a concrete slab (part of the raft foundations), insulated on the underside with extruded polystyrene boards. The intermediate floor is constructed with 248mm-thick CLT panels (fabricated from spruce), which rest on the timber-frame panels and/or the timber post-and-beam system. On top of the panels is an acoustic layer, covered with a screed and PVC flooring.

The four corner roofs with a truncated-pyramidal shape are constructed of spruce trusses. Here the diagonals play a major role: they support purlins, which, in turn, support smaller rafters laid in the direction of the slope. Each diagonal is supported at the foot by the external timber-framed walls (*see* Fig. 4.100) and at the top by three members (one vertical and two oblique) that rest on a horizontal frame positioned at ceiling level. These trusses are insulated with a double layer of glass wool. The roof covering consists of zinc sheets laid on battens. The ceiling is timber-framed and concealed with different types of lining products, depending on the room type: plasterboard (perforated sheets under solid ones) in the waiting rooms, acoustic wood-fibre panels in the corridors, and timber panels in the offices.

Environmental sustainability

MAAJ Architectes wished to offer Taverny's community an environmentally sound building that would be well integrated into its context. For this reason, they specified timber sourced from local French forests. The few openings on the exterior façades limit the noise disruption coming from the nearby motorway and contribute to patients' privacy. The central patio provides natural ventilation and constitutes a source of light for the waiting rooms and circulation space on both floors. The four corner pavilions have a skylight at the top, which provides further light and natural ventilation.

The building is equipped with a Canadian well[6] (also referred to as a Provençal or climatic well, or a geothermal air-to-ground heat exchanger): this is a geothermal system that can be used for space cooling or heating by taking advantage of the thermal

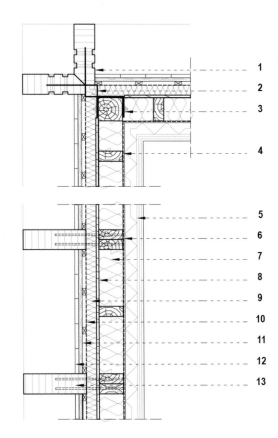

1	external Douglas fir stud
2	metal fastener
3	timber stud (140x140mm)
4	timber stud (70x140mm)
5	sound-absorbing panel
6	vapour barrier
7	glass-wool quilt (140mm)
8	OSB/3 sheet (15mm)
9	flexible, glass-wool mat (60mm)
10	breather membrane
11	batten & counterbatten (22x40mm)
12	vertically-laid Douglas fir board (21mm)
13	external Douglas Fir stud (120x360mm)

Fig. 4.98. Constructional detail of the external walls (horizontal section). (Drawing: adapted and translated from MAAJ Architectes)

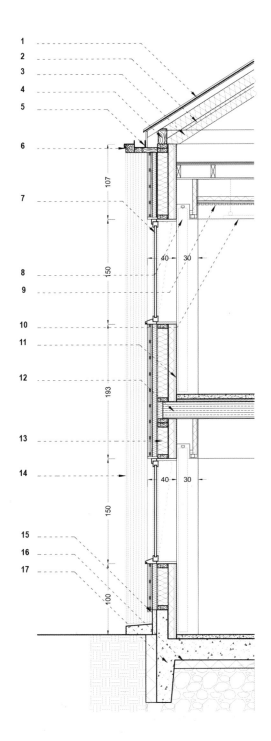

1   zinc roofing sheet on 60x80mm battens and rafters
2   timber rafter & ceiling tie (140x120mm)
3   flexible glass-wool mats, double layer (160+160mm)
4   rim joist (120x220mm)
5   gutter (100x150mm)
6   Douglas fir batten (120x120mm)
7   timber tilt-and-turn window
8   manually-operated sunblind
9   false ceiling: perforated plasterboard + cavity (200mm) + mineral wool (60mm)
10 suspended, radiant heating panels
11 plasterboard: double layer on SW & SE walls, triple layer on NE & NW walls
12 PVC flooring + screed (70mm) + mineral-wool insulation (40mm) + CLT panel (248mm)
13 timber-framed panel
14 external Douglas fir stud (120x360mm)
15 zinc flashing
16 PVC flooring + screed (60mm) + acoustic underlay + raft foundation (300mm) + XPS boards (120mm) + hardcore (600mm)
17 foundation rib

Fig. 4.99. Constructional detail (in vertical section) of the external wall and its junctions with the roof, ground floor and first floor. (Drawing: adapted and translated from MAAJ Architectes)

Fig. 4.100. The CLT panels of the intermediate floor rest on the timber-framed walls on the outer perimeter of the building and on timber columns closer to the courtyard. In the background, the timber-framed panels have been installed and externally sheathed with OSB/3 sheets. In the upcoming construction stages, glass-wool quilts will be fitted between the studs. (Photo: MAAJ Architectes)

Fig. 4.102. One of the pyramidal roofs under construction. The four diagonals that run along the edges of the pyramid have an important structural role: they support the purlins, which, in turn, support smaller rafters laid in the direction of slope. (Photo: reduced from MAAJ Architectes)

Fig. 4.101. A timber framework is constructed at ceiling level: this defines the ceiling itself and carries the load coming from the top of the pyramidal roof. Since at the apex of the pyramid is a skylight, an opening is formed in the ceiling to allow natural light to pass through and illuminate the first floor. The membrane laid over the walls is the vapour-control layer. (Photo: MAAJ Architectes)

inertia of the soil near a building. Fresh air (taken from outside the building) is made to circulate in a conduit buried into the ground and thus exchanges heat with the soil, through the surface of the pipe. At the end of the conduit, the air is then pumped into the building, contributing to the adjustment of the interior temperature. The efficiency of a Canadian well depends on several factors, such as weather conditions, soil type, aeration rate and flow speed through the conduit.

Taverny Medical Centre has been rated by EFFINERGIE[7], a French association established in 2006 with the goal of ensuring high levels of energy efficiency in new-build and refurbishment projects. Thanks to its low energy consumption, the Centre has been granted the 'EFFINERGIE+' label, which is reserved for buildings whose average primary-energy consumption is no more than 50kWh/(m²year).

The Centre also complies with French code RT2012 (*Réglementation Thermique*[8], first adopted in 2013), which sets the maximum energy consumption for both residential and non-residential buildings to 40–65kWh/(m²year), depending on location and altitude.

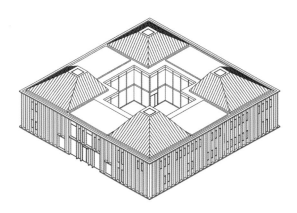

Fig. 4.103. Reference to Louis Kahn's Trenton Bath House (1955) is clearly visible in MAAJ Architectes' design of the four pyramidal roofs with a skylight at the apex. (Drawing: MAAJ Architectes)

Fig. 4.104. The skylight at the top of the pyramidal roof, surrounded by white, reflective surfaces, contributes to natural illumination of the first floor. (Photo: François-Xavier Da Cunha Leal)

Fig. 4.105. One of the waiting rooms on the first floor, simply decorated with a limited colour palette: clean white walls and ceilings, grey PVC flooring and natural wood colours. Patients can enjoy a view of the cross-shaped courtyard through the glazed surfaces. (Photo: François-Xavier Da Cunha Leal)

Notes

(1) The reader is invited to consult TRADA's publications for further information; particularly Lancashire and Taylor (2011) and Hislop et al. (2018).

(2) An extensive illustration of intermediate floors with high acoustic performance can be found in the documents that accompany building regulations (and provide recommended details), in *Robust Details* (ca.2020) and in TRADA's publications, especially Lancashire and Taylor (2011).

(3) In-depth information on trussed-rafter systems is offered in the publications by the Trussed Rafter Association (TRA) and by Gang-Nail Systems listed in the Bibliography.

(4) Jenks, 1994

(5) *Architects' Journal*, 2021; This building marked a change in Kahn's career. In a 1970 interview with a *New York Times* reporter, he said: 'If the world discovered me after I designed the Richards [Medical Research] towers building, I discovered myself after designing that little concrete-block bathhouse in Trenton' (Braudy, 1970).

(6) Touzani and Jellal, 2015

(7) Effinergie, ca.2012

(8) Ministère de la Transition écologique, 2020

Chapter Five

Designing with Structural Insulated Panels

Overview

Structural insulated panels (SIPs) are sandwich panels consisting of a thermal-insulation core between two skins of wood-based sheet material, generally OSB, or – less frequently – plywood or particleboard. The insulation core can be made of different materials: polyurethane, expanded polystyrene (EPS), extruded polystyrene (XPS) or polyisocyanurate (PIR), which all have comparable thermal conductivities and produce SIPs with similar structural performance. A proportion of recycled material can be used for the fabrication of the facings.

SIPs are based on a simple structural concept: that the two skins enable the panels to withstand the loads to which building elements are subjected, by virtue of their mechanical properties. The thickness of the insulating core keeps the two skins apart, thus providing more stability to the panels.

The development of SIPs dates back to the 1930s, when the Forest Products Laboratory in Madison (Wisconsin) started conducting research on new panelized systems towards better and more efficient use of timber and timber-based products. This research strand was further pursued by private companies, especially The Dow Chemical Company, which created the first SIP with a foam core. Frank Lloyd Wright used SIPs in some of his Usonian houses, designed for middle-income families during the 1930s and 1940s in the USA. In the 1990s, the SIP industry commenced utilizing CNC technology to fabricate SIPs; this, in conjunction with advancements in computer-aided design (CAD), meant that SIPs could easily be cut by transferring CAD information to CNC machinery. This innovation generated great advantages in terms of efficiency and productivity, which resulted in lower fabrication costs and thus made SIPs more competitive with other structural methods available on the market. Further growth in the SIP sector occurred when OSB manufacturers started producing larger sheets, which facilitated the fabrication of big SIP elements to be installed by crane.

SIPs are used especially for low- and mid-rise buildings, in the residential, civic and commercial sectors. In the UK, SIP-constructed buildings do not generally exceed four storeys in height. SIP construction is very versatile, in that it lends itself to several roof and wall configurations and can very easily be integrated with other timber structural systems. For instance, SIPs can be combined with timber-frame panel construction when they form part of the primary structure of a building; alternatively, they can be used as infill walls (secondary structure) in a building with a post-and-beam system (this is especially done in mid-rise buildings). In a similar manner, SIPs can be utilized in conjunction with other types of structural methods, such as steel-framed systems. The breadth of application of SIPs varies geographically. In the UK, SIPs are mostly employed for walls (especially external walls) and roofs (both flat and pitched); in other countries (for example the USA), they are also used for floors.

Like in any other types of buildings, wooden components in areas that might be temporarily exposed to moisture should previously have been treated with preservatives (as recommended in BS 8417). Timber members with a structural function should be kept away from moisture and be at least 150mm above

OPPOSITE: **Fig. 5.1.** House in the Woods in Hampshire, designed by Alma-nac, London. (Photo: Jack Hobhouse)

finished-ground level, as was also seen for TF panel construction in Chapter 4.

The total thickness of SIPs ranges from 100 to 250mm. The OSB facings are typically 11mm thick, but they can be thicker if necessary (for example 15 or 18mm).

Walls can be built up of:

- small panels, which follow the standard size of OSB sheets (typical dimensions: 1.2 × 2.4m);
- large panels (up to 6m long), which utilize multiple standard-size OSB sheets or just one larger-format OSB sheet.

Thanks to their light weight, small SIPs can easily be handled and lifted on site by two operatives and positioned manually. Bigger panels offer the advantage of faster construction time but are more reliant on large machinery, such as cranes, for installation purposes.

There exist two main methods to produce SIPs. A jig can be used to keep the two outer sheets at the necessary distance, then liquid foam is poured between the sheets: when the foam expands, it fills the whole gap and also bonds to the sheets. Alternatively, the core can be fabricated independently and then bonded on either side to the wooden sheets, with structural adhesive.

Manufacturing firms can pre-cut bespoke SIP elements in their facilities following the designers' specification for a given project and provide assistance with the engineering side of the design when requested. Manufacturers can then deliver a kit of panels and accessory components to the construction site, for assembly. Moreover, large manufacturing companies have developed whole building systems based on SIPs, complete with compatible and integrated solutions for the walls, floors and roof of an entire building.

Like all timber-based structural components, SIPs can exhibit creep behaviour over time, which needs to be accounted for in the structural design as well as in the detailing, to avoid damage coming from this type of time-dependent, mechanical response (*see* Chapter 1). Effects of shear stresses also need to be evaluated, since they are resisted by the OSB skins only, and not by the insulation core. In structural calculations, when SIPs are sized for roof or floor applications, deflection tends to be the predominant criterion.

External Walls

SIP walls do not differ widely from timber-frame walls (dealt with in Chapter 4) and can be finished, both internally and externally, with the same range of techniques and materials as was seen for TF panels. The exact thickness and make-up of the chosen SIP will depend both on the loading configuration and on the target level of thermal insulation. An important factor is whether the only insulation layer within the wall make-up is the foam contained in the SIPs themselves or an additional layer is to be introduced, generally on the outside. If an insulation jacket is added to attain the desired U-value, then a check to assess condensation risk should be performed.

When a SIP wall is compared to a TF one with solid timber studs (the simplest type of section), the

Fig. 5.2. Types of splines to connect adjacent SIPs: solid-timber spline and insulated spline, which consists of two OSB facings and an insulation core, like the SIPs. (Drawing and manufacturing: Hemsec Manufacturing Ltd)

former generally exhibits lower thermal bridging, because its build-up contains fewer timbers that can transfer heat between the two faces of the wall. However, SIP walls might also have solid timber splines, therefore thermal bridging should be assessed and, if necessary, attenuated with additional insulation layers, for instance an insulation jacket or insulating material inserted into the service void.

Foundations should be level before the installation of SIPs commences. Where SIPs rest on a concrete sub-structure (for example a reinforced-concrete, ground-bearing slab), a sole plate is first fixed to it. This plate is made from treated timber, and has the same width as the SIPs and minimum thickness of 38mm. When the sole plate is being laid, galvanized- or stainless-steel levelling shims can be used and injectable grout added to fill any gaps. A damp-proof course is interposed between the concrete surface and the sole plate.

A bottom rail (also referred to as bottom plate or locator plate) is placed on top of the sole plate; this component is also made from treated timber and has the same width as the insulation core of the SIPs, as it needs to fit between the two OSB skins at the feet of the panels. Holding-down bolts can be used to secure the structural connections between the SIPs and the concrete base: they pass through the sole plate and the bottom rail and penetrate the concrete slab. Both on the inside and outside, the SIPs are connected to the bottom rail with galvanized-steel, ring-shank nails. However, it is worth mentioning that there are different methods to connect the SIPs to the wall plate, and a bottom rail is not always inserted at the interface between the sole plate and the SIP, in which case the SIP slots into the sole plate, with its OSB facings over the sides of the plate. The technique adopted to connect SIPs, bottom plate, sole plate and sub-structure affects the panels' racking resistance.

Splines can be inserted between adjacent SIPs, in order to create a stronger structural connection. Two types of splines are available:

- solid splines, generally made from a solid length (but engineered timber could also be used when necessary);
- insulated splines, which have a very similar composition to the SIPs themselves: they consist of an insulation layer sandwiched between two wood-based skins.

Of these two types, the latter performs better from a thermal point of view, in that it allows for continuity of the insulation layer along the wall. Solid splines on the other hand offer much greater structural capacity and, in some cases, might be the only viable option.

Irrespective of whether solid or insulated splines are utilized, their thickness will need to be such that they can slot into the gap between the facings of the SIPs to be connected. Splines are fixed by means of nails, screws or bolts through the OSB skins, and then sealed. Expanding foam needs to be sprayed to fill the gaps between the SIPs and the spline: this will improve the thermal performance and airtightness of the wall. Splines are used not only to join two consecutive panels, but also at the end of wall runs. SIP manufacturers offer different proprietary systems to make the structural connection between their panels.

Where a SIP wall is subjected to high concentrated loads (for instance, those transferred from a girder truss, rafter or beam), *ad hoc* local reinforcement can easily be arranged by inserting a post between two SIPs, either of solid or engineered timber. Above the post, a pocket can be formed to accommodate the end of the beam, rafter or truss.

SIPs at corner junctions are joined with very long screws (for example 300mm), which can run through the end of one panel and the main side of the other, then they are sealed with expanding-foam glue or flexible mastic. SIPs must be connected by a continuous top rail (also referred to as a header or top plate) positioned in the gap between the OSB facings at the top of the panels. The top rail is screwed to the panels and fulfils an important role: it evenly distributes the

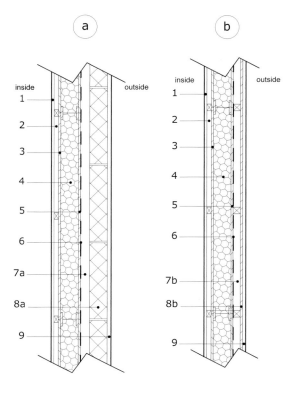

a			b		
inside	outside		inside	outside	
1			1		
2			2		
3			3		
4			4		
5			5		
6			6		
7a			7b		
8a			8b		
9			9		

1	plasterboard		7a	vented cavity
2	timber battens & service void		7b	timber battens & ventilated cavity
3	inner OSB skin (SIP)		8a	concrete blocks
4	foam core (SIP)		8b	render-carrier board
5	outer OSB skin (SIP)		9	render
6	breather membrane			

Fig. 5.3. Build-up of external walls constructed of SIPs, clad in blocks (a), or with render on carrier board (b). (Drawing: after Sanna, 2018)

loads transferred from intermediate floors and roofs between the SIPs that make up the wall.

In order to avoid interstitial condensation within the build-up of the walls, a vapour-control layer needs to be installed or, as an alternative, a lining product can be specified that offers sufficient resistance to vapour penetration (this could be plasterboard with incorporated vapour check: for instance, foil-backed plasterboard).

It is advisable not to run cable or pipes within the thickness of SIPs, as this practice would compromise their integrity and, ultimately, their structural capacity. It is recommended to form a service void on the inside of walls instead. The void is created with timber battens fixed to the skins of the SIPs and with a lining product such as plasterboard or wooden boards. Battening for dry-lining products can be built with solid timber battens, OSB/3 strips or metal rails. When it is necessary to run pipes or cables through an external wall, care should be taken to seal the gap around these. In addition, the portion of electrical cables penetrating SIPs should preferably be protected with *ad hoc* sleeves, to prevent the risk of leaching.

During wall erection, SIPs are kept in their intended position and stabilized by means of temporary braces. On-site installation of SIPs is generally a rather fast process (even more so if large panels are prefabricated in the factory), which means that the building becomes weather-tight quickly.

Openings

Openings can be formed in two ways: either by removing material from a large SIP in the factory (pre-cut openings), or by arranging smaller SIPs around the openings, on site or offsite.

Numerous options are available to construct lintels over openings in a SIP wall: a SIP panel, a solid-timber section, a glulam section or a flitch beam. Timber studs should be inserted on the sides of the openings, to provide a fixing support for the door/window frame. If the opening is a window, then a timber should also be inserted at sill level.

The number, area and position of openings affect the structural behaviour of a panel, in terms of strength, stability (of the individual panel and the structure as a whole) and racking resistance.

External cladding

Whether a light- or heavyweight cladding system is specified, it is important to consider and assess how this could perform in the event of fire. Suitable cavity barriers/fire-stops must be inserted into the constructions to prevent spread of flame, smoke and hot gases, especially from one storey to the ones above or from one fire compartment to another. Cavity barriers can be manufactured from a variety of materials, including solid timber, mineral wool (generally reinforced with metal wire) and intumescent substances. In SIP buildings, particular care must be taken for the correct positioning of cavity barriers: these must be mounted onto solid timbers (such as the timbers around the perimeter of openings or joists in an intermediate floor). This is because, if a barrier is mounted onto the SIPs, fire might spread through their insulation core and thus bypass the barrier itself.

Lightweight cladding

The choice of a cladding type should take into account meteorological aspects such as wind-driven rain in the building's area. The durability of the loadbearing SIP leaf will depend on the correct design and formation of joints. SIP walls are able to support a lightweight cladding system, without the need for this to rest on the foundations. This results in smaller foundations, with lower consumption of concrete and reduced environmental impacts arising from cementitious materials. The fixings used to secure the cladding to the SIPs must provide sufficient pull-out resistance through the OSB facings alone. The external cladding should not be mounted directly onto the SIPs, but onto battens inserted into a ventilated and well-drained cavity. The outer surface of the SIPs must be protected with a breather membrane, to prevent any incidental moisture that has penetrated the cladding screen from reaching and damaging the SIPs and the associated timber members (such as sole plates, top and bottom rails or splines).

The types of external cladding suitable for SIP-constructed walls are the same as those seen in Chapter 4 for TF panels: timber boarding, metal sheets, render on carrier-boards and so on.

Heavyweight cladding

If a heavyweight cladding system is designed, the wall build-up needs to be arranged as a cavity wall. The cavity (about 50mm) must be sufficiently ventilated (with open perpends or ventilators at suitable distances) and drained with weep holes. A breather membrane is installed on the outside of the SIP leaf, to protect it from moisture penetration and ensure durability in the long term. The outer masonry leaf needs efficient protection from rising moisture, with the installation of a damp-proof course.

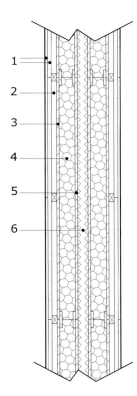

1   plasterboard (double layer)
2   timber battens & service void
3   inner OSB skin (SIP)
4   foam core (SIP)
5   outer OSB skin (SIP)
6   sound-absorbing layer: unfaced, wire-reinforced mineral-wool quilt (fixed to one leaf only)

Fig. 5.4. Make-up of a SIP-constructed separating wall. (Drawing: after Sanna, 2018)

The masonry leaf needs to be secured to the inner (loadbearing) leaf to provide sufficient overall rigidity to the wall. *Ad hoc* wall ties complete with screw fixings for SIP-masonry walls should be utilized: these can be fastened directly to the OSB skin. Stainless steel should be specified for wall ties and screws.

Different elements of a SIP building can expand or contract at different rates after completion. While SIPs themselves do not undergo major dimensional changes, other parts are likely to do so, for instance solid-timber rails, plates, splines and solid or engineered-timber joists. Therefore, suitable differential-movement gaps should be introduced in the masonry cladding, near window sills and floors, so as to avoid damage to the constructions. Additionally, expansion joints might be necessary in large walls, to allow the heavyweight cladding to expand without getting damaged or causing damage to other building components.

Internal Walls

Internal walls can be built with SIPs, but this is not a conventional choice. TF panels are often used instead, with the advantage that services can be run within their thickness, while a SIP wall would require a cavity service between the structural panel and the internal lining.

Party Walls

A SIP party wall is generally constructed with two, independent SIP leaves with a cavity in the middle (around 50mm thick). Appropriate inner lining should be specified to provide the wall with the level of fire resistance prescribed by local building regulations. The lining needs to be fixed to the SIPs via timber battens. If for instance sixty-minute fire resistance is required, this can be attained by installing two staggered layers of 15mm-thick sheets of gypsum plasterboard with improved core adhesion at high temperatures (type-F plasterboard, as defined by Standard BS EN 520).

Intermediate Floors

Beside their high compressive strength (in the longitudinal direction), SIPs also possess good bending strength, and thus can be used as flexural members to form floors. However, this type of application is rather unusual, especially in the UK.

Intermediate floors can be supported by SIP walls in two ways:

- the floor joists rest on top of the wall of the lower storey (more precisely, on their top rail). This arrangement is repeated at every floor and is typical of platform construction. It is common practice to introduce a rim beam perpendicular to the joists, which contributes to supporting the SIPs of the upper storey. The rim beam can be fabricated from solid or engineered timber;
- the floor joists hang from the inside of the walls, thanks to joist hangers fixed to the head of the wall (nailed, screwed or bolted to the head plate). This type of arrangement is typical of balloon construction, and the wall panels can be two-storeys high.

Typically, floors supported by SIP walls employ engineered joists (open-web joists, I-joists and so on) but solid joists or floor cassettes are also possible solutions – *see* Chapter 4 for timber-framed intermediate floors.

Flat Roofs

Cold-deck roofs

Flat roofs built with SIPs are classified as cold roofs and therefore require suitable ventilation between the SIPs and the deck on which the waterproofing layer is laid. A ventilation void can be formed by laying tapered battens (furrings) on the SIPs. Openings should be created at opposite ends of

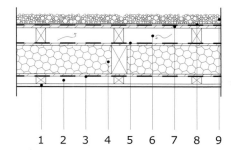

1 internal lining (e.g., plasterboard)
2 timber battens & service void
3 vapour-control layer (VCL)
4 SIPs & solid timber splines
5 breather membrane
6 timber furrings & ventilated cavity
7 decking
8 waterproofing layer
9 pebble ballast *[optional]*

Fig. 5.5. SIP-constructed flat roofs are classified as cold roofs; therefore they require a ventilated air space above the structural deck.

the roof, to facilitate ventilation through the void. The thickness of the ventilation void should be commensurate with the length of the roof and not less than 50mm.

The furrings support a deck laid to falls, made of OSB/3, plywood, particleboard or similar sheet material. A breather membrane needs to be interposed between the SIPs and the furrings. The deck must be overlaid with a waterproofing layer, for instance, bitumen-based membranes or a single-ply membrane.

An additional (and continuous) thermal-insulation layer can be applied underneath the SIPs, not only to improve the overall thermal resistance of the construction, but also to reduce thermal bridging through the splines or other solid timbers that might have been inserted between the SIPs to improve the strength and rigidity of the roof.

A vapour-control layer can be added to the underside of the SIPs, to prevent any water vapour produced indoors from penetrating the construction and condensing. If there are any service runs to be accommodated, a service void needs to be formed between the SIPs and the internal lining.

Pitched Roofs

SIP pitched roofs are classified as cold roofs (like their flat counterparts, as discussed above) and, consequently, need suitable ventilation between the SIPs and the covering. A continuous ventilation gap (from the eaves to the ridge) can be formed by laying the horizontal tiling battens not directly on the SIPs, but on top of counterbattens that run in the direction of slope. Counterbattens should be fabricated from treated softwood and fixed to the SIPs with stainless-steel screws. Openings of adequate area should be formed at both eaves and ridge level, to permit sufficient air flow through the ventilation gap.

SIP roofs are typically constructed with large panels, complete with openings, which are craned into position. Different structural configurations can be designed to support roof panels, the main two being the following:

- the roof panels span in the direction of slope, and rest on the heads of the wall SIPs, on timber purlins and/or on ridge beams. Within

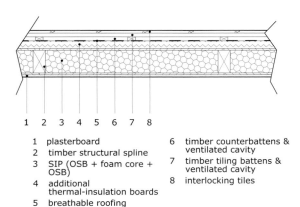

1 plasterboard
2 timber structural spline
3 SIP (OSB + foam core + OSB)
4 additional thermal-insulation boards
5 breathable roofing underlay
6 timber counterbattens & ventilated cavity
7 timber tiling battens & ventilated cavity
8 interlocking tiles

Fig. 5.6. Construction of a SIP pitched roof (section perpendicular to the plane of slope). A continuous layer of insulation boards can be laid above the SIPs so as to reduce thermal bridging through the timber splines that provide strength and rigidity to the roof. (Drawing: after Sanna, 2018)

Fig. 5.7. A multi-family residential building, whose external walls are constructed in SIPs (by Hemsec Manufacturing Ltd). The SIPs at the gable end (1) have been cut to fit the pitch of the roof; solid timber splines have been inserted between the SIPs (2). The internal walls (3) are built with timber-frame panels. The intermediate floor employs engineered joists supported by a glulam beam (4) and has a particleboard deck (5). (Photo: annotated and adapted from Hemsec Manufacturing Ltd)

Fig. 5.8. Construction of the lower storey contained in the roof space, in the same building shown in Fig. 5.7. The roof's slopes (1) have been constructed in SIPs (by Hemsec Manufacturing Ltd), and timber battens (2) have been installed to receive the internal lining. The intermediate floor employs metal-web joists (3) fixed to a timber member (4) inserted into the web of a steel I-beam (5). Timber-framed panels are erected for the full-height walls (6) and the dwarf walls (7) along the outer perimeter. (Photo: annotated from Hemsec Manufacturing Ltd).

this configuration, an unobstructed (without trusses) and habitable space under the roof is created;

- the roof panels span horizontally, and are supported by gable walls and/or internal walls.

In either case, special timber fillets are needed to join up the wall heads with the roof SIPs, and very long screws can be used that are able to pass through a roof SIP and the supporting member(s) underneath it. For instance, on top of the head plate, a special wall plate can be laid, which is angled to match the roof pitch.

A breather membrane should be laid over the roof panel. SIP roofs can employ any type of covering suitable for pitched roofs, ranging from metal sheets, to slates and concrete or clay tiles. Openings in roof panels (for example for skylights) can be formed in the same way that was discussed above for wall panels.

Fig. 5.9. External view of the roof of the building shown in Figs. 5.7 and 5.8. The roof is composed of SIPs that span in the direction of slope and are supported at three levels (lower floor, upper floor and ridge). The openings for the skylights have been lined in solid timber lengths. At the foot, the roof has a different pitch, formed with small timber trusses. (Photo and manufacturing: Hemsec Manufacturing Ltd)

Case Study 6: House in the Woods

Location: South Downs National Park, Hampshire, UK
Building type: residential – single-family house
Completion date: 2016
Design Team:
    Architect: Alma-nac, London, UK – Tristan Wigfall, Caspar Rodgers, Chris Bryant
    Structural engineer: Heyne Tillett Steel, London, UK – Mark Goobrand, Jonathan Flint
    Building-services engineer: Integration, London, UK – Dan Brooks, Julio Vale
    Landscape design: KR Garden Design, London, UK – Karen Rogers
Client: Jenny Stevinson
Gross floor internal area: 240m^2
Keywords: SIPs, glulam, hydrothermally modified wood, timber I-joists, rural, single-family home

Fig. 5.10. The western façade of House in the Woods is clad in timber and overlooks woodland. The wide openings on the ground floor are those of the kitchen, dining room and lounge. The windows and terrace on the first floor visually connect the bedrooms with the surrounding landscape. (Photo: Jack Hobhouse)

Brief and design process

House in the Woods is located in an area of outstanding natural beauty within the South Downs National Park in Hampshire, UK. It is built on the footprint of a pre-existing bungalow that was demolished, to minimize impact on the surrounding trees and landscape. The client wished to retain a similar approach to the site to that of the bungalow, while opening up views on the woodlands in which it is located. The programme needed to be flexible to accommodate the different functions envisaged by the client, with a focus on communal spaces for family gatherings and socializing. The living room (extending from east to west) and kitchen with a dining area (occupying the south-west part of the ground floor), split by a central fireplace, are the heart of the house. Alma-nac Architects envisaged the kitchen and dining areas to have full-height ceilings, enhanced by the duopitch roof and lightened up by a row of openings on the western façade. The location of the communal areas maximizes the views and access to the garden, as well as solar gain during the day. The northern part of the house accommodates the guest bedrooms on the ground floor and a separate staircase, which leads to the master bedroom and guest bedroom on the first floor. Such separation of spaces allows the client to close the guest wing, with a sliding door, and create a more intimate space when desired.

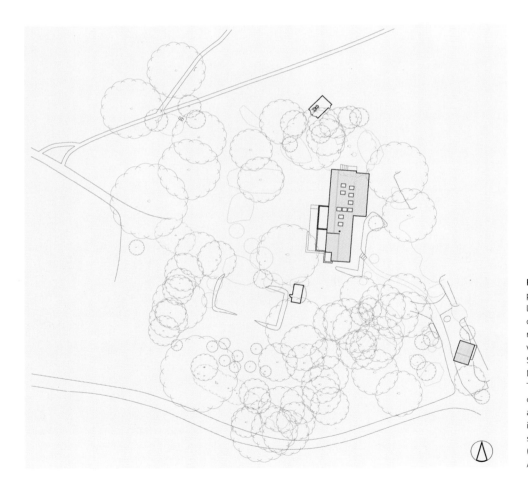

Fig. 5.11. Location plan. The house is located in an area of outstanding natural beauty within Hampshire's South Downs National Park. The building is overall rectangular and orientated in a north-south direction. (Drawing: Alma-nac, London)

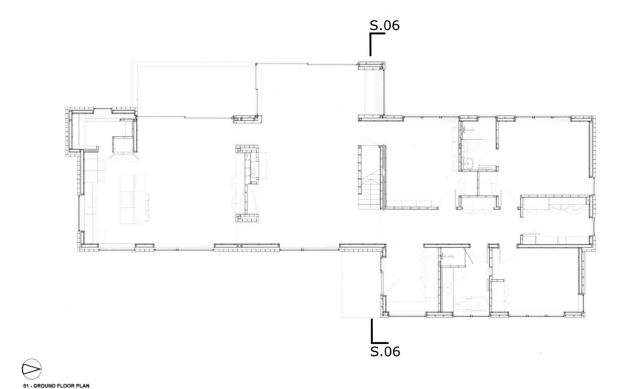

S.06

S.06

01 - GROUND FLOOR PLAN
1:50 @ A1 / 1:100 @ A3

Fig. 5.12. The design fulfils the client's desire to dedicate half of the ground floor to communal and socializing spaces such as the kitchen, dining area and living room. These spaces benefit from direct access to the garden. (Drawing: Alma-nac, London)

Fig. 5.13. A key aspect of House in the Woods is its strong connection with the landscape. Alma-nac made this possible through large openings on the communal spaces such as this large window in the dining room, looking out onto the landscape. (Photo: Jack Hobhouse)

Fig. 5.14. In the eastern façade, the most 'public' side of the house, the building seems to be lower than it actually is. The upper floor, indeed, is clearly visible only in the western façade, the more private part of the house. (Photo: Jack Hobhouse)

Key to House in the Woods' design is the relationship with the surrounding landscape. It was achieved through enhancing the best views identified from the old bungalow and adding extensive glazing that fronts onto the woodland situated west of the house. The openings allow for direct access to the garden from the communal areas of the house. On the first floor, Alma-nac designed a terrace that overlooks the garden and woodland.

Not only is the new building footprint very close to that of the old bungalow, but the size of the building remains modest. The house appears, on approach, as a single-storey building with a duopitched roof, while it reveals its two-storey wing only if seen from the private garden on the western side.

Construction

> **Structural system:**
> **Foundations:** concrete strip foundations
> **Vertical supports:** SIPs
> **Ground floor:** suspended beam-and-block floor
> **Intermediate floor:** timber I-joists
> **Roof:** SIPs and glulam members (for example ridge beam)
> **Thermal insulation:** rigid urethane foam (within wall and roof SIPs); rigid thermoset polyisocyanurate (PIR) boards (ground floor)

The house is largely constructed of SIPs, used for the walls and the pitched roof. These were transported to the building site on the back of two lorries and assembled over ten days. The SIPs used were made out of a urethane insulation core, sandwiched between two layers of 15mm (OSB)[1]. In this project, adjacent panels were connected through insulated splines, which are comparable to small SIP panels in themselves. This type of spline maintains the insulation layer intact and reduces thermal bridging and air leakage.

The design fully shelters the SIPs from the elements, thus ensuring their durability over time. The SIPs are indeed covered and protected by (from the inside out) a breather membrane, a wall cavity and exterior cladding. Two different types of external cladding are used for the perimeter walls. The north, south and east walls are clad with hand-cut bricks; while the west façade is clad with timber boards that have undergone hydro-thermal treatment in the factory, aimed to improve their durability and dimensional stability. In both cases, the gutters and downpipes are concealed and cannot be seen from the outside. The gutters are aluminium channels located behind the top of the brick skin or of the timber boards. The downpipes, instead, are positioned inside the wall cavity. The walls are internally finished with plasterboard (with integrated vapour check) and a 25mm service cavity is left between the SIPs and the plasterboard.

The duopitch roof is also constructed with SIPs, which span between the external walls and glulam beams running parallel to the façade. The roof over the entrance is clad in timber, while the main roof is covered with natural-slate tiles, which blend with the organic colours of the surroundings thanks to their varying tones. The internal finish is plasterboard separated from the SIPs by a 100mm void.

The SIPs were manufactured as storey-height panels in the factory, where windows and door openings were also pre-cut. Once the SIP superstructure had been fully erected in situ, doors and windows were added and sealed, to ensure optimum airtightness of the building envelope. The external wall cladding, the roof covering and all internal finishes were installed on site.

The ground floor was constructed using a beam-and-block system, and completed with rigid foam boards and a sand-cement screed with mesh reinforcement and underfloor heating system. The intermediate floors, conversely, use a lightweight system, based on timber I-joists.

Fig. 5.15. The walls and the roof were entirely built out of SIP panels, which were transported on site by lorries and assembled in just ten days. The SIP panels that make up the roof span between glulam beams that run along the ridge and the edges. (Photo: Alma-nac, London)

Fig. 5.16. Construction of the external walls: the SIPs are cut to follow the exact geometry of the gable ends and the roof profile. In this building, adjacent SIPs are connected by means of insulated splines (which are small SIPs in themselves). (Photo: Alma-nac, London)

Fig. 5.17. Detailed section through an external SIP wall clad in bricks. The gutters are realized as an aluminium channel concealed behind the brick skin. The rainwater pipe is also incorporated into the wall make-up: it runs inside the cavity between the brickwork and the SIPs. The roof is covered with natural slate tiles fixed to the SIPs by means of battens and counterbattens made from treated timber. (Drawing: adapted from Alma-nac, London)

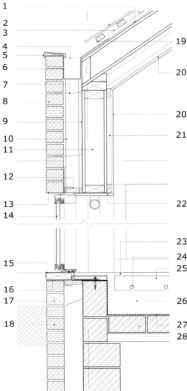

1 breather membrane
2 natural-slate roof tiles
3 25x50mm battens & counterbattens (preservative-treated timber)
4 continuous leaf-guard fitted to top of gutter
5 polyester-powder-coated aluminium coping
6 pressed-aluminium gutter
7 brick ties
8 grey bricks
9 breather membrane
10 concealed rainwater downpipe within wall cavity
11 SIPs
12 insulated cavity closer
13 steel lintel
14 patio door
15 pressed-aluminium sill
16 damp-proof course (DPC)
17 open perpends (to ventilate & drain cavity)
18 frost-resistant engineering bricks
19 insect mesh
20 plasterboard with integrated vapourcheck
21 service void
22 plasterboard taken into window reveal
23 hardwood flooring
24 underfloor heating system
25 85mm sand:cement screed
26 150mm thermal-insulation boards
27 damp-proof membrane (DPM)
28 suspended beam-and-block flooring system

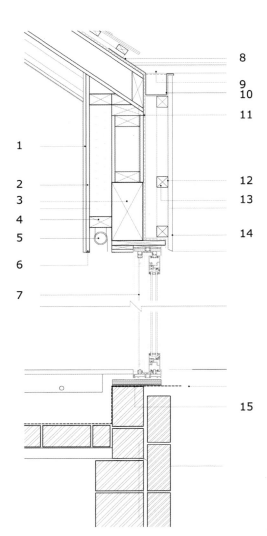

Fig. 5.18. Detailed section through an external SIP wall clad in vertical boards of hydrothermally modified wood. The boards are connected to the SIP leaf through a system of horizontal battens and vertical counterbattens of treated timber. A continuous insect mesh is fitted behind the cladding boards. (Drawing: adapted from Alma-nac, London)

1   plasterboard with integrated vapourcheck
2   15mm plywood
3   glulam beam
4   softwood studs
5   concealed automated blind
6   plaster skim taken up to edge bead
7   sliding glazed doors
8   insect mesh
9   continuous leaf-guard
10   polyester-powder-coated aluminium gutter and coping
11   breather membrane
12   continuous insect mesh
13   50x50mm horizontal & vertical battens (preservative-treated timber)
14   vertical cladding boards (thermally-modified timber)
15   damp-proof course lapped with damp-proof membrane

Environmental sustainability

SIPs were chosen for their thermal efficiency and air-tightness. The high level of insulation and the sealed junctions reduce heating requirements in the winter and can achieve comfortable levels of indoor temperature in the summer by means of passive ventilation through the windows and rooflights.

The beam-and-block system was chosen for the ground floor to give it more thermal mass and regulate temperature fluctuations throughout the year.

An air-source heat pump services the under-floor heating on the ground floor, localized radiators on the upper floor, a small hot-water cylinder for low-volume use and a booster tank that is only required when there is a full household.

As a consequence of the airtight design, there is a risk that indoor air might become stale or moisture-loaded. For this reason, the interior of the house is mechanically ventilated when the windows are closed through a heat-recovery unit, which extracts the heat from the exhausted air and pumps warm, pure air back into the house.

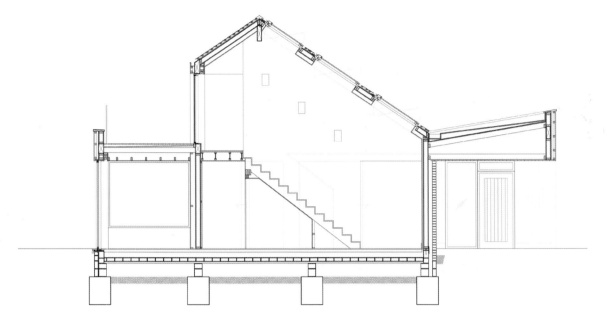

Fig. 5.19. Cross-section of the house through the staircase (looking north). Three rooflights illuminate the flight of steps. The ground floor is suspended and adopts a beam-and-block system. (Drawing: Alma-nac, London)

Fig. 5.20. The south-facing gable side of the dwelling, with its glazing. The elevated patio on the left includes a dining area, partially protected by an overhang. (Photo: Jack Hobhouse)

Notes

(1) The urethane core was attached to the OSB boards by means of auto-adhesion. The liquid chemicals that made up the foam were sprayed between the boards and their reaction resulted in an expanded, rigid foam with high insulation properties.

Chapter Six

Designing with Solid Timber Panels

Overview

Cross-laminated timber (CLT, also referred to as crosslam or X-lam) is a structural material that has gained increasing attention over the last two decades, at global scale. In the UK, for instance, the first CLT building was constructed in 2004 and since then many other CLT projects have been completed, attracting the attention of clients, designers, professional bodies and contractors alike. CLT panels can be employed for a variety of building elements, such as walls, floors, roofs, stairs and lift shafts.

Similarly, other structural systems based on massive timber panels have been developed, rediscovered or rethought in recent times; these include nail-laminated timber, dowel-laminated timber and log construction.

Cross-Laminated Timber

Fabrication and characteristics of the panels

Key properties

CLT panels consist of different layers of timber boards (lamellae) glued together to form a solid object. In each layer, the boards are laid at 90-degree angles with respect to the adjacent layers (hence the term 'cross-lamination'): this fundamental characteristic means that CLT panels span in two directions. The

OPPOSITE: **Fig. 6.1.** La Borda apartment block, Barcelona, designed by Lacol. The cantilevering walkways act as horizontal circulation space and provide access to the apartments, the staircase and the lift. (Photo: Lluc Miralles)

layers are usually in odd numbers (typically three, five or seven, but nine or more is also possible); which results in panels having a predominant direction of span:

- in longitudinal panels, the boards of the majority of layers are orientated lengthwise;
- in transversal panels, the boards of the majority of layers are orientated crosswise.

Cross-lamination provides enhanced mechanical and physical properties to the final product relative to the base material. In particular, cross-lamination:

- distributes the high mechanical properties that wood exhibits along the grain in two directions;
- makes the final material much more dimensionally stable (less susceptible to shrinkage and swelling as a result of changes in environmental conditions). Moisture movement is about 0.01 per cent change in moisture content on panel plane (both longitudinally and transversally), and around 0.20–0.25 per cent change in moisture content perpendicular to panel plane (in the thickness direction);
- reduces the effect of natural defects. Knots, for instance, can be present in the lamellae, but they are discontinuous and do not coincide in subsequent layers.

CLT is, in most cases, fabricated from softwoods: generally spruce or alternatively Douglas fir or larch. Hardwoods can also be employed, but this is a much rarer choice. Different types of adhesives can be utilized, either individually or mixed: polyurethane (PUR), melamine urea formaldehyde (MUF) and emulsion polymer isocyanate (EPI). The quantity of adhesive used is small relative to that of timber and amounts to about 0.6 per cent of the overall panel weight.

Fig. 6.2. Example of seven-layer CLT panels, typically utilized for floor or roof applications. In each layer, the timber boards are arranged at right angles to those of the adjacent layers. (Photo: Ying Liu, Haibo Guo, Cheng Sun and Wen-Shao Chang, CC BY 4.0)

Moisture content of CLT elements is usually around 12 per cent on delivery. Key thermophysical properties of a CLT panel as a whole are very close to those of the raw material used. For a panel made from spruce, density is around 470kg/m³ (at 12 per cent moisture content) and thermal conductivity 0.12W/(m·K).

Dimensions and layup of panels

Ordinary CLT panels range between 50 and 300mm in thickness, but much larger panels can be manufactured if needed (up to 500mm). The maximum length and width of the panels depend mostly on the constraints posed by transportation from the factory to the site and the possibility of using tall cranes on site. For these reasons, panels rarely exceed 13.5m in length and 3m in width. Panels are generally flat, but curved panels can also be fabricated in advanced manufacturing facilities.

Normally, the width of the sawn boards that make up the panels is approximately 150mm, while their thickness varies between 20 and 45mm. The cross-section of a CLT panel is symmetrical around the main axis of the central layer. Within the same

panel, different layers can have different thicknesses, to optimize structural performance. In panels to be used as flexural members (such as floor or roof panels), wood is concentrated in the longitudinal layers (in the panels' main direction of span), which are thicker than the transverse layers. For instance, a 150mm-thick panel for floor or roof applications can be built up of layers of the following thicknesses (from one outer surface to the other): (40+20+30+20+40) mm. In order to increase the amount of wood with the grain oriented in one direction, pairs of adjacent lamellae might have the same orientation. In these special configurations optimized for flexural members, the overall number of lamellae can therefore be even, while the number of layers remains odd.

It is important to stress that there is currently little standardization in the CLT industry: different manufacturers have developed products with different layups and formats, and adopt different fabrication processes. This has important implications for designers when they are preparing the specifications for a CLT project or estimating its cost.

Fabrication process

CLT panels are produced to order, for individual projects.

The main phases of a typical fabrication process can be summarized as follows:

- parts with large defects (such as knots or fissures) are removed from the timber boards and the ends of abutting boards are finger-jointed;
- the boards are planed, to enhance surface bonding in the subsequent phases;
- the boards are arranged horizontally to form the first layer of the panel, and the adhesive is evenly applied over them;
- the boards of the second layer are placed on top of the first layer (typically, at right angles). Adhesive and subsequent layers are added as needed;

- the panel is inserted into a mechanical press and subjected to high compressive loads (0.6–0.8 N/mm^2) for up to thirty minutes. Pressure is exerted perpendicular to the main surfaces of the panel, but it can also be exerted laterally, on the four sides, to ensure that there are no gaps left between the boards that make up every layer;
- the panels are trimmed and the edges are given the intended geometry with CNC machines;
- openings (if any) are formed by removing material from the panels;
- chases for services are milled (if specified);
- surface treatment is performed (if specified), for instance fire-retardant coatings.

Pre-cut openings and building services

Typically, CLT panels are cut in the factory with CNC machines, and cutting on site is not advisable, since it is time-consuming, expensive and might have repercussions on the structural capacity of the panels. The openings formed offsite can be for doors, fenestration, service penetration and so on.

Building services can be accommodated in *ad hoc* voids on the inside of walls and roofs, and in suspended ceilings. Alternatively, it is possible to run small services such as electrical wires in routes milled in the factory along the joints between adjacent panels or in chases on one side of the panels. These latter arrangements allow reducing the overall thickness of building elements but require more coordination between different aspects of the design (and between the respective professionals) and rely on more advanced manufacturing techniques.

Fire safety

In order to protect CLT buildings from rapidly collapsing in the event of fire, two main options are available to designers:

- the CLT panels are protected by adequate lining (for example gypsum plasterboard), as was seen in Chapters 4 and 5 for timber-frame and SIP constructions, respectively;
- the panels are produced in thicknesses that exceed those required for structural purposes under normal circumstances. In the event of fire, the faces of the panels exposed to flame will char and thus protect the timber behind the charring layer, which will remain intact and continue to fulfil its structural function, at least for a given length of time. In other words, the extra timber added to the panels will act as a sacrificial layer in case of fire. An indicative measure of the charring rate is 0.7mm/min.

Fire-retardant coatings can be applied to the surfaces of the panels, either in the factory or on site, after the panels have been erected.

Appearance and surface treatment

Building standards regulate surface quality and define different classes of visual appearance. In Europe, standard EN 13017-1, *Solid wood panels. Classification by surface appearance. Part 1: softwood,* introduces the following appearance classes (from highest to lowest):

- class 0. Appearance must be well balanced in colour and texture. Coarse texture is not permitted. Discolouration is not permitted;
- class A. Appearance must be well balanced in colour and texture. Coarse texture is permitted. Discolouration is not permitted;
- class B. Appearance must be largely balanced in colour and texture. Coarse texture is permitted. Slight discolouration is permitted;
- class C. No requirements on appearance or on texture. Discolouration is permitted;
- class S. No requirements on appearance or on texture. Discolouration is permitted.

Natural defects (such as knots, resin pockets, bark pockets and fissures) are permitted increasingly from class 0 to class S. Similarly, the standard regulates other characteristics of the panels for each appearance class (thickness of glue line, presence of blemishes, quality of panels' edges and ends, presence of finger-joints and so on).

However, manufacturing companies tend to use their own terminology to define the same or similar finishes. Classes 0 and A correspond to what manufactures tend to define as 'visible quality' (or similar wording), class B to 'industrial visual quality', and classes C and S to 'non-visual quality'.

If CLT panels are manufactured from softwoods and the surfaces are untreated, they will yellow over time when exposed to artificial and especially natural light, since ultraviolet (UV) radiation damages the lignin contained in the wood. Yellowed areas of a CLT panel can be sanded and thus regain their original, paler appearance, but this can be very impractical or inconvenient in occupied buildings.

In order to avoid UV-related aging, the exposed surfaces of CLT elements can be treated with substances that will make them less reactive to UV light, thus allowing them to maintain their initial pale colour. Other treatments are also available that can give the surfaces of the panels the desired hue and level of opacity or gloss. Not all manufacturers offer these types of surface treatments, so they are often conducted on site. When applying a coating on the side of a CLT panel, it is worth keeping in mind that the transverse lamellae will respond differently to the same treatment, because the end-grain will tend to absorb more product than the long grain. Similarly, the effect of the same coating can be different over knots, finger-joints or deviated grain.

The exposed surface of a CLT panel will tend to change appearance as a response to fluctuations in environmental conditions (especially after the first year and heating season). For example, small fissures or gaps between adjacent boards might appear on the surface, due to shrinkage and swelling of the wood in the outer layer. Cracks are particularly likely to form near heat sources, because the higher temperature will cause the wood to lose more moisture and, as a consequence, to shrink more than in other areas of the building.

Some manufacturers offer the option of gluing an extra layer of wood onto the exposed face of a CLT panel, for aesthetic or decorative reasons. In this additional layer, the grain is oriented as in the lamellae immediately behind.

Reinforcement and connections

When the spans of flexural components such as roof or floor panels are noticeable, either the thickness of the panels is increased so as to achieve the necessary structural capacity, or a hybrid solution is chosen, with the introduction of glulam or metal intermediate beams. The latter option requires lesser use of timber and results in the building element being lighter in weight.

CLT panels are connected to one another by means of long screws or steel brackets. There are various types of techniques to join panels; the edges can be square or more complex: notched, rebated, or profiled for half-lapped joints. If CLT is combined with other wood-based products, making the connections is generally straightforward and can be done with screws, nails and/or bolts. Connecting CLT panels to concrete, masonry or steel components is, conversely, more burdensome. It is also worth keeping in mind that wood-based components will respond to changes of environmental conditions in a similar way and to a comparable extent.

The most straightforward and economical fixing method (numerous screws and brackets) has very little aesthetic appeal, but this does not constitute a problem when the CLT panels are lined. If, instead, CLT panels are exposed, then connections should be carefully studied and specified; screws and other fixing types can be concealed and used on the back faces of the panels, if these are accessible. When both faces of a CLT panel are exposed (for example in internal walls), concealing the fixings in a successful manner becomes more difficult. In order to hide the connections, designers can opt for panels with rebated or slotted edges, or for plugs or cover plates to be applied to the exposed surfaces after the fixings have been inserted.

On-site assembly

After transportation to site, CLT panels can be erected very quickly, which means that subsequent operations, such as the installation of non-structural components, can be performed promptly.

Different proprietary systems have been developed to lift CLT panels during transport and erection: these can be based, for example, on slings or metal anchors inserted into blind holes or through-holes.

It is important for designers to remember that when CLT panels (especially large ones) are transported to site and then manoeuvred and lifted for installation, their corners and edges can be damaged easily, particularly if they are not simple, square edges, but more complex ones (for example rebated or slotted). Therefore, when specifying the geometry and finish of panels, designers should factor in the practicalities of transport and erection and the overall size of the panels, in order that the final output reasonably matches the expectations set at the design stage.

Constructions

External walls

CLT panels can sit directly on a concrete slab, without the interposition of any timbers. For levelling purposes, the panels can be mounted on non-shrink grout, or, alternatively, this can be injected at a later stage into any gaps between the foot of a panel and the slab. Metal shims can be used if the slab surface presents some irregularities. It is good practice to treat the feet of the wall panels with end-grain sealant, which prevents them from absorbing moisture from the grout or from the ground.

Alternatively, CLT panels can be laid on a timber sole plate fixed to the concrete substructure. The sole plate can be fabricated from durable or moderately durable species (for example larch) and fixed to the concrete slab via bolts. The CLT panel is then fixed to the plate with inclined screws. A long, metal fastener can be used to connect all three elements (panel, sole plate and slab). A damp-proof course needs to be laid underneath the sole plate. Some CLT manufacturers offer the option of a rebated sole plate that matches a rebated foot in the CLT panels.

Steel angle brackets are used to fix the panel locations, typically at 1.0–1.5m centres. The brackets are screwed into the timber and bolted into the concrete slab. Self-adhesive, compressible strips can be used between abutting panels (lined up or at an angle), to improve airtightness and acoustic performance.

Numerous solutions are possible to form the joints between panels, and each manufacturing company tends to have its preferred method. Abutting panels can have square edges, or rebated edges. When two CLT walls abut at right angles, long screws are used, which are inserted perpendicular to the main surface of the panel through which they pass, or at an angle to both panels, to avoid entering a lamella in the direction of the grain (where the connection would be weaker).

If a wall is subjected to high concentrated loads at certain locations, the designer can either increase the thickness of the whole CLT panel, or introduce *ad hoc* strengthening locally, where it is most needed. The latter option can be executed by adding structural members of solid timber, engineered timber or other materials (for example metals) to complement the CLT panels.

CLT walls can be clad with light- or heavyweight systems, although the latter are less common. The range of suitable cladding materials is the same as for timber-framed and SIP buildings. Timber cladding (boards or panels) is a frequent choice for CLT walls.

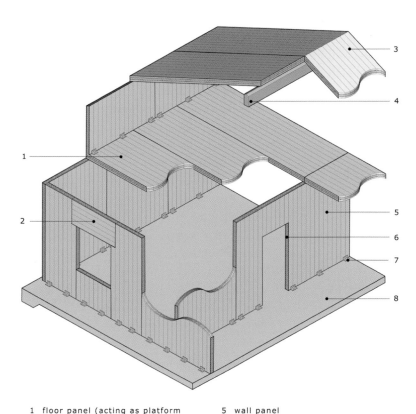

Fig. 6.3. Main structural components of a two-storey CLT building with a duopitch roof. The openings can be formed either by punching a panel (6), or by arranging various panels around them, including a lintel member (2), which is generally orientated perpendicular to the other wall panels.

1 floor panel (acting as platform   5 wall panel
  for upper floor)   6 punched opening
2 lintel panel   7 steel bracket
3 roof panel   8 reinforced-concrete slab
4 glulam ridge beam

Fig. 6.4. Metal brackets that connect CLT wall panels to a floor have a twofold function: to locate the panels and to resist the shear forces to which they are subject.

In mid- and high-rise buildings, fire safety becomes of paramount importance; therefore, adequate fire-stops need to be inserted into the constructions (such as around openings), to prevent fire from spreading from one storey to those above.

With CLT walls, the most practical position for the thermal-insulation layer is on the outside of the panels. This means that the inner face of the CLT panels can be exposed (in which case, visual quality will need to be specified) or completed with a service void, typically with timber battens and lining sheets. Semi-rigid or rigid insulation boards can be fixed to the panels with special anchors screwed into the CLT. Alternatively, timber battens can be fixed to the outside of the CLT panels and the insulant fitted between them (in this case, quilts could also be specified). This solution, however, might create thermal bridging along the battens and therefore needs to be designed attentively. The thermal-insulation layer is externally covered in breather membrane, which protects the integrity of the insulant and, more importantly, of the wooden structure. In principle, it is also possible to position the thermal insulant on the inside of the CLT panels (an inner thermal jacket), but this precludes the possibility of exposing the CLT internally and causes thermal bridging at the level of intermediate floors.

In the case of masonry cladding, the designer will need to ensure that the outer leaf of the wall is well integrated into the overall construction system.

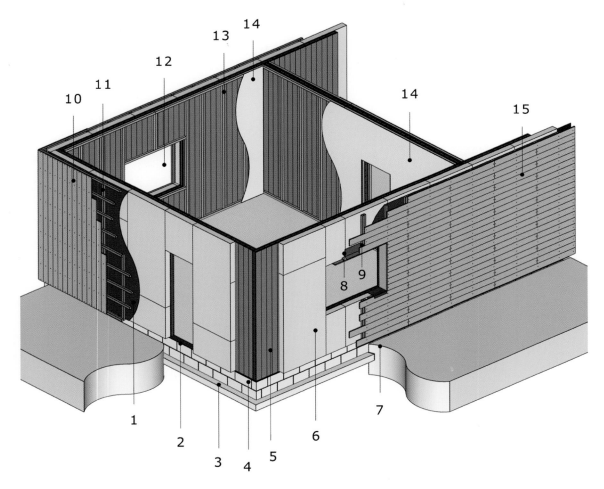

Fig. 6.5. Construction of a CLT building with timber cladding: vertical boards on battens and counterbattens (left), or horizontal boards on vertical battens (right). Note: vertical battens (9) and counterbattens (11) are fixed to the CLT panels with long fasteners that pass through the insulation boards (6).

1 breather membrane	10 external cladding: vertical timber boards on horizontal battens
2 damp-proof course (DPC)	11 vertical counterbatten
3 foundation footing	12 punched opening
4 foundation wall	13 timber batten (service void)
5 CLT panel	14 plasterboard
6 thermal-insulation board	15 external cladding: horizontal timber boards on vertical battens
7 finished ground level	
8 metal flashing	
9 vertical batten	

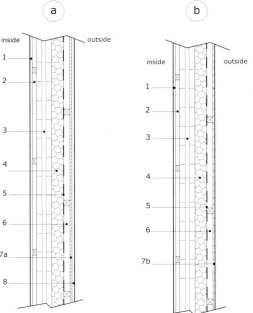

a   b

inside   outside

1
2
3
4
5
6
7a
8

inside   outside

1
2
3
4
5
6
7b

1   plasterboard
2   timber battens & service void
3   CLT panel
4   rigid insulation board
5   breather membrane
6   timber battens & ventilated cavity
7a render-carrier board
7b horizontal timber boards
8   render

Fig. 6.6. Examples of solutions for external walls made of CLT panels, with two types of lightweight cladding: render on carrier board (a) and horizontal timber boards (b). (Drawing: after Sanna, 2018)

In particular, it is important to remember that the CLT structure and the masonry cladding will respond differently to variations in environmental conditions over time. Although CLT has greater dimensional stability than natural wood – as was seen above – some movement is likely to happen in the CLT structure

Fig. 6.8. A double-leaf internal wall designed to meet high acoustic-insulation requirements: the cavity between the CLT panels has been partially filled with mineral-wool quilts.

Fig. 6.7. It is common practice in CLT buildings to use some steel structural members where very high stresses need to be resisted. In this case, a steel section forms the lintel over a large aperture in the façade and supports the CLT panels of the intermediate floor.

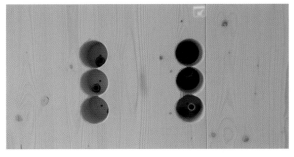

Fig. 6.9. CLT panels for wall applications can be milled to accommodate electrical services.

and at a different rate than in the masonry cladding. A cavity is necessary between the CLT panels and the masonry leaf: this will need to be adequately ventilated and drained. Wall ties must be installed to stabilize the outer skin of the wall.

With lightweight cladding, a ventilated cavity is necessary. The cladding components (for example, timber boards, or timber/metal sheets) are mounted on timber battens (and counterbattens, if necessary) or metal rails, which, in turn, are fixed to the CLT panels (passing through the insulation layer, if this is on the outside of the CLT leaf). Thanks to the continuity of the CLT substrate, it is easier to position fixing points for the cladding than in timber-framed walls, in which the fixing points must coincide with stud locations. The weight of the outer cladding is generally carried by the CLT structure; therefore, the cladding does not sit on the foundations.

Internal walls

Internal walls are constructed in CLT especially when they have a loadbearing function; otherwise, different systems such as timber-framed panels can complement the CLT primary structure. For internal walls with high acoustic requirements, good insulation levels can be achieved by interposing a layer of acoustic insulant between two skins of CLT.

Party walls

There are two main ways of building a CLT party wall: with a single or a double CLT leaf. In both cases, fire safety and acoustic insulation become key aspects of the detailing and material specification. When there are two CLT leaves, these are structurally separated, and the cavity between them can be fully or partially insulated with materials such as mineral wool, which will provide both acoustic performance and increase fire safety. The panels can be protected from fire on the inside with fire-resistant materials such as gypsum plasterboard, which can be fixed directly to the panels or to timber battens. The void between the battens can be filled with insulant. In order to prevent transmission of impact sound, resilient strips can be interposed between the CLT surface and the battens.

When there is a single CLT leaf, fire-safety and acoustic requirements will be fulfilled completely by the layers on either side of the panels, which therefore need to be detailed very attentively. Battens can be attached to the panels to provide support for a sufficiently thick layer of plasterboard or other fire-resistant material. The space behind the lining is filled with insulation of adequate thickness and density. Resilient strips at the interface between the battens and the CLT surfaces can greatly reduce the passage of impact vibration between the two properties.

Intermediate floors

With CLT, both platform construction and balloon construction are possible. For high-rise buildings, platform construction is advisable, while for low-rise buildings the two options are equally viable. This poses an advantage over timber-frame construction, as CLT wall panels can be longer than their timber-frame counterparts. In techniques close to balloon construction, the floor panels can be supported:

- by steel angle brackets screwed to the wall panels. Depending on the fire-protection requirements set by building regulations, the metal brackets might need to be lined with fire-resistant materials. The floor panel can be notched where it meets the horizontal flange of the bracket;
- by edge beams (solid or glulam) fixed to the wall panels.

In either case, a resilient, compressible strip can be inserted between the floor panels and their metal or timber supports.

In platform construction, floor panels bear upon the wall panels below (to which they are screwed) and, in turn, support the wall panels of the upper storey. Angle brackets at the foot of the upper wall panels are screwed to both the wall and the floor panels. In a T-junction between an external wall and an intermediate floor, a perforated metal plate can be inserted on the outside of the wall: this is nailed to both wall panels. Self-adhesive, resilient strips can be inserted between the floor panel and the wall panels (both upper and lower), to limit the transmission of impact and airborne sound between the two storeys.

Separating floors have higher requirements in terms of acoustic insulation and fire protection than floors within the same property, residential unit or fire compartment. An attentive study of the build-up is necessary to achieve satisfactory acoustic performance, especially to minimize the transmission of impact sound (which proves more difficult than in separating walls). Various measures can be taken, in different combinations, to enhance the acoustic behaviour of a separating intermediate floor:

- adding mass to the construction with high-density layers, such as in situ screeds, 'dry screeds' with gypsum boards, timber-based decks, or loose gravel;
- inserting resilient layers;
- inserting soft acoustic insulation;
- creating floating floors (by combining the measures above);
- forming a suspended ceiling, with acoustic insulation, and preferably with appropriate fasteners to decouple the ceiling and the CLT panels;
- choosing a soft floor finish (for example carpet).

These options are effective thanks to two main mechanisms: they either increase the mass of the build-up or create acoustic discontinuity between its components.

Intermediate floors can be constructed with dry or wet methods. A floating screed on an insulation layer is recommended for acoustic purposes. A 50–70mm in situ screed can be created on top of the CLT panels, which can incorporate the service runs. This type of solution entails involving wet trades and might extend construction time. The screed can be based on cement or calcium sulphate. A thin polyethylene layer should be interposed between the screed and the substrate.

The alternative to a traditional screed is a dry form of construction – dry screed – with high-density boards. These can be manufactured from gypsum (and achieve a density of around 1,600kg/m³), with a thickness of 20–25mm, and have rebated or tongue-and-groove edges for ease of installation. The boards can be fixed to one another with adhesive (for example PUR-based glue) and/or steel screws or clips. These boards are also marketed with an insulating layer laminated on the underside of the gypsum panel (of mineral wool, wood-fibre or polystyrene).

A similar dry solution involves laying timber battens that support a timber-based deck (such as plywood, OSB or particleboard) or a gypsum-based deck, using the same products as discussed above. The battens can be decoupled from the CLT substrate by means of resilient strips or resilient cradles that prevent the transmission of impact vibrations between storeys (similar to what was described in Chapter 4 for timber-framed floors). The construction can then be finished with the desired type of flooring.

Flanking transmission of both impact and airborne sound can be mitigated with the insertion of strips along all the edges of the floor (where it abuts the walls), in both wet and dry techniques. These strips – which can be made of different materials, for instance, mineral wool or rubber – need to isolate the whole thickness of the floor, including the floor finish. For this reason, it is advisable to remove the excess part of the strips after the entire floor has been constructed.

Small-diameter gravel can be used to add further mass to the floor. If the gravel is mixed with a cementitious binder and water, then the density and compressive strength of this layer will increase.

If the underside of the CLT panels is not exposed, it can be completed with suitable lining (such as plasterboard sheets), mounted directly onto the CLT

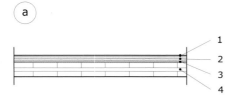

(a)

1 floor finish
2 floating floor: double layer of board
  (e.g., wood- or gypsum-based)
3 resilient layer
4 exposed CLT panel

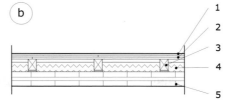

(b)

1 floor finish
2 floating floor: double layer of board
  (e.g., wood- or gypsum-based)
3 resilient batten (i.e., timber batten on
  resilient strip)
4 mineral-wool quilt
5 exposed CLT panel

Fig. 6.10.
Examples of
build-ups of
intermediate floors
constructed of CLT
panels exposed
on the underside.
The non-structural
layers above
the deck can be
built with dry
techniques (a & b)
or wet techniques
(c & d).

(c)

1 floor finish
2 screed (e.g., cement or calcium
  sulphate)
3 resilient layer
4 exposed CLT panel

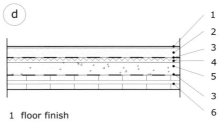

(d)

1 floor finish
2 self-levelling screed
3 separating/protective layer
4 impact-sound insulation layer
5 screed with coarse aggregate
6 exposed CLT panel

Fig. 6.11.
Intermediate floors
constructed of CLT
panels concealed
by ceiling linings
of different types:
the non-structural
layers above the
CLT deck employ
dry techniques.
Impact-sound
insulation is
achieved with a
continuous resilient
layer (a & b) or with
resilient battens (c
& d). The ceiling
is either directly
attached to the
CLT deck (a & c) or
suspended (b & d).

(a)

1 floor finish
2 floating floor: double layer of board
  (e.g., wood- or gypsum-based)
3 resilient layer
4 CLT panel
5 plasterboard

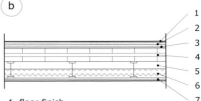

(b)

1 floor finish
2 floating floor: double layer of board
  (e.g., wood- or gypsum-based)
3 resilient layer
4 CLT panel
5 void
6 mineral-wool quilt
7 suspended ceiling: double layer of
  plasterboard

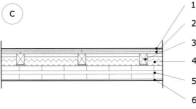

(c)

1 floor finish
2 floating floor: double layer of board
  (e.g., wood- or gypsum-based)
3 resilient batten (i.e., timber batten on
  resilient strip)
4 mineral-wool quilt
5 CLT panel
6 plasterboard

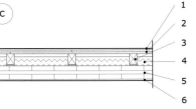

(d)

1 floor finish
2 floating floor: double layer of board
  (e.g., wood- or gypsum-based)
3 resilient batten (i.e., timber batten on
  resilient strip)
4 mineral-wool quilt
5 CLT panel
6 void
7 suspended ceiling: double layer of
  plasterboard

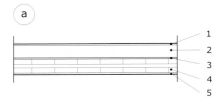

a

1 floor finish
2 screed (e.g., cement or calcium sulphate)
3 resilient layer
4 CLT panel
5 plasterboard

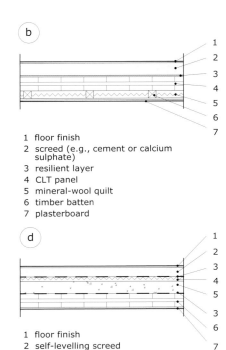

b

1 floor finish
2 screed (e.g., cement or calcium sulphate)
3 resilient layer
4 CLT panel
5 mineral-wool quilt
6 timber batten
7 plasterboard

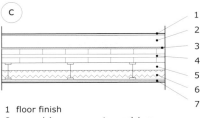

c

1 floor finish
2 screed (e.g., cement or calcium sulphate)
3 resilient layer
4 CLT panel
5 void
6 mineral-wool quilt
7 suspended ceiling: double layer of plasterboard

d

1 floor finish
2 self-levelling screed
3 separating/protective layer
4 impact-sound insulation layer
5 screed with coarse aggregate
6 CLT panel
7 plasterboard

Fig. 6.12. Intermediate floors constructed of CLT panels concealed by ceiling linings of different types: the non-structural layers above the CLT deck employ wet techniques. In order to improve acoustic performance, it is beneficial to add mass to the build-up by laying one screed (a, b & c) or two screeds (d).

Fig. 6.13. Service hole formed within a CLT intermediate floor. The area is sufficient to accommodate the ducts of the heating, ventilation and air-conditioning system.

members or in a suspended ceiling. It is preferable to acoustically decouple the suspended ceiling from the CLT floor, with *ad hoc* clips that mitigate the transmission of impact vibrations from the floor to the lower storey. The depth of the cavity between the deck and the ceiling needs to be attentively optimized: if the cavity is not deep enough, it will have negligible effect; if it is too deep, it will cause resonance. Mineral wool or other types of acoustic insulants need to be inserted into the cavity to prevent it from acting as a resonance chamber (drum effect).

High-quality workmanship on site and attentive supervision during the whole construction process are fundamental to achieving the intended level of acoustic performance.

Flat roofs

In CLT buildings, flat roofs are generally arranged as warm roofs, with a continuous layer of insulation laid above the CLT deck (with the interposition of a vapour-control layer, if necessary). One

Fig. 6.14. An internal staircase entirely constructed in CLT. The sloping panels span between those making up the floors and the intermediate landings, which, in turn, are supported by CLT wall panels and steel sections.

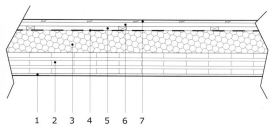

1 2 3 4 5 6 7

1 plasterboard
2 CLT panel
3 rigid insulation boards
4 breathable roofing underlay
5 timber counterbattens & ventilated cavity
6 timber tiling battens & ventilated cavity
7 interlocking tiles

Fig. 6.16. Construction of a CLT pitched roof with plasterboard lining on the underside (section perpendicular to the plane of slope). (Drawing: after Sanna, 2018)

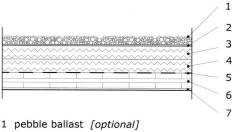

1 pebble ballast *[optional]*
2 waterproofing layer
3 rigid thermal-insulation board (tapered)
4 rigid thermal-insulation board (constant thickness)
5 vapour-control layer (VCL)
6 CLT panel
7 internal lining (e.g., plasterboard)

Fig. 6.15. Example of a typical build-up for a CLT flat roof, arranged as a warm-deck roof. The waterproofing layer is laid on a slightly sloping surface achieved by means of tapered insulation boards.

way to create a gradient for water drainage is to lay two courses of rigid insulation boards: the lower boards have constant thickness, while the upper boards are tapered and thus form the desired slope. On top of the upper boards, the waterproofing layer is installed: this can be based on a single-ply system (such as PVC membranes) or multi-ply system (for example bituminous membranes), as was seen in Chapter 4 for other structural systems. The waterproof membrane can be left exposed or protected with other components, such as pebble

ballast or tiles. The underside of the CLT panels can be exposed (if of visual quality) or lined with sheet materials, with or without the creation of a service void.

Pitched roofs

In pitched roofs, CLT panels are supported by external or internal walls and possibly purlins or ridge beams. Depending on the pitch of the roof, the CLT panels will exert greater or smaller lateral thrust at the eaves, which needs to be adequately withstood by the structural system for overall stability. The top floor can act as a diaphragm and resist the lateral loads coming from the roof.

The thermal-insulation layer is generally placed on top of the CLT panels, and then protected by a breather membrane. On top of the membrane, timber battens can be laid in the direction of slope or, if necessary for the chosen type of covering, sloping counterbattens with horizontal battens on top can be added. If there is a risk of interstitial condensation through the thermal insulant, and depending on the type of insulant, a vapour-control layer might be necessary. If the underside of the CLT panels is not exposed, then a service void with battens and lining can be formed.

Nail- and Dowel-Laminated Timber

Nail-laminated and dowel-laminated timber panels are largely produced in central Europe, especially in Austria, Switzerland and Germany, with the largest companies having manufacturing facilities dotted throughout this region. Over the last decades, the market has been expanding into neighbouring countries such as Italy and France. Norway also has a growing market for these construction methods.

DLT and NLT are almost exclusively fabricated from softwoods: especially white and red spruce. Manufacturers can also utilize other species on the client's request. The advantage of nail- and dowel-lamination is that no glues are used, which also means that the panels do not release the volatile organic compounds (VOCs) typically associated with structural adhesives (although these are in minimal quantity, as explained in the sections above on CLT). NLT and DLT panels can be manufactured in great lengths (up to 16m). In these cases, finger-jointing is performed to fabricate the long lamellae.

Both DLT and NLT elements can be integrated with other timber techniques, such as framed panels and glulam members. In buildings with long spans, it is not unusual to rely on hybrid systems; for instance the massive floor panels can easily rest on the flanges of steel I-beams.

Fig. 6.17. Example of a DLT wall, showing, from left to right: internal plasterboard lining, structural DLT panel (with voids to accommodate service runs), OSB sheathing, double layer of wood-fibre insulation boards with rebates, and external render. The side of the DLT panel in the foreground shows the positions of the hardwood dowels used to connect its softwood lamellae. (Photo: James Henderson, CC BY-SA 3.0)

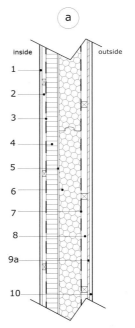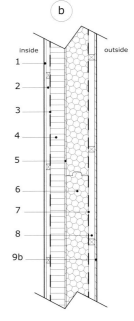

1	plasterboard
2	timber battens & service void
3	vapour-control layer (VCL)
4	NLT or DLT panel
5	OSB sheathing layer
6	rigid insulation boards
7	breather membrane
8	timber battens & ventilated cavity
9a	render-carrier board
9b	horizontal timber boards
10	render

Fig. 6.18. Details of external walls constructed of NLT or DLT panels. Two different cladding systems are proposed: render on carrier board (a) and horizontal timber boards (b). (Drawing: after Sanna, 2018)

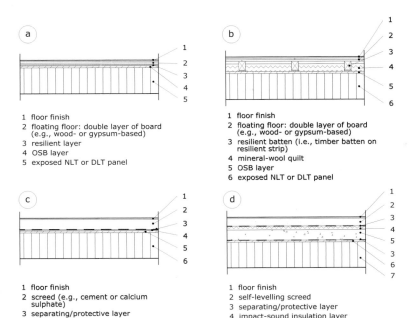

a

1 floor finish
2 floating floor: double layer of board (e.g., wood- or gypsum-based)
3 resilient layer
4 OSB layer
5 exposed NLT or DLT panel

b

1 floor finish
2 floating floor: double layer of board (e.g., wood- or gypsum-based)
3 resilient batten (i.e., timber batten on resilient strip)
4 mineral-wool quilt
5 OSB layer
6 exposed NLT or DLT panel

c

1 floor finish
2 screed (e.g., cement or calcium sulphate)
3 separating/protective layer
4 resilient layer
5 OSB layer
6 exposed NLT or DLT panel

d

1 floor finish
2 self-levelling screed
3 separating/protective layer
4 impact-sound insulation layer
5 screed with coarse aggregate
6 OSB layer
7 exposed NLT or DLT panel

Fig. 6.19. There are many possible arrangements for intermediate floors constructed of exposed NLT or DLT panels. The layers laid above the structural deck can either use dry techniques (a & b) or wet techniques (c & d).

When designing with NLT and DLT, it is important to remember that they maintain the typical anisotropic and hygroscopic characteristics of solid timber (Chapter 1), which instead become much less accentuated in cross-laminated elements. Therefore, when designing and specifying panels, this should be done in a way that permits dimensional changes during the construction and operational phases of a building. It is equally important to ensure good workmanship, weatherproofing and attentive supervision of construction sites, so as to ascertain that the panels are adequately stored and installed, and that direct absorption of water is prevented.

Nail-laminated timber

NLT was invented in the 1970s in Germany for mining and railway applications, and to use lower-grade timber. After the development and uptake of DLT, NLT became less popular. In recent years, NLT has been rediscovered, especially in North America.

In their simplest configuration, NLT panels are formed by timber planks stacked together in the same orientation and connected by steel nails. In order to improve the panels' mechanical properties, one layer is often added on one side, and nailed to the planks, to act as a diaphragm; this can be made of OSB sheets, gypsum-based boards, or timber boards positioned diagonally to the planks. This additional layer, useful for wall and floor applications alike, particularly improves racking performance and airtightness.

Dowel-laminated timber

DLT can also be referred to as dowellam. It was largely employed in North America in industrial and agricultural buildings in the nineteenth and early twentieth centuries, especially in conjunction with post-and-beam systems. Noticeable examples are the Globe Elevators – grain silos – in Duluth (Minnesota), completed in 1887, with walls built up of horizontal timber planks; or Toronto's multi-storey warehouses, which employed solid-timber floors for their high

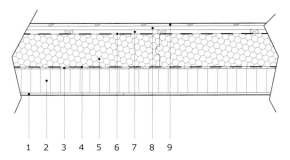

1 2 3 4 5 6 7 8 9

1 plasterboard
2 NLT or DLT panels
3 OSB sheathing
4 vapour-control layer
   (VCL)
5 rigid insulation boards

6 breathable roofing
   underlay
7 timber counterbattens &
   ventilated cavity
8 timber tiling battens &
   ventilated cavity
9 interlocking tiles

Fig. 6.20. Construction of a pitched roof supported by NLT or DLT panels (section perpendicular to the plane of slope). The desired level of thermal insulation can be obtained by installing rigid insulation boards on top of the structural panels, resulting in a warm-roof configuration. (Drawing: after Sanna, 2018)

performance in the event of fire (they were indeed referred to as 'fire-resisting floors').

In the UK, the very first DLT building is Acharacle Primary School (Scotland), designed by Gaia Group and completed in 2009; but the first project with massive panels manufactured from home-grown timber (Sitka spruce and Douglas fir) is the extension to the Coed-y-Brenin Forest Park Visitor Centre (Wales), designed by Architype and completed in 2013.

The applications of DLT panels range from walls (*Brettsperrholzwand*) to floors and roofs (*Brettsperrholzdecke*). DLT panels can have at least three types of layups:

- all the boards have the same orientation. This is the simplest form and is also referred to as *Brettstapel* in German-speaking countries;
- each layer is at right angles to the adjacent layers. This arrangement is very similar to CLT, but no glue is used to connect the boards;
- the lamellae are oriented in three different directions: parallel, perpendicular and diagonal to the main axis of the panel.

In *Brettstapel*, the dowels are generally inserted perpendicular to the stacked planks; however, it is also possible to insert them at an angle to improve structural performance (especially shear performance).

The dowels are generally fabricated from hardwoods (for example beech) and kept at lower moisture content than the planks. After insertion, as they reach equilibrium moisture content, they will absorb moisture and expand; as a result, they will exert pressure on the surfaces of the drilled holes and thus make the connection tighter and stronger. To the same end, the holes drilled into the planks can have a slightly smaller diameter than the dowels.

The form of the dowels can also vary, the most common type having a fluted end and ridged surface. Some manufacturers use dowels with a threaded surface, which means that the holes drilled into the timber planks need to be compatible. This latter type of connection is therefore more similar to that of a screw.

Panel profiles and visual quality

The range of possible profiles for the lamellae is wide, from simple butt joints to half-lapped or tongue-and-groove joints. Interlocking profiles offer some advantages: during the fabrication process, they facilitate alignment of the lamellae; once installed, they can improve distribution of loads. The sides of the panels can be grooved, so that loose tongues can be inserted between adjacent panels.

NLT panels can be exposed on one side, especially when used for floor construction. If the underside of the floor panel is visible, it can be completely flat or employ planks of different depths that can be alternated. This option can generate various panel configurations that can be desirable for both aesthetic and acoustic reasons. Sometimes, 'shadow gaps' are formed along the joints between the lamellae on the exposed underside of the panels: these tend to make effects of dimensional movement (especially shrinkage) less noticeable. For acoustic purposes, bigger voids can be formed above the shadow gaps, which will affect the way in which the ceiling reflects and absorbs sound waves. The use of exposed panels in walls is rare.

Log Construction

Log construction is a very ancient technique, characterized by rich variations through the centuries and the geographical regions where it developed. It is founded on a simple principle: walls can be formed by arranging logs horizontally and shaping and notching their ends in such a way that they interlock. Roof and floor elements can be built using other timber-based methods.

In Europe, log construction was widespread in vast areas of Finland, Scandinavia, Russia and the Baltic countries. In all these regions, it was possible to procure long and straight logs from the local coniferous forests. Log construction was exported to North America when Europeans settled there. Over the centuries and across geographical regions, log construction was adopted for a large variety of buildings: from agricultural sheds to houses, civic and commercial buildings, especially in rural settings. In Europe and North America in the 1930s and 40s, log construction was replaced by other forms of timber construction (such as timber frame) or by different structural materials altogether, and its use became limited to holiday homes and wood cabins. Over the last decades, log-constructed buildings have been rediscovered and, in some countries with a strong timber industry, such as Finland, they have been used again for non-residential purposes.

In traditional log construction, the logs were debarked and then notched by hand, often using simple tools. The way in which the cross-section of the logs and their ends were notched varied geographically and chronologically, generating a broad range of techniques and products. For example, the 'flat-on-flat' method involves flattening both the top and bottom of the logs, in order to easily stack them one on top of the other.

Shrinkage becomes very important during the lifespan of log buildings, especially in the first years after completion. As the wood dries out, it contracts; in particular, the cross-section of the logs changes due to shrinkage in the radial and tangential directions (in which wood exhibits the least dimensional stability, as seen in Chapter 1). Depending on the species and the variation in internal moisture content, the height of a log wall can undergo a substantial change of 10–15mm per metre. Typically, internal walls shrink less than external walls, due to the different conditions to which they are exposed and the consequent levels of moisture content.

Nowadays, while there are still companies that employ handcrafted logs, industrialized methods are readily available and the logs can be quickly and precisely milled (or 'machine-processed') in a factory. With advanced machinery the logs can be given complex profiles, which make longitudinal and corner joints much tighter and more effective.

A further evolution of the market has been facilitated by the production of engineered logs. It is possible to form logs by gluing wood lamellae and thus obtaining a final product that possesses enhanced properties with respect to solid sawn wood. Laminated logs can be very long if the lamellae are finger-jointed. The shrinkage rate in engineered logs is noticeably less than in their sawn counterparts. Proprietary systems can include:

- the use of steel fixings (for example bolts or dowels) to increase the strength and rigidity of the constructions where necessary;
- ancillary components, such as self-adhesive gaskets, that can make the joints very tight (along the logs and at corner junctions alike), with improved thermal and acoustic performance.

An example of a state-of-the-art log house is illustrated in Case Study 10, at the end of this chapter.

Fig. 6.21. St Severin's Old Log Church in Clearfield County (Pennsylvania) was built by German settlers in the 1840s. The walls are constructed of square-hewn, white pine logs. The corners feature dovetail and half-dovetail joints. The longitudinal joints between the logs are filled with mortar (chink). (Photo: Public Domain)

Case Study 7: La Borda Apartment Block

Fausto Sanna & Annalaura Fornasier

Location: Constitució 85–89, Barcelona, Catalonia, Spain

Building type: residential – block of apartments

Completion date: October 2018

Design Team:

Architect: Lacol SCCL (Pol Massoni, Cristina Gamboa, Mirko Gegundez and Eliseu Arrufat), Barcelona, Spain

Structural engineer: Miguel Nevado, Barcelona, Spain

Building services engineer: Arkenova, Barcelona, Spain

Environmental consultant: Societat Orgànica, Projecte d'Arquitectura I Sostenibilitat (Coque Claret and Dani Calatayud), Barcelona, Spain

Acoustic consultant: Àurea Acústica (Grisella Iglesias), Barcelona, Spain

Client: La Borda Cooperativa d'habitatges en cessió d'ús

Gross floor internal area: 2,950m²

Awards:

Winner – Ciutat de Barcelona Award, 2018

Winner – Barcelona Building Construmat Award, category of built work – architecture, 2019

Winner – European Responsible Housing Awards, special innovation award, 2019

Winner – Premis Catalunya Construcció, category: construction management (Xavier Aumedes and Gemma Rius), 2019

Key words: CLT, high-rise, residential, apartments, courtyard, *corralas*, passive solar design

Fig. 6.22. La Borda's southern façade within its urban context. (Photo: Lacol)

Brief and design process

The project originated as an initiative by La Borda Cooperativa, a housing cooperative founded in 2012 by a group of neighbours in Barcelona. The group decided to collectively tackle the need for affordable housing, in the context of Barcelona's housing crisis. Its mission centres on the need to create a community-living model that could act as an alternative to the jointly public-private or fully private building developments in the Catalonian capital.

Lacol cooperative of architects was involved from the outset in this project led by La Borda, a six-storey residential block of twenty-eight apartments (of varying sizes: 40, 60 and 75m²), between the neighbourhood of La Bordeta and the industrial area of Can Batlló. The building is erected on council land, with a seventy-five-year leasehold. It is collectively owned by the members of the cooperative and has been funded with their individual contributions, along with bank loans, grants and a micro-lending campaign,

which reached a total budget of €2.4 million. The cooperative cedes the right of use of the apartments to its members. The innovative living model aspires to place value upon use and quality of space.

The plot lies in a compact urban area between two existing buildings. Building regulations for the plot strictly dictated the maximum allowed volume, number of storeys and area. The regulations also mandated the construction of a car park, but the architects persuaded the relevant authority to waive this requirement, so as to reduce the economic cost and the environmental impact of the scheme and, at the same time, encourage a shift in urban transport towards greater use of bicycles.

La Borda's goals comprise collective property, community life, self-development, active participation of end-users and adaptation of buildings to their needs, economic affordability and environmental sustainability (in particular, the promotion of buildings with minimal impact upon the environment during the construction and occupation stages).

All these aspects had to be considered by Lacol when they started developing a design strategy. One of La Borda's aspirations was to enhance social relations between users, as well as to promote a housing model (and associated living style) that would reduce the apartments' areas by 10 per cent, thanks to a set of shared spaces such as laundry facilities, guest rooms and storage closets. Active user participation was integrated into all phases of the project, from design and construction to management of the building during occupancy. Reciprocal trust and an open, fruitful dialogue between Lacol architects and La Borda led them to take experimental and brave structural decisions, in spite of all the challenges they entailed.

In the design process, the architects were inspired by SAAL (*Serviço Ambulatório de Apoio Local*), an initiative funded by the Portuguese government in 1974 to give a voice to the communities living in substandard housing[1]. SAAL required professionals to work *with*, rather than *for*, the residents, enabling an inclusive approach to architecture. In design and programmatic terms, Lacol was inspired by *corralas*: a traditional, collective form of housing

Fig. 6.23. A traditional *corrala* building in Spain. This residential building type has the two distinguishing communal spaces that can be observed here: a courtyard and a walkway on the upper floor, which provides access to the individual apartments. (Photo: Santiago López-Pastor; CC BY-ND 2.0)

that can be found in Madrid and southern Spain, especially Malaga and Sevilla. Numerous origins are attributed to *corralas*, from ancient Roman villas and Islamic courtyard houses, to monastic and military architecture. Nevertheless, *corrala* developments increased with the demographic growth in Spanish cities from the eighteenth century onwards[2], and played a key role in accommodating the rising population. *Corrala* architecture is defined by two types of communal spaces: a central courtyard (*patio*), where occupants spent a large proportion of their time, and a passageway (*corredor*) located on each floor and structured as a balcony, open on the courtyard side. Traditionally, the materials employed in these

Fig. 6.24. Plan of the second floor, which accommodates six apartments, all accessible via a balcony-like walkway around the communal courtyard. (Drawing: Lacol)

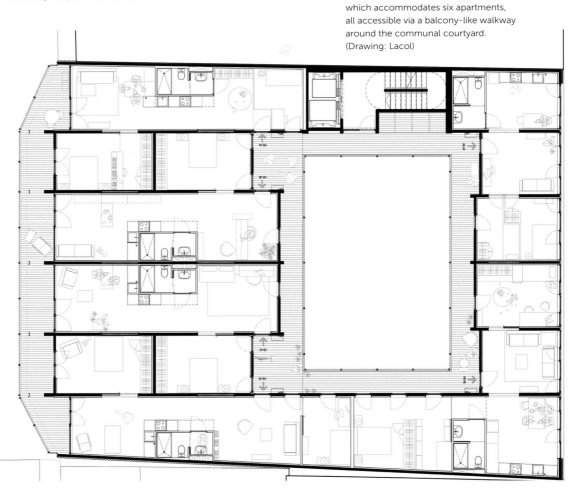

Fig. 6.25. Cut-away view of the building, showing how the layout of the various floors revolves around the all-important courtyard. (Drawing: Lacol)

Fig. 6.26. On the first floor is a communal, double-height space, located between the courtyard and the northern, translucent façade. (Photo: Lluc Miralles)

Fig. 6.27. Among the numerous communal spaces of this apartment block is a large terrace on the fifth floor, which overlooks the urban area north of the building. (Photo: Lluc Miralles)

Fig. 6.28. The staircase is completely realized in CLT panels. (Photo: Lluc Miralles)

buildings were timber for the supporting structure, and adobe and bricks for infill walls.

Lacol architects see architecture as a tool for social, environmental and economic change, and their values reflect La Borda's ethos, whereby a residential project means building a community. In fact, Lacol believe that the community model promoted by La Borda has made it possible to overcome major limitations (often encountered in architectural projects) and has offered them an opportunity to propose

Fig. 6.29. Interior of an apartment, with kitchen, dining and living area. This room gives access to a deep balcony, which can easily accommodate a table and some chairs. (Photo: Institut Municipal de Habitatge i Rehabilitacio de Barcelona)

unconventional design solutions, towards a more responsible way of building.

Construction

Structural system:
> **Foundations:** 600mm-thick reinforced-concrete raft foundations
> **Vertical supports:** ground floor: 250 × 400mm reinforced-concrete columns; first to sixth floor: 100–120mm-thick CLT panels
> **Ground floor:** beam-and-block floor and reinforced concrete slab
> **Intermediate floors:** 120mm-thick CLT panel floors (exposed ceiling structure)
> **Roof:** 120mm-thick CLT panels (flat roof)

Thermal insulation: mineral wool
Acoustic insulation: mineral wool

Cross-laminated timber (CLT) was chosen for being a lightweight and sustainable construction material. This was regarded as an innovative approach in Spain at the time of construction (February 2017– October 2018), when La Borda became the tallest CLT timber building in the country. The construction process was divided into two phases, to minimize the initial investment: in the first phase, minimum living conditions were achieved for residents to move in; in the second phase, the community could independently complete the design, by adapting the interior layout of individual apartments to users' needs.

The lowest storeys of the building have a reinforced-concrete structure, consisting of both a skeleton and some solid walls and ground-bearing slabs. The remainder of the building is completely made of CLT panels, used both vertically and horizontally, for the intermediate floors and the two types of flat roofs (a terrace and a green roof). The floors of the south-facing balconies and the walkways around the courtyard are also made of CLT panels (which cantilever from their vertical supports).

Unlike most CLT buildings of similar height, La Borda does not have a loadbearing core of other materials from the first storey upwards. This means that the CLT structure achieves sufficient overall rigidity on its own, without relying on concrete-built lift shafts, staircases or service cores, as is often the case. The loadbearing structure consists of 100 × 200mm-thick CLT timber panels, used from the first to the sixth floor, supported by 600mm reinforced-concrete foundations and 250 × 400mm reinforced-concrete columns on the ground floor. All CLT panels were fabricated from radiata pine grown in northern Spain. An empty plot adjoining the site facilitated the unloading and storing of materials, and accommodated the crane by means of which all the prefabricated elements were lifted and assembled, including a prefabricated CLT staircase core. The external walls are insulated with mineral wool of variable thickness, depending on the orientation (126mm in northern walls, 450mm in southern and courtyard walls).

Inside the building, the first floor accommodates a double-height communal space, which sits on the concrete structure of the ground floor and hosts glulam portals. The upper storeys have 120mm-thick CLT panel floors, with a 20mm-thick acoustic insulation mat (200kg/m²) and a 70mm concrete screed. The acoustic insulation disconnects the screed from the CLT structure and helps minimize noise and vibration transmission between different storeys. In the internal walls of the apartments, the CLT panels are covered with 45mm-thick mineral-wool mats and plasterboard, which provide acoustic insulation between adjacent apartments.

The main roof (over the sixth-floor apartments, *see* Fig. 6.31) is flat and supported by the same 120mm CLT panels that make up the rest of the structure. In addition, there is a flat, green roof on the northern side of the building (over the fourth-floor apartments), with a 100mm-thick soil substrate for vegetation. A lightweight canopy protects the central courtyard; this is a curved, steel frame covered in translucent polycarbonate sheets and completed, underneath, with an adjustable sun-blind, which can be operated remotely. This central greenhouse-like canopy was an innovative strategy chosen by the architects to optimize natural lighting and temperature inside the building, throughout the year.

Environmental sustainability

Lacol architects focused on two main strategies in response to climate change. On the one hand, they aimed to reduce energy consumption during the construction phase, by avoiding building

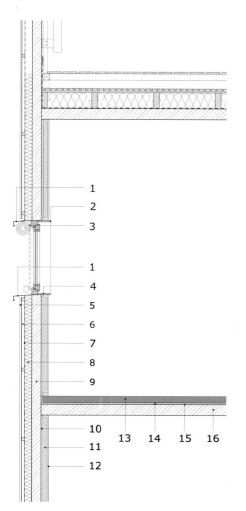

1   galvanised-steel flashing (1.5mm)
2   varnished pine reveal (15mm)
3   sunblind anchors
4   pine sill (15mm)
5   corrugated steel sheet
6   ventilated cavity & galvanised-steel tubular
7   breather membrane
8   mineral-wool insulation layer (80mm)
9   CLT panel (100mm)
10 plasterboard (15mm)
11 mineral-wool insulation (45mm, 0.036W/(m·K)) between metal studs
12 plasterboard (15mm)
13 polished concrete screed (70mm)
14 acoustic-insulation layer (20mm, 200kg/m³)
15 plastic separation layer
16 C24-graded CLT panels, with exposed underside (120mm)

Fig. 6.30. Detailed section showing construction of the north-facing external wall and the intermediate floor. (Drawing: translated and re-drawn from Lacol)

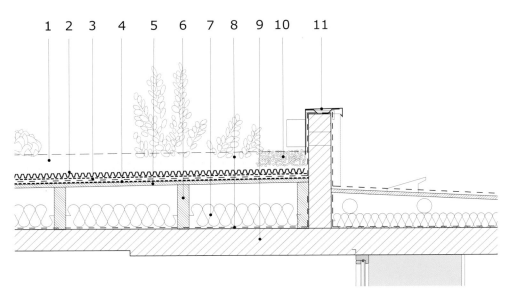

Fig. 6.31. Detailed section showing construction of the green roof. (Drawing: translated and re-drawn from Lacol)

1 sedum (100mm)
2 protective layer + draining membrane + filtering membrane
3 PVC membrane (1.2mm)
4 geotextile membrane (150g/m^2)
5 OSB/4 decking (22mm)
6 pine battens (62mm x variable depth)
7 mineral-wool insulation (150mm)
8 breather membrane
9 C24-graded CLT panels (150mm)
10 draining gravel
11 galvanised steel flashing (1.5mm)

Fig. 6.32. An adjustable, motorized sun-blind filters the light that floods into the courtyard through the translucent roof. (Photo: Gabriel López)

underground and specifying prefabricated timber panels for the main structure. Since Spain does not have a tradition of, or professional expertise in, timber construction, it proved challenging to demonstrate compliance with regulations when proposing a timber building. However, Lacol had previously realized some other projects in timber and the housing cooperative's desire to build using sustainable materials allowed them to overcome these difficulties. On the other hand, the architects designed the building with passive energy strategies, to reduce energy consumption during the occupational phase.

An example of a passive measure is the orientation of the apartments: twenty-four out of twenty-eight apartments have openings in the southern façade, to take advantage of solar radiation in winter, while still having balconies sheltered from it in summer. For this reason, secondary spaces, such as communal and utility areas, are located along

Fig. 6.33. The southern façade during construction. The balconies are supported by cantilevering CLT panels. (Photo: Lluc Miralles)

Fig. 6.34. Construction of the communal, double-height space on the first floor. The third floor (above this space) consists of CLT panels supported by a series of glulam portal frames, whose columns are mechanically fixed to the first-floor reinforced-concrete slab. (Photo: Lacol)

Fig. 6.35. The completed CLT structure. The wall panels are fixed to the floor panels by means of steel angles and bolted connections. The lintels over the wide openings are realized with glulam members, spanning between CLT walls. (Photo: Lacol)

Fig. 6.36. The staircase was prefabricated in multiple sections, which were positioned inside the building by means of a tower crane. (Photo: Lacol)

the northern façade and on the ground floor. The central courtyard, inspired by traditional *corralas*, is another important element of the passive design strategy. The courtyard functions as a collective heating mechanism, maximizing heat gains from solar radiation in winter and allowing for cross-ventilation in summer for cooling purposes. Some of the panes that make up the canopy and the thin, lightweight walls underneath it are motorized and openable.

Furthermore, to increase the thermal mass of the intermediate floors, a 70mm concrete screed was added on top of the CLT deck, balancing the temperature between day and night. The building's occupants have reported that the internal spaces are very comfortable thanks to these passive strategies, which allow for mild temperatures even in winter, without resorting to the heating system. La Borda also has a centralized thermal-generation system for water-heating, space-heating and air-conditioning, which serves all its apartments and includes a biomass boiler.

While it was not possible to introduce a rainwater collection system due to budgetary constraints, photovoltaic panels were installed on the green roof to reduce La Borda's consumption of electrical energy from the grid. Thanks to all these environmental measures, La Borda achieved 'A' standard according to the Spanish energy-rating system for the building sector (known as EPC).

Case Study 8: Three Sisters Footbridge

Location: Saint-Charles River, linking Bourdages Street to Victoria Park, Québec City, Quebec, Canada
Building type: footbridge
Completion date: 2016
Design Team:
  Architect: ABCP Architecture, Canada
  Structural engineer: EMS
  Electrical consultant: SGTR
Client: Ville de Québec
Span: 53m
Deck area: 420m²
Awards:
  Winner – Cecobois Excellence Award (innovative-solutions category), 2016
  Winner – Wood Design & Building Awards (North-American category), 2018
Key words: cable-stayed bridge, CLT, glulam, cables, masts

Fig. 6.37. View of the Three Sisters Footbridge over the Saint-Charles River, in Québec City. (Photo: Gino Pelletier)

Brief and design process

The Three Sisters Footbridge (*Passerelle des Trois-Soeurs*, in French), located in Québec City, crosses the Saint-Charles River and connects Vanier residential area to Victoria Park (in the Saint-Sauveur district). It stands out for its shape, original design solution and materiality.

The construction of this footbridge had been long awaited and debated: citizens' committees had gathered numerous times to identify the best location for the structure. They had discussed several issues, such as preservation of the trees in Victoria Park, site accessibility (due to high traffic in the residential area, especially in summertime), the presence of old foundations on site and how to construct on the riverbanks.

ABCP Architecture were engaged by the municipality, Ville de Québec, to design the footbridge. This firm, also based in Québec City, aims to produce designs that respect the environment and respond directly to their contexts. For this project, they were asked by the client to explore the possibility of incorporating wood into the design. They then decided to construct most of the structure (the masts and deck) from this material. While this key choice posed several challenges, it also contributed to the harmonious integration of the bridge into its surroundings.

The accesses at both ends of the bridge were also designed with particular care and sensitivity to the place, in a way that minimized their footprint. The concrete abutments follow the form of the riverbanks and thus blend gently with the landscape.

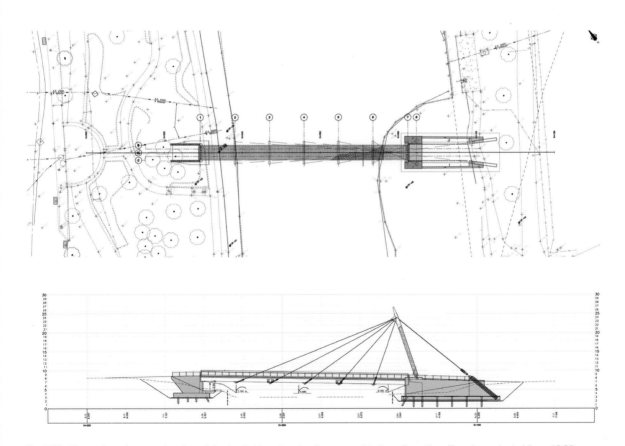

Fig. 6.38. Plan and south-west elevation of the footbridge, showing its asymmetrical configuration. (Drawing: adapted from ABCP architecture)

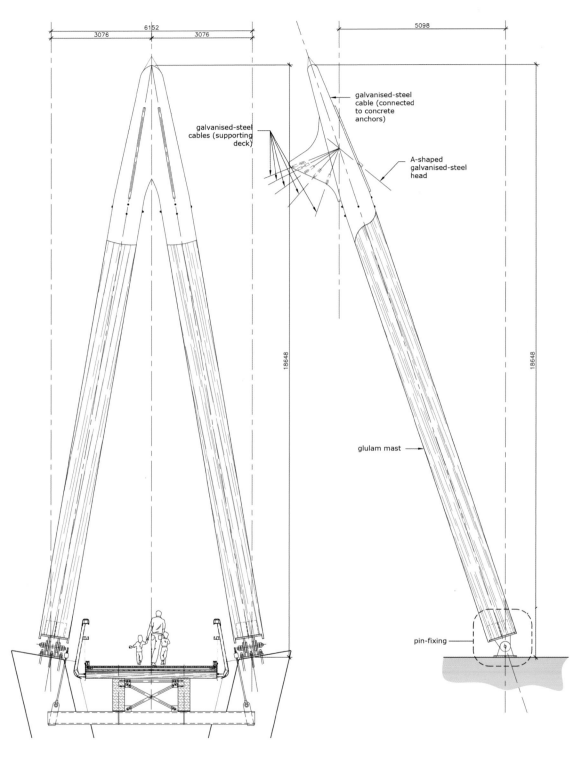

Fig. 6.39. Front and side elevations of the timber masts and the steel, A-shaped head on top of them, to which all the cables are connected. (Drawing: adapted and translated from ABCP architecture)

Fig. 6.40. Access to the bridge from Victoria Park (right side of the river). The two masts and the A-shaped steel cap that joins them are recognizable from a distance and visually act as a gateway. (Photo: Gino Pelletier)

Fig. 6.41. Eye-level view of the bridge towards the timber masts. The guardrail is composed of thin steel spindles, and the floor of diagonal timber boards. (Photo: Gino Pelletier)

Fig. 6.42. The bridge in wintertime, under a blanket of snow. (Photo: ABCP architecture)

Construction

Structural system:

   Bridge type: asymmetric, A-shaped, cable-stayed footbridge

   Foundations: piles and reinforced-concrete anchors

   Vertical supports: glulam masts and galvanized-steel cables

   Deck: steel beams (circular hollow sections), glulam beams and CLT panels

The design aimed to limit as much as possible the number of wood-based members exposed to the elements, in the interests of long-term durability of the bridge as a whole. Hence, the two masts are the only timber structural elements exposed to the weather. The deck has a glulam and CLT structure that is fully protected by waterproof membranes. The details were attentively studied to allow for good water drainage and ventilation of the components.

This is a cable-stayed bridge with an asymmetric configuration, in that the spans on either side of the masts are different. The two masts are the primary loadbearing members that transmit the bridge loads to the ground. They are made from glued laminated spruce and are about 900mm in diameter. The lower ends of the masts are connected to the concrete foundations by means of steel hinges. The upper ends are joined by a sizable steel head, which creates an A-shape and signposts the entrance to the bridge from the park.

The cables (made from galvanized steel) all connect to the steel head placed on top of the masts, in a fan-like arrangement. This means that each couple of cables (one for each side of the bridge) has a different length and a different inclination. Where the cables meet at the top, they are sufficiently spaced from one another to facilitate this structural connection, adequate protection from the weather elements, and good access to individual cables during maintenance operations. The steel head is a white, sculptural component that acts as a visual clue and sharply contrasts with the wooden structure; it springs up through the trees to surprise and attract pedestrians, and to invite them to the bridge access.

Two types of cables connect to the steel head: on one side of the masts, the cables that support the deck; on the other side, the cables that counterbalance the former, by connecting the steel head (and thus the masts) to the concrete anchors built into the ground.

The deck consists of several members that have a different place in the structural hierarchy and load-transfer system. CLT panels create the deck proper and are supported by 1.8m-deep glulam beams that run parallel to the main axis of the bridge. These glulam beams transfer the loads to tubular steel beams connected to the masts through the cables. Above every tubular beam is a steel, cross-bracing system, whose role is to provide the whole structure with transversal rigidity and to stabilize the longitudinal glulam beams, keeping them in their correct position. The guard rails are composed of curved steel plates and thin spindles. The plates in the lower part of the rails also serve the function of concealing the different layers that the deck is composed of.

The creation of a cable-stayed bridge with both masts and deck made from timber was an innovation in itself. In addition, the combined use of different structural materials – glulam, CLT and steel elements – required fine coordination during both the design and construction phases.

All timber and steel members were entirely fabricated offsite: the only operations carried out in situ were the construction of the foundations and the assembly of the prefabricated elements. The two longitudinal glulam beams (under the deck) were split into three sections for practical reasons. The sections were installed on-site one at a time, starting from the one closest to the masts and then proceeding towards the opposite riverbank. Bolted

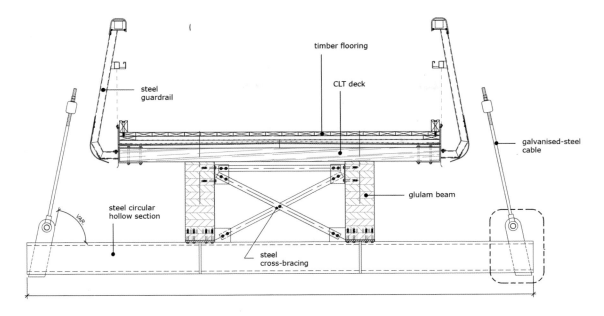

timber flooring

CLT deck

steel guardrail

galvanised-steel cable

steel circular hollow section

glulam beam

VAR

steel cross-bracing

Fig. 6.43. Detailed cross-section of the bridge, illustrating its hybrid timber-steel structural system. (Drawing: adapted and translated from ABCP architecture)

Fig. 6.44. The steel head that joins the two masts is connected to all the steel cables (the ones supporting the deck and the ones transferring its overall load to the concrete anchors). (Photo: Gino Pelletier)

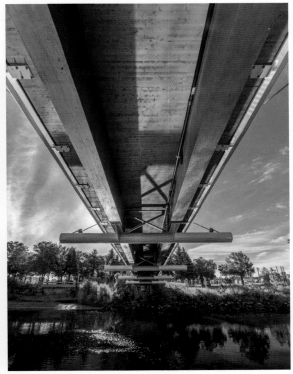

Fig. 6.45. Underside of the bridge deck. The most important members of the structure are all recognizable in this view: the transversal steel beams (hanging on the cables), the longitudinal glulam beams, the cross-bracing and the CLT panels. (Photo: Gino Pelletier)

Fig. 6.46. Installation of the prefabricated upper panels of the deck, by crane. (Photo: ABCP architecture)

Fig. 6.47. The deck was divided lengthwise into three sections, which were installed one at a time. In this view, the first two sections have been installed. The abutting segments of the longitudinal glulam beams were joined together by bolted connections, with the interposition of steel inverted-T sections (visible in the foreground, in white). (Photo: ABCP architecture)

connections were used between abutting sections of the glulam beams, with the insertion of a steel inverted T-section (which had been pre-perforated for the bolts). Thanks to the structural system adopted, the operations conducted on site became relatively simple and, during the assembly process, each section of the beams could be immediately supported by the cables connected to the masts.

In the Three Sisters Footbridge, not only the cables, but also the masts are mostly subjected to axial primary forces: tension in the cables and compression in the masts (and no bending moments). The masts have connections at both ends very close to perfect hinges: these impede the generation of bending moments inside the masts, which are then subjected to compressive forces only[3]. Among the main structural components, therefore, the only flexural members are the longitudinal glulam beams and the transverse steel beams (in that the loading configuration causes internal bending moments in them).

The fortune and popularity of cable-stayed bridges (both pedestrian and vehicular) have gone through highs and lows since their invention. They have gained new prominence over the last decades for moderate spans, since – with the materials and machinery currently available – they allow structural and economic benefits in comparison with other bridge types (for example, suspended or arched bridges). Cable-stayed systems also permit very expressive and compelling solutions, as is well exemplified by the Three Sisters Footbridge.

Environmental sustainability

The use of wood for the main structure of the footbridge was also preferred from a climate-change perspective. In addition to the advantages associated with carbon sequestration (explained in Chapter 3), the wood used in this project was locally grown, which limited transport distances and associated greenhouse-gas emissions.

The attentive design of several construction details aims to ensure the durability of the bridge over time, in order to fit this project into a logic of sustainable development. Finally, the election of a cable-stayed system over other available structural options negated the need to build the bridge foundations in the riverbed, which would have affected the aquatic flora and fauna.

Case Study 9: 111 East Grand Avenue

Fausto Sanna & Annalaura Fornasier

Location: Des Moines, Iowa (IA), USA

Building type: mixed-use building (offices and retail)

Completion date: 2019

Design Team:

Architects: Neumann Monson Architects, IA, USA

Structural engineer: Raker Rhodes Engineering, Des Moines, IA, USA; StructureCraft Builders Inc., Abbotsford, BC, Canada

Building-services engineer: Baker Group, Ankeny, IA, USA

Client: 111 East Grand LLC (joint venture between JSC Properties, Rypma Properties, Christensen Development, and Ryan Companies)

Gross floor internal area: 6,039m²

Awards:

Winner – AIA Iowa Design Honor, 2019

Winner – AIA Central States Region Design Honor, 2019

Winner – WoodWorks Wood Design Award (Commercial Mid-Rise), 2020

Keywords: dowel-laminated timber, glulam, mixed-use building, office, retail

Fig. 6.48. 111 East Grand became the tallest dowel-laminated-timber building in North America, as of 2019. It is located in Des Moines' East Village and is part of its redevelopment and growth process, which has led to the creation of several office and commercial spaces. (Photo: Mike Sinclair)

Brief and design process

This mixed-use building was commissioned by 111 East Grand LLC, a joint venture with which Neumann Monson Architects had previously worked on similar developments and parking facilities. This established working relationship gave the architects more confidence in suggesting the use of mass timber for the project: a four-storey building, comprising a commercial space at street level and flexible office spaces above.

Located in Des Moines' East Village, 111 East Grand is in a central area of the city that has undergone a regeneration process through several new developments, with apartments, offices and retail spaces. This is an urban-infill project, and 111 East Grand functions as a liner building: it abuts the unsightly car park located in the centre of the block, thus concealing it from the main road. A market study, carried out by the client, revealed that prospective tenants – mainly retailers and firms of professionals – were looking for retail or office space located in a central and dynamic part of town where they could welcome their clients. The choice of a high-quality, mass-timber building seemed appropriate – to both the client and the architects – to reflect the mood and lively location of the project.

Neumann Monson Architects had pursued the idea of a mass-timber building in the past, but the high cost had been a primary deterrent, to the advantage of other construction methods. On this occasion, however, the established relationship with the client made timber construction a viable option. The design team visited the T3 office building in Minneapolis (which employs NLT panels and was designed by Michael Green Architecture and DLR Group), to better understand the structural complexity and spatial qualities of solid-timber buildings, which also helped the client assess the advantages of this construction method. Just like T3, most previous mass-timber developments had used cross-laminated timber or nail-laminated timber. However, after

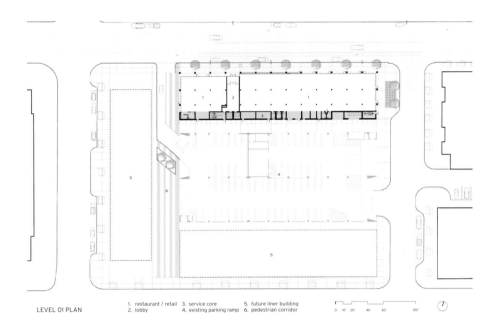

Fig. 6.49. Ground-floor plan. 111 East Grand is the first of three liner buildings to be constructed around a car park in the centre of the block. (Drawing: Neumann Monson Architects)

LEVEL 01 PLAN

1. restaurant / retail
2. lobby
3. service core
4. existing parking ramp
5. future liner building
6. pedestrian corridor

0' 10' 20'   40'   60'   100'

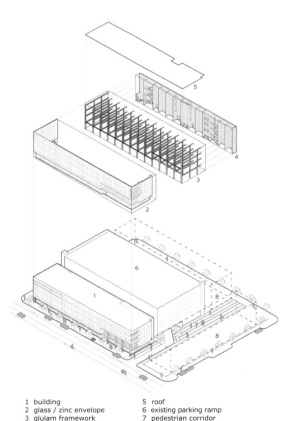

1 building
2 glass / zinc envelope
3 glulam framework
4 precast-concrete core
5 roof
6 existing parking ramp
7 pedestrian corridor
8 future liner building

extensive research and meetings with suppliers, the architects chose to pursue DLT, a less widespread option in the USA. The fact that the timber supplier had already worked with DLT eased the client's concerns over the possible risks associated with using a less-known structural system. In 2019, 111 East Grand became the tallest DLT building in North America.

The project is also innovative in that the design team followed an Integrated Project-Delivery approach. At the design stage, the architects shared the Building Information Model (BIM) with the timber supplier, who was tasked with creating detailed drawings for each timber element. Subsequently, the model was shared with the

Fig. 6.50. The site is an urban infill, and 111 East Grand conceals the car park behind. The south-facing part of the building (which lines the car park) is a service core, made of precast concrete, with stairs, lifts and other ancillary spaces. The main volume of the building, which accommodates retail activities on the ground floor and offices on the upper floors, has a glulam skeleton frame and employs DLT panels for the floors and the roof. (Drawing adapted from: Neumann Monson Architects)

Fig. 6.51. The commercial space on the north-west corner is sheltered by the overhanging first floor, which allows visitors to comfortably access the building on a rainy day and offers shelter from the sun in the summer. The architects chose to leave the DLT structure visible internally, to prevent tenants from using toxic paints and to ensure a coherent interior aesthetic. (Photo: Cameron Campbell Integrated Studio)

Fig. 6.52. The large, open-plan floors of the three office storeys have three glazed façades, while the rear elevation is blank. The western façade offers views onto the nearby Des Moines River and the city centre. As is the case on the commercial ground floor, the DLT floor panels have been left exposed, and lighting, fire-extinguishing and ventilation systems are all visible. (Photo: Mike Sinclair)

general contractor, who then combined it with the consultants' models. The design team carried out virtual design and construction meetings that allowed them to identify conflicts between the different systems involved. Prior to construction, the timber engineers provided assembly and installation drawings.

As regards the programme, the two main functions, retail space and offices, are accommodated on the ground floor and on the upper floors, respectively. A large space, now used as a restaurant, is located on the north-west corner of the building and is sheltered by an overhanging roof. The west-facing aspect of the building has balconies with views over the river and Des Moines' centre.

Construction

Structural system:
    Foundations: concrete footings
    Vertical supports: spruce glulam columns and precast concrete core
    Ground floor: slab on grade
    Intermediate floor: DLT timber panels
    Roof: DLT timber panels
Thermal insulation: mineral wool within and outside cavity (external walls); tapered rigid boards made of a core of isocyanurate foam and cellulosic-felt facers (flat roof)

Fig. 6.53. View of the construction site after the glulam posts and beams had been erected and the DLT panels installed. (Photo: Neumann Monson Architects)

Fig. 6.54. The prefabricated and very long floor panels are lifted with a tower-crane and then laid on the supporting glulam beams. (Photo: StructureCraft)

In the glulam skeleton (the primary structure), the beams are very deep, to achieve the necessary strength and rigidity. The beam-to-column connections are of the mortise-and-tenon type, while the one-storey-high segments of the columns are joined with metal dowels. The intermediate floors are built up of DLT panels completed on top with OSB sheets, an acoustic mat and a concrete screed (the underside of the panels being unclad and exposed). A small portion of the panels is cut out where they abut the columns. The timber planks are less thick on the long edges, to create a channel for electrical services and light fixtures. Most panels are supported by three glulam beams (one at either end and one at midspan), attaining the configuration of a continuous slab on three supports. The panels of the westernmost bay follow a different structural configuration: each of them is supported by two beams and cantilevers from the one located along the west edge of the building, thus forming balconies.

The DLT panels were prefabricated in a factory, and, once the glulam framework had been erected, they were transported to site and rapidly installed by crane.

Environmental sustainability

The use of DLT was a first step towards a sustainable structural approach. Since this material uses hardwood dowels to connect the prefabricated timber planks, it greatly reduces consumption of glues and the associated off-gassing during fabrication, compared to CLT (in which the wooden planks are joined with structural adhesives). The DLT superstructure is exposed on the inside, which discourages tenants from re-decorating or using chemically impregnated finishing products, thus maintaining the organic and uniform interior appearance.

Ventilation ducts and electrical cabling fit between the exposed structural timber panels and are not visually intrusive. The power plant is located at the rear of the site, within a concrete core. The office spaces can be naturally ventilated, since each structural bay is equipped with operable windows in order that tenants can manually adjust the internal temperature as desired.

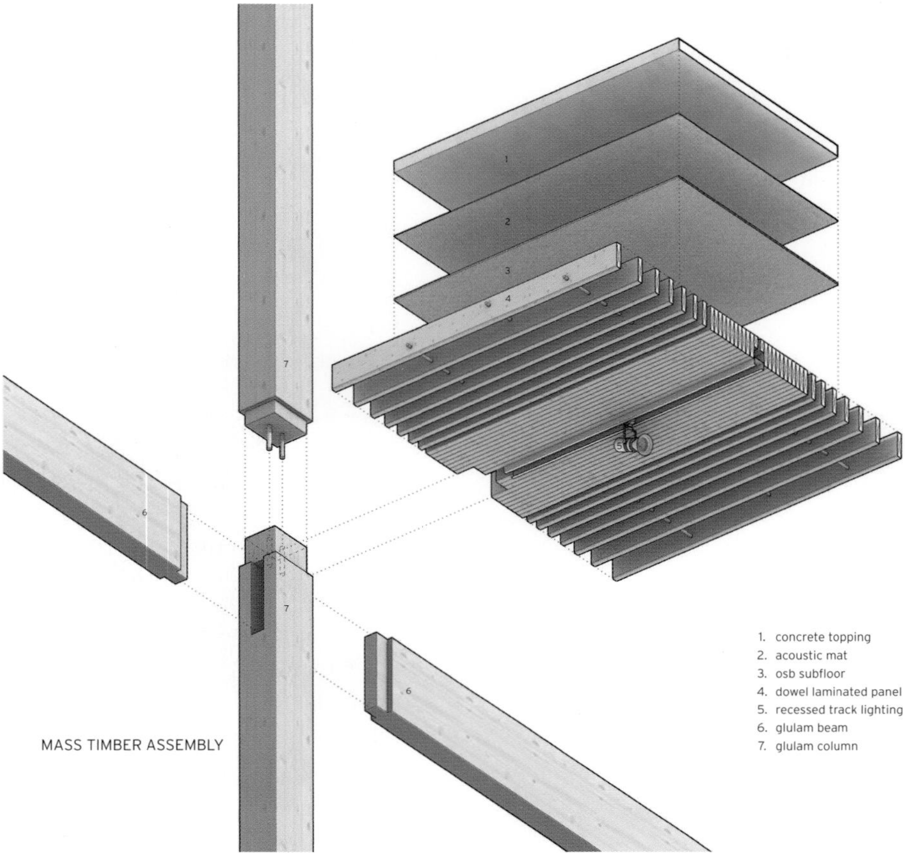

Fig. 6.55. Exploded axonometric view illustrating the make-up of the DLT floor panels and their connection to the glulam skeleton frame. (Drawing: Neumann Monson Architects)

MASS TIMBER ASSEMBLY

1. concrete topping
2. acoustic mat
3. osb subfloor
4. dowel laminated panel
5. recessed track lighting
6. glulam beam
7. glulam column

Fig. 6.56. The primary structure of the building is a glulam skeleton with very deep beams, which support the long-spanning DLT floor panels. (Photo: StructureCraft)

Fig. 6.57. The north-east corner of the building viewed from the main road. On the ground floor, the glulam columns (which sit on a concrete base and are thus elevated from street level) are left exposed. The upper floors are clad with a black rainscreen and their fenestration consists mainly of evenly spaced windows and a curtain wall on the top floor. (Photo: Mike Sinclair)

Fig. 6.58. The façade of 111 East Grand has been designed in such a way as to attract the visitor's eye to its double-height entrance, away from the car park located at the rear. (Photo: Mike Sinclair)

Case Study 10: House in Haute-Nendaz

Fausto Sanna & Annalaura Fornasier

Location: Haute Nendaz, Canton of Valais, Switzerland

Building type: residential – single-family house

Completion date: 2016

Design Team:

Architect: Jean-Michel Martignoni (Ma Maison Bois, Switzerland)

Structural engineer: Paul Glassey SA/Kontio®, Finland

Building-services engineer: Ma Maison Bois SARL, Switzerland

Environmental consultant: Technica Architecture, Switzerland

Contractor: Kontio®, Finland

Client: Jean-Michel Martignoni

Gross floor internal area: 240m²

Key words: engineered logs, log construction, glue-lamination, roof trusses, house, Switzerland, vernacular, *mayens*

Brief and design process

When designing his future home in the Valais Alps, Swiss architect Jean-Michel Martignoni reinterpreted the vernacular log house in a contemporary way, adapting it to current needs and using new technologies. The reference to rural architecture, along with the use of timber, creates a connection between built and natural landscape, conferring a sense of belonging within the Alpine context. Wood was also chosen for the atmosphere it creates, evoking scents, tactile experiences and wellbeing.

The architect drew inspiration from traditional *mayens*[4], examples of which date back to the early sixteenth century (*see* Fig. 6.60). *Mayens* are traditional small shelters for farmers erected in the Canton of Valais, located in uplands above villages, in areas suitable for animal pasture. They were used by families during transhumance, from May to November, and functioned as shelters for men, animals and crops.

Mayens are built into the ground on the uphill side. They have a stone-built ground floor, designated for animal stables, a stone or timber structure for the first floor, and a timber pitched roof covered with stone slates. Larch, spruce or Swiss pine logs are

Fig. 6.59. The north- and east-facing aspects of the house. The walls are clad in reclaimed wood boards with chromatic nuances. (Photo: Franck Paubel, Ma Maison Bois, Switzerland & Kontio, Finland)

utilized to build the superstructure and are hand-cut with an axe into 140/160mm-diameter logs. *Strick-bau*[5], typical of Canton Valais, is the construction method employed, whereby logs are connected by hand-cut dovetail joints. *Mayens* only have few or no windows and a small door, to limit cold draughts into the building. In addition, it was a popular belief that few openings would help keep evil spirits out of the house.

A compositional language similar to that of *mayens* was used by Martignoni in the design of this house, which includes a concrete basement, an engineered-log structural system and a timber pitched roof. The two-storey house sits on a steep slope at an altitude of 1,535m. The house consists of two wings, connected by a central, concrete core, where the circulation space and entryway are located (*see* Fig. 6.61). The entryway is on the first floor, where the slope meets the external footpath, reflecting the local *mayens* tradition of accessing interior spaces from the upper storey. The central core also acts as a buffer zone between the more private area (smaller wing) and the communal area (larger wing). The former accommodates the bedrooms, while the latter the living room, kitchen, relaxation spaces (including a sauna and, outside, a hot tub) and terraces.

Fig. 6.60. Local vernacular architecture: traditional *mayens* built on the steep hillsides of Valais. (Photo: reduced from Xavier Von Erlach on Unsplash)

Construction

Structural system:
   Foundations: 430mm-thick raft foundations
   Basement: reinforced concrete
   Vertical supports: engineered (cross-laminated) pine logs
   Ground floor: reinforced concrete
   Intermediate floors: pine joists and engineered logs, with concrete topping
   Roof: pine trussed rafters
Thermal insulation: wood-fibre boards

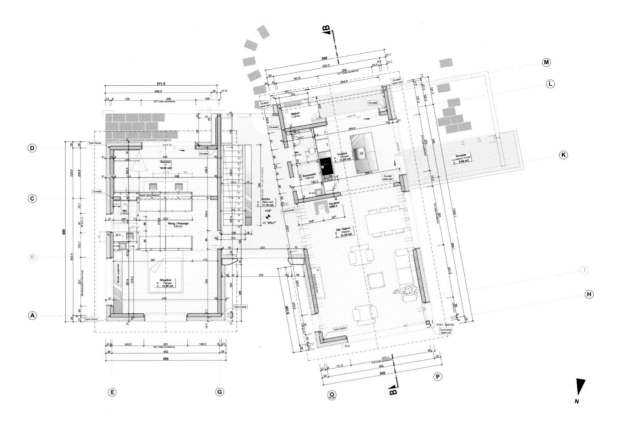

Fig. 6.61. Plan of the first floor. The main access into the building is located at this level, on the uphill side of the central core. (Drawing: adapted and translated from Jean-Michel Martignoni, Ma Maison Bois, Switzerland)

Fig. 6.62. View from the core window onto the mountains across the valley. (Photo: Franck Paubel, Ma Maison Bois, Switzerland & Kontio, Finland)

Architect Martignoni chose a log structural system[6] for this project, as he is the founder of Ma Maison Bois, the Swiss reseller of Finnish manufacturer Kontio, which specializes in the production of prefabricated log houses.

The house sits on a concrete basement. Inspired by the traditional *mayens* structure, Martignoni designed a partly sunken lower storey, which adapts to the 4m difference in height between the front and the rear. The southern wall (on the uphill side) is made of concrete, in a way not too dissimilar to the traditional stone-built walls of *mayens'* lower storeys.

Fig. 6.63. Engineered prefabricated logs. (Photo: Franck Paubel, Ma Maison Bois, Switzerland & Kontio, Finland)

The walls of the upper storeys are built from engineered logs, each made of five pine lamellae glued crosswise in the factory, under high pressure. This fabrication system results in long, laminated logs as a final product, and reduces their swelling and shrinking, thus ensuring higher dimensional stability and offering broader design opportunities. Dovetail joints have been pre-machine-cut in the factory and resemble the axe-cut traditional dovetail joints used in *mayens*. The logs are fixed to one another on site, by means of timber dowels of different sizes and placed in different locations. Each log has two perforations

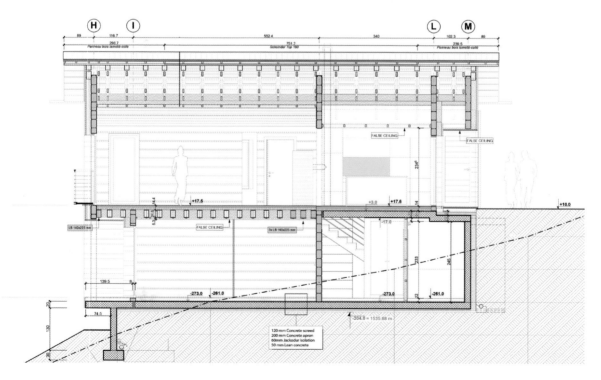

Fig. 6.64. Cross-section of the dwelling, showing how it sits on the steep site. The lower storey is partly sunk into the ground, on the uphill side. (Drawing: adapted and translated from Jean-Michel Martignoni, Ma Maison Bois, Switzerland)

Fig. 6.65. Close-up of the dovetail joints of two internal walls. The difference in texture and colour of the logs' cross-sections is due to their being engineered components, obtained from cross-lamination of pine lamellae. (Photo: Franck Paubel, Ma Maison Bois, Switzerland & Kontio, Finland)

(pre-made in the factory), so that dowels can connect the logs stacked up vertically to form the wall. Where two walls intersect at right angles, the dovetail ends are also perforated and completed with the insertion of dowels. Airtightness is achieved in the massive walls thanks to different types of self-adhesive tapes that function as gaskets (*see* Fig. 6.68). These tapes are positioned along the grooves of the logs, to fill the gaps between juxtaposed logs. In the 'eagle corners', where dimensional tolerances are larger, expansive tapes are used: these, once applied, can significantly increase in volume and easily fill the corner gaps by adapting to their size and shape.

Fig. 6.66. The roof structure consists of a series of parallel trusses whose timber components have been joined by means of punched metal plates. (Photo: Franck Paubel, Ma Maison Bois, Switzerland & Kontio, Finland)

The façade is externally clad with horizontal slats of old barn wood, discoloured by sunlight over the years. The use of these repurposed slats confers an aged look on the building, as if it had been there for a very long time. The external walls are insulated with a 160mm-thick layer of wood fibre, placed on the outside of the engineered pine logs. The intermediate floor is made of timber joists, with wood-fibre fitted between the gaps, a 140mm screed and a wooden floor finish. The joists are not exposed, but concealed by timber ceiling panels; this results in all sides of the interior spaces being of the same material and having similar appearance. The roof planes have a 21.8-degree (40 per cent) pitch and are covered with traditional larch shingles, known as *tavaillons* in French. With adequate maintenance, roofs covered with *tavaillons*, each crafted and placed by hand, can last up to a century despite the harsh Alpine weather. The supporting structure of the roof is made of trussed rafters and has a 320mm-thick wood-fibre insulation layer. The roof trusses are internally concealed by timber panelling.

The central core is supported by engineered pine log walls on the sides, while its northern and southern walls are made of in situ concrete, which is exposed externally and insulated on the inside. The core's

Fig. 6.67. North façade of the reinforced concrete core, overlooking the valley. (Photo: Franck Paubel, Ma Maison Bois, Switzerland & Kontio, Finland)

Fig. 6.68. In order to achieve the desired level of tightness, various gasket tapes are used between interlocking logs. Two tapes run along the grooves of each log. Each corner joint (eagle joint) is wrapped in two strips of expansive insulation tape, which has an adhesive surface. Wooden dowels are inserted into holes pre-drilled in the middle of each eagle joint and in the main body of the logs. (Photo: Franck Paubel, Ma Maison Bois, Switzerland & Kontio, Finland)

intermediate floor is realized as an exposed concrete slab. The core has a flat roof, which contrasts with the more organic and vernacular forms of the wings. This flat roof is supported by 42 × 290mm timber joists, insulated with a 280mm wood-fibre layer and covered with gravel.

Overall, the construction process was eased and sped up by the prefabrication of the logs and joints, which only required their assemblage on site, on top of the concrete foundations poured in situ. The log structure was in fact built over a period of two weeks and the whole project was completed in nine months.

Environmental sustainability

The building is accredited by *Minergie*[7], which is a registered, voluntary quality label for low-energy buildings in Switzerland, established in 1998 and supported by the Swiss Confederation, the Swiss cantons and the local construction industry. It primarily focuses on the residential sector (but is now slowly expanding to other sectors), and its main aim is to ensure comfortable living and working solutions for a building's end-users. *Minergie* requires a high-performing building envelope, controlled air exchange, low energy consumption and maximization

Fig. 6.69. View of the lounge, on the first floor. The wide opening on the left of this space leads to the central core, where the staircase is located. The log walls are internally exposed and their appearance is matched by that of the flooring and ceiling panelling. (Photo: Franck Paubel, Ma Maison Bois, Switzerland & Kontio, Finland)

Fig. 6.70. The bedroom has two windows, which overlook the valley. (Photo: Franck Paubel, Ma Maison Bois, Switzerland & Kontio, Finland)

of renewable-energy use. It also demands that buildings exceed by 20 per cent the energy requirements set by the Swiss Cantonal Energy Prescriptions Model (MoPEC 2014)[8].

In order to support a sustainable living environment, the architect decided to disconnect the electrical network of the private spaces from the rest of the house. In this way, all electrical sources and associated electromagnetic fields can be manually switched off, to prevent harmful waves on the residents at night.

The pine-log structure was identified as a sustainable design solution, by virtue of the carbon stored in the woody material (*see* Chapter 3 for carbon sequestration) and the calorific value that can be used to produce energy at the end of its life-cycle. In addition, logs were chosen as they are considered by some among the systems that require the least amount of energy consumption in the construction of a wall[9]. Finally, the utilization of prefabricated logs accelerates the construction process and reduces material wastage.

Notes

[1] Sealy, 2016

[2] Sánchez Sanz, 1979

[3] This simplified description of the structural system focuses on primary forces and neglects secondary forces, which are small compared to the former.

(4) Mariétan, 1952

(5) Ombellini, 2009

(6) The main proprietary system developed by Kontio ® (Finland) that was used in this project is Massive SmartLog™.

(7) Association Minergie, ca 2020

(8) Conférence des Directeurs Cantonaux de l'Énergie, 2020

(9) Alasaarela, 2009

ABCP architecture (ca.2015) *3 Sisters Pedestrian Bridge*. Available at: https://www.abcparchitecture.com/en/projects/urban-design/3-sisters-pedestrian-bridge (Accessed: 25 July 2021).

Alasaarela, M. (2009) *Eco-competitiveness of a Log Wall*. Hirsitalo Teollisuus: Vuokatti.

Alma-nac (ca.2015) *House in the Woods*. Available at: http://www.alma-nac.com/houseinthewoods (Accessed: 25 July 2021).

American Institute of Timber Construction and Linville, J.D. (eds) (2012) *Timber Construction Manual*. 6th edn. Hoboken: Wiley.

Architects' Journal (2016) 'Great Detail: Alan Dunlop on Louis Kahn's Trenton Bath House', *The Architects' Journal*, 8 September. Available at: https://www.architectsjournal.co.uk/buildings/great-detail-alan-dunlop-on-louis-kahns-trenton-bath-house (Accessed: 29 August 2021).

Association Minergie (ca.2020) *Qu'est-ce que Minergie?* Available at: https://www.minergie.ch/fr/a-propos-de-minergie/en-bref/?l (Accessed: 25 April 2020).

Barker, K. (2006) *A Review of Housing Supply. Delivering Stability: Securing Our Future Housing Needs. Final Report: Recommendations*. Available at: http://www.andywightman.com/docs/barker_housing_final.pdf (Accessed: 21 August 2021).

Bejder, A.K. (2012) *Aesthetic Qualities of Cross Laminated Timber*. Aalborg: River Publishers.

Benedetti, C. (ed.) (2010) *Timber Building. Low-Energy Construction*. 2nd edn. Bolzano: Bozen-Bolzano University Press.

Binderholz (ca.2020) *Processing Manual Binderholz CLT BBS*. Available at: https://www.binderholz.com/fileadmin/user_upload/pdf/products/bbs-processing-manual.pdf (Accessed: 2 September 2019).

Binderholz and Saint Gobain Rigips (2019) *Solid Timber Manual 2.0*. Available at: https://www.binderholz.com/fileadmin/user_upload/books/en/solid_timber_manual_2/ (Accessed: 2 September 2019).

BM TRADA (2016) *Hybrid Construction. Timber-Based Solutions to Structural Challenges*. High Wycombe: BM TRADA.

BM TRADA (2017) *Cross-Laminated Timber. Design and Performance*. High Wycombe: BM TRADA.

BM TRADA (2019) *Procuring Engineered Timber Buildings. A Client's Guide*. High Wycombe: BM TRADA.

BM TRADA (2020) *Designing Timber Structures. An Introduction*. High Wycombe: BM TRADA.

BM TRADA (2020) *Wood Information Sheet 2/3-68. Structural Insulated Panels (SIPs): Introduction for Specifiers*. High Wycombe: BM TRADA.

BM TRADA (2020) *Wood Information Sheet 2/3-69. Structural Insulated Panels (SIPs): Structural Principles*. High Wycombe: BM TRADA.

Boustead, I. (1996) 'LCA – how it came about', *International Journal of Life Cycle Assessment*, 1(3), p.147. Available at: https://link.springer.com/article/10.1007/BF02978943 (Accessed: 9 August 2021).

Braudy, S. (1970) 'The Architectural Metaphysic of Louis Kahn'. *The New York Times*, 15 November. Available at: https://www.nytimes.com/1970/11/15/archives/the-architectural-metaphysic-of-louis-kahn-is-the-center-of-a.html (Accessed: 29 August 2021).

British Standards Institution (2001). *BS EN 13017-1:2001: Solid Wood Panels. Classification By Surface Appearance. Part 1: Softwood*. London: British Standards Institution.

British Standards Institution (2011) *BS EN 15978:2011: Sustainability of construction works. Assessment of environmental performance of buildings. Calculation method*. London: British Standards Institution.

British Standards Institution (2014) *BS 8417:2011+A1:2014: Preservation of Wood. Code of Practice*. London: British Standards Institution.

British Standards Institution (2014) *BS EN 16485:2014: Round and sawn timber. Environmental Product Declarations. Product category rules for wood and wood-based products for use in construction*. London: British Standards Institution.

British Standards Institution (2016) *BS EN 338:2016: Structural Timber. Strength Classes*. London: British Standards Institution.

British Standards Institution (2016) *BS EN 350:2016: Durability of Wood and Wood-based Products. Testing and Classification of The Durability to Biological Agents of Wood and Wood-based Materials*. London: British Standards Institution.

Brownell, B. (2016) 'T3 Becomes the First Modern Tall Wood Building in the U.S'. *Architect*, 8th November. Available at: https://www.architectmagazine.com/technology/t3-becomes-the-first-modern-tall-wood-building-in-the-us_o (Accessed: 3 September 2021).

Bryan, T. (2010) *Construction Technology: Analysis and Choice*. 2nd edn. Chichester: Wiley-Blackwell.

Building Research Establishment (2021) *BREEAM*. Available at: https://www.breeam.com/ (Accessed: 18 August 2021).

Buildoffsite (2017) *Buildoffsite Review 2014–2015*. Available at: http://www.buildoffsite.com/content/uploads/2015/03/bos_yearbook_2014_Nonmembers.pdf (Accessed: 21 August 2021).

Canadian Forest Service (2020) *Statistical Data*. Available at: https://cfs.nrcan.gc.ca/statsprofile/ (Accessed: 12 August 2021).

Charlett, A.J. and Maybery-Thomas, C. (2013) *Fundamental Building Technology*. 2nd edn. Abingdon: Routledge.

Conférence des Directeurs Cantonaux de L'énergie (2020) *MoPEC*. Available at: https://www.endk.ch/fr/politique-energetique/mopec (Accessed: 25 April 2020).

Connor, S.W. (2009) 'Wisconsin's flying trees: the plywood industry's contribution to World War II', *Wisconsin Magazine of History*, 92(3), pp.16-27. Available at: https://content.wisconsinhistory.org/digital/collection/wmh/search/ (Accessed: 16 August 2021).

Crawley, N. (2021) *Cross Laminated Timber. A Design-Stage Primer*. London: RIBA Publishing.

Dauksta, D. (2014) *Brettstapel*. Powys: Wales Forest Business Partnership.

Davies, I. (2013) *Moisture Conditions in External Timber Cladding: Field Trials and their Design Implications*. Thesis (PhD). Edinburgh Napier University. Available at: http://researchrepository.napier.ac.uk/Output/4702 (Accessed: 11 September 2021).

Department for Environment, Food and Rural Affairs (2013) *Timber Procurement Policy (TPP): Prove Legality and Sustainability*. Available at: https://www.gov.uk/guidance/timber-procurement-policy-tpp-prove-legality-and-sustainablity (Accessed: 10 August 2021).

Dixon, D.M. (1975) 'Timber in Ancient Egypt', *The Commonwealth Forestry Review*, 53(3), pp.205-209. Available at: https://www.jstor.org/stable/42605377 (Accessed: 16 August 2021).

Dow Jones Architects (ca.2019) *New Maggie's Cancer Centre at Velindre Hospital, Cardiff*. Available at: https://www.dowjonesarchitects.com/projects/maggies/ (Accessed: 25 July 2021).

Eco Platform (2013) *Regulations and By-laws*. Available at: http://www.eco-platform.org/the-organization.html (Accessed: 01 November 2016).

Effinergie (ca.2012) *Le Label Effinergie+*. Available at: https://www.effinergie.org/web/les-labels-effinergie/le-label-effinergie-plus (Accessed: 29 August 2021).

Feilden Fowles (ca.2016) *Feilden Fowles Studio*. Available at: https://www.feildenfowles.co.uk/feilden-fowles-studio/ (Accessed: 25 July 2021).

Food and Agriculture Organization of the United Nations (2018) *Global Forest Products, Facts and Figures*. Rome: Food and Agriculture Organization of the United Nations. Available at: http://www.fao.org/3/ca7415en/ca7415en.pdf (Accessed: 10 August 2021).

Food and Agriculture Organization of the United Nations (2020) *The State of the World's Forests*. Available at: http://www.fao.org/state-of-forests/en/ (Accessed: 12 August 2021).

Forest Products Laboratory (2010) *Wood handbook – Wood as an engineering material. General Technical Report FPL-GTR-190*. Madison, WI: U.S. Department of Agriculture, Forest Service, Forest Products Laboratory.

Forest Research (2012) *Roundwood Imports and Exports*. Available at: https://www.forestresearch.gov.uk/tools-and-resources/statistics/statistics-by-topic/timber-statistics/uk-wood-production-and-trade-provisional-figures/ (Accessed: 10 August 2021).

Forest Research (2019) *Number of Sawmills by Type of Wood Sawn*. Available at: https://www.forestresearch.gov.uk/tools-and-resources/statistics/statistics-by-topic/timber-statistics/uk-wood-production-and-trade-provisional-figures/ (Accessed: 10 August 2021).

Forest Research (2021) *Forestry Statistics 2021*. Available at: https://www.forestresearch.gov.uk/tools-and-resources/statistics/forestry-statistics/forestry-statistics-2020/ (Accessed: 10 August 2021).

Forest Research (2021) *UK Wood Production and Trade: Provisional Figures*. Available at: https://www.forestresearch.gov.uk/tools-and-resources/statistics/statistics-by-topic/timber-statistics/uk-wood-production-and-trade-provisional-figures/ (Accessed: 10 August 2021).

Forest Stewardship Council (ca.2021) *FSC*. Available at: https://fsc.org/en (Accessed: 18 August 2021).

Forestry Commission (2017) *The UK Forestry Standard*. London: Forestry Commission. Available at: https://www.gov.uk/government/publications/the-uk-forestry-standard (Accessed: 12 August 2021).

Forestry Commission (2020) *Forestry Statistics: Chapter 1 Woodland Area and Planting*. London: Forestry Commission. Available at: https://www.forestresearch.gov.uk/documents/7769/Ch1_Woodland_FS2020_cgadFu3.pdf (Accessed: 12 August 2021).

Franco, A. and Chiapparini, C. (2013) *Alp House: Cultura e Ecologia dell'architettura Alpina*. Available at: http://www.alphouse.eu/medien/medienpool/Cultura-ed-ecologia-VEN.pdf (Accessed: 23 August 2021).

Gang-Nail Systems Ltd. (2021) *The Trussed Rafter Manual*. Available at: https://wilsonrooftruss.co.uk/wp-content/uploads/2014/07/Trussed-Rafter-Manual.pdf (Accessed: 23 August 2021).

Goodier, C. and Gibb, A. (2007) 'Future opportunities for offsite in the UK', *Construction Management and Economics*, 25(6), pp.585-595. Available at: https://doi.org/10.1080/01446190601071821 (Accessed: 21 August 2021).

Goss, R. (2001) *Roofing Ready Reckoner: Metric and Imperial Dimensions for Timber Roofs of any Span and Pitch*. 3rd edn., revised by Chris N. Mindham. Oxford: Blackwell Science.

Guinée, J.B., Gorrée M., Heijungs R., Huppes G., Kleijn R., de Koning A., van Oers L., Wegener Sleeswijk A., Suh S., Udo de Haes H.A., de Bruijn H., van Duin R., Huijbregts M.A.J., Lindeijer E., Roorda A.A.H. and Weidema B.P. (2001) *Handbook on Life Cycle Assessment. Writing an Operational Guide to the ISO Standards for LCA and Related Sub-Projects*. Leiden: Centre of Environmental Science (Universiteit Leiden). Available at: https://www.universiteitleiden.nl/en/research/research-projects/science/cml-new-dutch-lca-guide (Accessed: 9 August 2021).

Hairstans, R. (2010) *Offsite and Modern Methods of Timber Construction: A Sustainable Approach*. High Wycombe: Timber Research and Development Association.

Hairstans, R. and Sanna, F. (2017) 'A Scottish perspective on timber offsite construction', in Smith, R.E. and Quale, J.D. (eds.), *Offsite Architecture: Constructing a Post-Industrial Future*. Abingdon: Routledge, pp.224-251.

Hamilton-MacLaren, F. (2013) *Alternative, More Sustainable, Wall Construction Techniques Than Brick and Block, for New Housing in England and Wales*. Thesis (PhD). Loughborough University. Available at: https://ethos.bl.uk/OrderDetails.do?did=1&uin=uk.bl.ethos.574225. (Accessed: 22 August 2021).

Hislop, P. and O'Leary, P. (2012) *External Solar Shading with Wood. A Design Guide for Architects*. High Wycombe: BM TRADA.

Hislop, P., Kaczmar, P. and Searle, A. (2018) *Timber Decking. The Professional's Manual*. 3rd edn. High Wycombe: BM TRADA.

Holzforschung Austria (2021) *Dataholz*. Available at: https://www.dataholz.eu/en.

House of Commons. Housing, Communities and Local Government Committee (ca.2019) *Modern Methods of Construction*. Available at: https://publications.parliament.uk/pa/cm201719/cmselect/cmcomloc/1831/1831.pdf (Accessed: 19 August 2021).

International Organization for Standardization (2000) *ISO 14020:2000: Environmental Labels and Declarations*. Geneva: International Organization for Standardization.

International Organization for Standardization (2006) *ISO 14025:2006: Environmental Labels and Declarations. Type III*

Environmental Declarations – Principles and Procedures. Geneva: International Organization for Standardization.

International Organization for Standardization (2006) *ISO 14040:2006: Environmental Management. Life Cycle Assessment. Principles and Framework.* Geneva: International Organization for Standardization.

International Organization for Standardization (2006) *ISO 14044:2006: Environmental Management. Life Cycle Assessment. Requirements and Guidelines.* Geneva: International Organization for Standardization.

International Organization for Standardization (2016) *ISO 14021:2016: Environmental Labels and Declarations. Self-declared Environmental Claims (Type II Environmental Labelling).* Geneva: International Organization for Standardization.

International Organization for Standardization (2018) *ISO 14024:2018: Environmental Labels and Declarations. Type I Environmental Labelling. Principles and Procedures.* Geneva: International Organization for Standardization.

Interpol (2019) *Global Forestry Enforcement. Strengthening Law Enforcement Cooperation against Forestry Crime.* Lyon: Interpol.

Jacobs, K. (2018) 'Anne Tyng and Her Remarkable House', *Architect*, the Journal of the American Institute of Architects. Available at: https://www.architectmagazine.com/design/anne-tyng-and-her-remarkable-house_o (Accessed: 29 August 2021).

Jenks, M.K. (1994) *A View from the Front Line.* Available at: https://www.maggies.org/about-us/how-maggies-works/our-story/ (Accessed: 3 September 2021).

Kim, T.H. and Chae, C.U. (2016) 'Environmental impact analysis of acidification and eutrophication due to emissions from the production of concrete', *Sustainability*, 8(6), pp.578-598. Available at: https://doi.org/10.3390/su8060578 (Accessed: 14 September 2021).

KLH (2020) *Cross Laminated Timber.* Available at: https://www.klhuk.com/wp-content/uploads/2019/10/cross-laminated-timber-072021-1.pdf (Accessed: 2 September 2019).

Klöpffer, W. and Grahl, B. (2014) *Life Cycle Assessment (LCA): A Guide to Best Practice.* Weinheim: Wiley-VCH.

Kollmann, F.F.P., Kuenzi, E.W. and Stamm, A.J. (1975) 'Veneer, plywood and laminate', in Kollmann, F.F.P., Kuenzi, E.W. and Stamm, A.J. (eds.), *Principles of Wood Science and Technology II: Wood Based Materials.* Dordrecht: Springer, pp.154-284.

Kontio (ca.2019) *Log Frame. Smartlog™ Eagle Corner Installation Instructions.* Pudasjärvi: Kontio.

Lacol, arquitectura cooperativa (ca.2019) *La Borda Habitatge Cooperatiu.* Available at: http://www.lacol.coop/projectes/laborda/ (Accessed: 25 July 2021).

Lancashire, R. and Taylor, L. (2011) *Timber Frame Construction. Designing for High Performance.* High Wycombe: TRADA Technology.

Lancashire, R. and Taylor, L. (2012) *Innovative Timber Construction. New Ways to Achieve Energy Efficiency.* High Wycombe: BM TRADA.

Lessaveur, A. (2015) 'Climate change', in Hauschild, M.Z. and Huijbregts, M.A.J. (eds.), *Life Cycle Impact Assessment.* Dordrecht: Springer, pp.39-50.

Liu, Y., Guo, H., Sun, C. and Chang, W.S. (2016) 'Assessing cross laminated timber (CLT) as an alternative material for mid-rise residential buildings in cold regions in China – A life-cycle assessment approach', *Sustainability*, 8(10), p.1047. Available at: https://doi.org/10.3390/su8101047 (Accessed: 19 August 2021).

Lu, N. and Liska, R. (2008) 'Designers' and General Contractors' Perceptions of Offsite Construction Techniques in the United States Construction Industry', *International Journal of Construction Education and Research*, 4(3), pp.177-188. Available at: https://doi.org/10.1080/15578770802494565 (Accessed: 19 August 2021).

Lundholm, P. and Sundström, G. (1985) *Resource and Environmental Impact of Tetra Brik Carton and Refillable and Non-refillable Glass Bottles.* Malmö: G. Sundström AB.

Luppold, William G., and Bumgardner, Matthew S. (2017) 'Changes in eastern US sawmill employment and estimated hardwood lumber production from 2001 to 2015', *Forest Products Journal*, 67(7-8), pp.408-415. Available at: https://doi.org/10.13073/FPJ-D-16-00066 (Accessed: 10 August 2021).

MAAJ Architectes (ca.2020) *Pôle Médical Pluridisciplinaire, Taverny.* Available at: http://www.maaj.fr/portfolio/pole-medical-pluridisciplinaire-taverny-95/ (Accessed: 25 July 2021).

Maggie's (ca.2019) *Architecture and design – Cardiff.* Available at: https://www.maggies.org/our-centres/maggies-cardiff/architecture-and-design/ (Accessed: 23 August 2021).

Maggie's (ca.2019) *Our Buildings.* Available at: https://www.maggies.org/about-us/how-maggies-works/our-buildings/ (Accessed: 23 August 2021).

Mariétan, I. (1952) 'Les "mayens" du Valais', *Bulletin de la Murithienne*, 69, pp.57-68. Available at: https://doc.rero.ch/record/23930/files/BCV_N_112_069_1952_057.pdf (Accessed: 23 August 2020).

McEvoy, T.J. (2012) *Positive Impact Forestry: a Sustainable Approach to Managing Woodlands.* Washington, D.C.: Island Press.

McMullin, P.W. and Price, J.S. (eds.) (2017) *Timber Design.* Abingdon: Routledge.

Miller, M., Miller, R. and Leger, E. (2004) *Audel Complete Building Construction.* 5th edn. Indianapolis: Wiley.

Ministère de la Transition Écologique (2020) *Réglementation Thermique RT2012.* Available at: https://www.ecologie.gouv.fr/reglementation-thermique-rt2012 (Accessed: 29 August 2021).

Ministry of Housing, Communities and Local Government (2019) *Modern Methods of Construction: Introducing the MMC Definition Framework.* Available at: https://www.gov.uk/government/publications/modern-methods-of-construction-working-group-developing-a-definition-framework (Accessed: 19 August 2021).

Ministry of Housing, Communities and Local Government and Esther McVey MP (2020) *Modern Methods of Construction: Speech given by the Minister of State for Housing at Legal & General's Modular Housing Factory.* Available at: https://www.gov.uk/government/speeches/modern-methods-of-construction (Accessed: 21 August 2021).

Mitchell, P. and Hurst, R.R. (2009) *Technology Assessment of Automation Trends in the Modular Home Industry. Report Number: FPL–GTR–188.* Available at: https://www.fs.usda.gov/treesearch/pubs/35058 (Accessed: 19 August 2021).

Moore, N. (2015) *Timber Utilisation Statistics 2014 & 2015 for the Forestry Commission.* Available at: https://www.forestresearch.gov.uk/documents/3592/Timber_Utilisation_Report_2015.pdf (Accessed: 19 August 2021).

National House Building Council (NHBC) (2020), *NHBS Standards 2021.* Milton Keynes: NHBC. Available at: https://www.nhbc.co.uk/builders/products-and-services/techzone/nhbc-standards/standards-2021 (Accessed: 23 August 2021).

Natural Resources Canada (2020) *Forest Land Ownership.* Available at: https://www.nrcan.gc.ca/our-natural-resources/

forests-forestry/sustainable-forest-management/forest-land-ownership/17495 (Accessed: 12 August 2021).

Neumann Monson Architects (ca.2019) *111 East Grand*. Available at: https://neumannmonson.com/111-east-grand/ (Accessed: 25 July 2021).

Ombellini, S. (2009) *Tradizione vs Immaginazione. Architettura Contemporanea nell'Area Alpina. 1981–2001*. Doctoral thesis. Università degli Studi di Parma. Available at: http://dspace-unipr.cineca.it/handle/1889/1048 (Accessed: 5 September 2021).

Oregon Forest Resources Institute (2016) *Oregon is Number One*. Available at: https://oregonforests.org/blog/oregon-number-one (Accessed: 10 August 2021).

Owen, J. (2007) *Kit and Modern Timber Frame Homes: The Complete Guide*. Ramsbury: Crowood Press.

Pacheco-Torgal, F., Cabeza, L.F., Labrincha, J. and de Magalhães, A. (eds.) (2014) *Eco-efficient Construction and Building Materials. Life Cycle Assessment (LCA), Eco-labelling and Case Studies*. Cambridge: Woodhead Publishing.

Park, W-J, Kim, R., Roh, S. and Ban, H. (2020) 'Identifying the major construction wastes in the building construction phase based on life cycle assessments', *Sustainability*, 12(19), pp.8096-8900. Available at: https://doi.org/10.3390/su12198096 (Accessed: 14 September 2021).

Partington. R. and Bradbury, S. (2017) *Better Buildings. Learning from Buildings in Use*. London: RIBA Publishing.

Pfeifer (2020) *Pfeifer CLT – Image Brochure*. Available at: https://www.pfeifergroup.com/en/downloads/product-information/ (Accessed: 25 July 2021).

Pliny the Elder, translated by John Healey (1991) *Natural History*. London: Penguin Classics.

Programme for the Endorsement of Forest Certification (2021) *PEFC*. Available at: https://www.pefc.org/ (Accessed: 18 August 2021).

Quarzazate, 10–13 December, pp.1-7. Available at: https://ieeexplore.ieee.org/document/7455023 (Accessed: 29 August 2021).

Riley, M. and Cotgrave, A. (2014) *Construction Technology 2: Industrial and Commercial Building*. 3rd edn. London: Palgrave MacMillan.

Riley, M. and Cotgrave, A. (2018) *Construction Technology 1: House Construction.* 2nd edn. London: Palgrave Macmillan Education.

Robust Details (ca.2020) Available at: https://www.robustdetails.com/ (Accessed: 3 September 2021).

Ross, P. (2011) 'The practicalities of designing with hardwoods', in *Designing with Timber*. Belfast: Forestry Commission, pp.39-40.

Ross, P., Hislop, P., Mansfield-Williams, H. and Young, A. (2012) *Concise Illustrated Guide to Timber Connections*. High Wycombe: BM TRADA.

Roux, A., Colin, A., Dhôte, J.F., and Schmitt, B. (eds.) (2020) *The Forestry and Wood Sector and Climate Change Mitigation: From carbon sequestration in forests to the development of the bioeconomy*. Versailles: Quae. Available at: https://hal.inrae.fr/hal-03121025 (Accessed: 12 August 2021).

Sánchez Sanz, M.E. (1979) 'Vivir en "una Corrala"', *Narria: Estudios de Artes y Costumbres Populares*, 13, pp.3-8. Available at: https://repositorio.uam.es/handle/10486/7995 [Accessed: 25 April 2020].

Sandaker, B.J., Eggen, A.P. and Cruveller, M.R. (2011) *The Structural Basis of Architecture*. 2nd edn. Routledge: Abingdon: Routledge.

Sanna, F. (2018) *Timber Modern Methods of Construction: A comparative study*. Doctoral Thesis. Edinburgh Napier University. Available at: https://www.napier.ac.uk/research-and-innovation/research-search/outputs/timber-modern-methods-of-construction-a-comparative-study (Accessed: 23 August 2020).

Sanna, F., Hairstans, R., Leitch, K., Crawford, D., Menéndez, J. and Turnbull, D. (2012) 'Structural optimisation of timber offsite modern methods of construction', in Quenneville, P. (ed.), *World Conference on Timber Engineering – WTCE 2012*. Red Hook, NY: Curran Associates, pp.368-377.

Schunck, E. (2003) *Roof Construction Manual: Pitched Roofs*. Basel: Birkhäuser.

Scottish Government (2011) *Homes Fit for the 21st Century. The Scottish Government's Strategy and Action Plan for Housing in the Next Decade: 2011–2020*. Edinburgh: Scottish Government.

Sealy, P. (2016) 'Review: The SAAL Process: housing in Portugal 1974–76', *Journal of the Society of Architectural Historians*, 75(1), pp.120-121. Available at: https://doi.org/10.1525/jsah.2016.75.1.120 (Accessed: 23 August 2020).

SIP Building Systems (ca.2012) *Design Guide. Part 1: Structural Design*. Available at: https://www.sipbuildingsystems.co.uk/pdf/SBS-Design-Guide.pdf (Accessed: 29 August 2021).

Slavid, R. (2005) *Wood Architecture*. London: Laurence King Publishing.

Sotirov, M., Pokorny, B., Kleinschmit, D. and Kanowski, P. (2020) 'International forest governance and policy: Institutional architecture and pathways of influence in global sustainability', *Sustainability*, 12(17), p.7010. Available at: https://www.mdpi.com/2071-1050/12/17/7010 (Accessed: 12 August 2021).

Steinhardt, D. and Manley, K. (2016) 'Adoption of prefabricated housing – the role of country context'. *Sustainable Cities and Society*, 22, pp.126-135. Available at: https://eprints.qut.edu.au/100065/ (Accessed: 19 August 2021).

Stevenson, F. (2019) *Housing Fit for Purpose*. London: RIBA Publishing.

Stora Enso (2020) *CLT by Stora Enso. Construction*. Available at: https://www.storaenso.com/en/products/wood-products/massive-wood-construction/clt/brochures-and-downloads (Accessed: 3 September 2021).

Structural Timber Association (2017) *Annual Survey of UK Structural Timber Markets*. Available at: http://www.forestryscotland.com/media/370371/annual%20survey%20of%20uk%20structural%20timber%20markets%202016.pdf (Accessed: 19 August 2021).

Studio Weave (ca.2017) *Belvue Woodland Classrooms*. Available at: https://www.studioweave.com/projects/belvue-school/ (Accessed: 25 July 2021).

Taylor, M.D. (2010) 'A definition and valuation of the UK offsite construction sector'. *Construction Management and Economics*, 28(8), 885-896. Available at: https://doi.org/10.1080/01446193.2010.480976 (Accessed: 19 August 2021).

Timber Design Initiatives (2020) *Why Dowel Laminated Timber?* Available at: https://www.build-back-rural.com/post/why-dowel-laminated-timber (Accessed: 2 November 2021).

Timber Design Initiatives (2021) *What Precisely Do We Mean by 'Dowel Laminated Timber' and How Is It Made?* Available at: https://www.build-back-rural.com/post/what-precisely-do-we-mean-by-dowel-laminated-timber-and-how-is-it-made (Accessed: 2 November 2021).

Timber Research and Development Association (TRADA) (2017) *Wood Information Sheet 2/3-63. Modified Wood Products*.

High Wycombe: BM TRADA. Available at: https://www.trada.co.uk/publications/wood-information-sheets/list-of-wood-information-sheets/ (Accessed: 3 September 2021).

Timber Research and Development Association (TRADA) (2021) *Wood Information Sheet 2/3-11. Specification and Use of Wood-Based Panels in Exterior and High Humidity Situations*. High Wycombe: BM TRADA. Available at: https://www.trada.co.uk/publications/wood-information-sheets/list-of-wood-information-sheets/ (Accessed: 3 September 2021).

Timber Research and Development Association (TRADA) (2021) *Wood Information Sheet 2/3–16. Preservative Treatment for Timber – a Guide to Specification*. High Wycombe: BM TRADA. Available at: https://www.trada.co.uk/publications/wood-information-sheets/list-of-wood-information-sheets/ (Accessed: 3 September 2021).

Timber Research and Development Association (TRADA) (2021) *Wood Information Sheet 4–7. Timber Strength Grading and Strength Classes*. High Wycombe: BM TRADA. Available at: https://www.trada.co.uk/publications/wood-information-sheets/list-of-wood-information-sheets/ (Accessed: 3 September 2021).

Touzani, N. and Jellal, J.E. (2015) 'Study of an air conditioning and heating system incorporating a Canadian well in continental areas, cases of Rabat', *2015 3rd International Renewable and Sustainable Energy Conference (IRSEC),* Marrakech and Trussed Rafter Association (TRA) (2007) *Creating Roofscapes with Trussed Rafters.* London: TRA. Available at: https://www.tra.org.uk/technical-advice-downloads/trussed-rafters/ (Accessed: 23 August 2021).

Trussed Rafter Association (TRA) (2007) *Examples of Basic Trussed Rafters Profiles and More Complex Trussed Rafters Profiles.* London: TRA. Available at: https://www.tra.org.uk/technical-advice-downloads/trussed-rafters/ (Accessed: 23 August 2021).

Trussed Rafter Association (TRA) (2019) *The Buyers' Guide To Trussed Rafters*. London: TRA. Available at: https://www.tra.org.uk/technical-advice-downloads/trussed-rafters/ (Accessed: 23 August 2021).

Trussed Rafter Association (TRA) (2020) *Introduction to the Storage and Installation of Trussed Rafters On Site*. London: TRA. Available at: https://www.tra.org.uk/technical-advice-downloads/trussed-rafters/ (Accessed: 23 August 2021).

U.S. Fish and Wildlife Service (ca.2008) *Lacey Act*. Available at: https://www.fws.gov/international/laws-treaties-agreements/us-conservation-laws/lacey-act.html (Accessed: 12 August 2021).

UK Structural Insulated Panel Association (2011) *Technical Bulletin 1: Structure*. Available at: https://www.sipbuildingsystems.co.uk/pdf/TB1_Structure.pdf (Accessed: 29 August 2021).

UK Structural Insulated Panel Association (2013) *Code of Practice. SIP Technology*. Available at: https://www.sipsindustries.com/wp-content/uploads/2018/08/UK-SIPs-Code-of-Practice.pdf (Accessed: 29 August 2021).

United Nations Climate Change (2012) *Kyoto Protocol. Targets for the First Commitment Period.* Available at: https://unfccc.int/process-and-meetings/the-kyoto-protocol/what-is-the-kyoto-protocol/kyoto-protocol-targets-for-the-first-commitment-period (Accessed: 9 August 2021).

United Nations Economic Commission for Europe (1999) *Protocol to Abate Acidification, Eutrophication and Ground-level Ozone (Gothenburg Protocol)*. Available at: https://unece.org/gothenburg-protocol (Accessed: 9 August 2021).

United Nations Environmental Programme (2020) *Emissions Gap Report 2020*. Nairobi: United Nations Environmental Programme. Available at: https://www.unep.org/emissions-gap-report-2020 (Accessed: 9 August 2021).

United Nations Environmental Programme (ca.2021) *About Montreal Protocol*. Available at: https://www.unep.org/ozonaction/who-we-are/about-montreal-protocol (Accessed: 9 August 2021).

United Nations, Department of Economic and Social Affairs (2019) *Global Forest Goals and Targets of the UN Strategic Plan for Forests 2030*. Available at: https://www.un.org/esa/forests/wp-content/uploads/2019/04/Global-Forest-Goals-booklet-Apr-2019.pdf (Accessed: 12 August 2021).

United States Forest Service (2021) *1905–2020 National Summary Cut and Sold Data and Graphs*. Washington, D.C.: United States Forest Service. Available at: https://www.fs.fed.us/forestmanagement/documents/sold-harvest/documents/1905-2020_Natl_Summary_Graph.pdf (Accessed: 10 August 2021).

van Uffelen, C. (2017) *Living in Wood: Architecture and Interior Design*. Salenstein: Braun.

Welsh Government (2020) *Re-imagining Social House Building In Wales: A Modern Methods Of Construction Strategy For Social Housing*. Available at: https://gov.wales/sites/default/files/publications/2020-02/social-house-building-strategy_0.pdf (Accessed: 21 August 2021).

Wilk, C. (2017) *Plywood: a Material Story*. London: Thames and Hudson.

Wilson, P. (2017) *The Modern Timber House in the UK. New Paradigms and Technologies*. Edinburgh: Arcamedia.

Woodproducts.fi (ca.2021) *Design Log Houses*. Helsinki: Puuinfo. Available at: https://www.woodproducts.fi/content/design-log-houses (Accessed: 3 September 2021).

Woodworking History (2016) *A History of Woodworking*. Available at: www.woodworkinghistory.com (Accessed: 16 August 2021).

Wright, F.L. (1908) 'In the cause of architecture', *The Architectural Record*, 23(3), pp.155-165. Available at: https://www.architecturalrecord.com/ext/resources/news/2016/01-Jan/InTheCause/Frank-Lloyd-Wright-In-the-Cause-of-Architecture-March-1908.pdf (Accessed: 23 August 2020).

ABCP architecture
300, rue Saint-Paul, bureau 412
Quebec City – Quebec – G1K 7R1
Canada
E: quebec@abcparchitecture.com
W: https://www.abcparchitecture.com/

Alma-nac
Unit 11 Waterloo Court – 10 Theed Street
London – SE1 8ST
United Kingdom
E: info@alma-nac.com
W: http://www.alma-nac.com/

BGLA architecture + urban design
50, Côte Dinan
Québec – QC G1K 8N6
Canada
E: http://www.alma-nac.com/contact
W: https://www.bgla.ca/

Catnic, a Tata Steel Enterprise
Pontypandy Industrial Estate
Caerphilly – CF83 3GL
United Kingdom
E: catnic.sales@tatasteeleurope.com
W: https://catnic.com/contact

Dietrich | Untertrifaller Architects
International
Gerlinde Jüttner, Head of Communications
Flachgasse 35-37 – 1150 Vienna,
Austria
E: gj@dietrich.untertrifaller.com
W: https://www.dietrich.untertrifaller.com/

Dow Jones Architects
10 Station Parade – Balham High Road

London – SW12 9AZ
United Kingdom
E: mail@dowjonesarchitects.com
W: https://www.dowjonesarchitects.com/

Feilden Fowles
8 Royal Street
London – SE1 7LL
United Kingdom
E: info@feildenfowles.co.uk
W: https://www.feildenfowles.co.uk/

Hemsec Manufacturing
Stoney Lane, Rainhill,
Prescot, Merseyside – L35 9LL
E: contact@hemsec.com
W: https://www.hemsec.com/

HK Architekten
Sportplatzweg 5,
6858 – Schwarzach
Austria
E: office@hkarchitekten.at
W: https://www.hkarchitekten.at/

Holzforschung Austria
(Austrian Forest Products Research Society)
Franz-Grill-Straße 7, A-1030 Vienna
Austria
E: hfa@holzforschung.at
W: https://www.dataholz.eu/en

Kontio Log Houses
Ranuantie 224
93100 – Pudasjärvi
Finland
E: export@kontio.fi
W: https://www.kontio.com/

Lacol | arquitectura cooperativa
Riera d'Escuder, 38, nau 2 planta 1
08028 – Barcelona
Spain
E: info@lacol.coop
W: http://www.lacol.coop/

MAAJ Architectes
36, rue Pradier
75019 – Paris
France
E: maaj@maaj.fr
W: http://www.maaj.fr/

Mirko Franzoso architetto
Via Don Luigi Borghesi 8
38023 Cles – Tn
Italy
E: info@mirkofranzoso.it
W: http://www.mirkofranzoso.it/

MRM Arquitectos
C/ Puente de Miluze, 12
31012 – Pamplona
Spain
E: mrm@mrmarquitectos.com
W: https://mrmarquitectos.com/

Neumann Monson Architects
221 East College Street, Suite 303
Iowa City – Iowa 52240
United States
E: info@neumannmonson.com
W: https://neumannmonson.com/

Scotts Timber Engineering Ltd
Bridge Street,
Thrapston – Northamptonshire – NN14 4LR
United Kingdom
E: thrapston@scottste.co.uk
W: https://www.scottste.co.uk/

Studio Botter
Viale Sommariva, 38
32021 – Agordo, Belluno
Italy

E: info@studiobotter.it
W: https://www.studiobotter.it/

Studio Bressan
Via Luigi Pastro, 21
31044 – Montebelluna, Treviso
Italy
E: info@studiobressan.net
W: https://studiobressan.net/

Studio Weave
217 Mare Street
London – E8 3QE
United Kingdom
E: hello@studioweave.com
W: https://www.studioweave.com/

Technische Universität Kaiserslautern – Department of Architecture
Pfaffenbergstrasse 95 – 67663 Kaiserslautern
Germany
W: https://design-build.space/ (project) and https://www.architektur.uni-kl.de/startseite/ (university)

Timber Research and Development Association (TRADA)
Stocking Lane – Hughenden Valley
High Wycombe – HP14 4ND
United Kingdom
E: membership@trada.co.uk
W: https://www.trada.co.uk

Trussed Rafter Association (TRA)
The Building Centre – 26 Store Street
London – WC1E 7BT
United Kingdom
E: info@tra.org.uk
W: https://www.tra.org.uk/

Woodknowledge Wales
Ffarm Moelyci
Felin Hen Road – Tregarth
Gwynedd – LL57 4BB
United Kingdom
E: info@woodknowledge.wales
W: https://woodknowledge.wales/